CONNECTED COMMUNITIES
Creating a new knowledge landscape

KV-030-368

CULTURAL INTERMEDIARIES CONNECTING COMMUNITIES

Revisiting approaches to cultural engagement

Edited by
Phil Jones, Beth Perry and Paul Long

First published in Great Britain in 2019 by

Policy Press
University of Bristol
1-9 Old Park Hill
Bristol
BS2 8BB
UK
t: +44 (0)117 954 5940
pp-info@bristol.ac.uk
www.policypress.co.uk

North America office:
Policy Press
c/o The University of Chicago Press
1427 East 60th Street
Chicago, IL 60637, USA
t: +1 773 702 7700
f: +1 773-702-9756
sales@press.uchicago.edu
www.press.uchicago.edu

© Policy Press 2019

British Library Cataloguing in Publication Data
A catalogue record for this book is available from the British Library

Library of Congress Cataloging-in-Publication Data
A catalog record for this book has been requested

978-1-4473-4499-5 hardback
978-1-4473-4501-5 paperback
978-1-4473-4500-8 ePdf
978-1-4473-4502-2 ePub
978-1-4473-4503-9 Mobi

The rights of Phil Jones, Beth Perry and Paul Long to be identified as editors of this work has been asserted by them in accordance with the Copyright, Designs and Patents Act 1988.

All rights reserved: no part of this publication may be reproduced, stored in a retrieval system, or transmitted in any form or by any means, electronic, mechanical, photocopying, recording, or otherwise without the prior permission of Policy Press.

The statements and opinions contained within this publication are solely those of the editors and not of the University of Bristol or Policy Press. The University of Bristol and Policy Press disclaim responsibility for any injury to persons or property resulting from any material published in this publication.

Policy Press works to counter discrimination on grounds of gender, race, disability, age and sexuality.

Cover design by Clifford Hayes
Front cover image: Communication network with assorted avatars © Freepik.com
Printed and bound in Great Britain by CMP, Poole
Policy Press uses environmentally responsible print partners

Contents

List of figures, tables and boxes

Figures

Tables

Boxes

Notes on contributors

Laura Ager is an independent researcher, freelance event organiser and film programmer, based in Leeds, UK. She programmes films and documentaries for the Leeds International Film Festival and curates and organises her own series of pop-up screenings under the name Film Fringe. She is the regional coordinator for the Scalarama film festival in Leeds and currently is working with the Hyde Park Picture House in Leeds on the development of their community cinema programme. She recently completed her PhD on festivals presented by UK universities at the University of Salford and she currently teaches part-time on the MA course in Culture, Creativity and Entrepreneurship at the University of Leeds. She wishes to thank the organisers of the Bristol Radical Film Festival for their participation in this research.

Mohammed Ali is an artist, educator and curator born and raised in the UK. He is best known for melding together his passion for street art from the early 1980s with Islamic script and geometric design that speaks to people of all faiths in multicultural cities across the world. Ali has pioneered his particular style, influencing artists the world over. His work has travelled across the globe from Australia to Canada, from Malaysia to South Africa. See: aerosolarabic.com

Orian Brook is Creative Economy Engagement Fellow at the University of Sheffield, collaborating with the National Theatre to look at audiences for Black theatre, and a Research Associate at the University of Edinburgh researching social mobility in creative employment. She is interested in social and spatial inequalities, especially in relation to culture, and has specialised in spatial modelling of the relationship between the distribution of cultural assets, social inequalities and cultural participation. She has a PhD from the University of St Andrews and worked in cultural organisations for many years in marketing and audience research.

Dan Burwood is a photographer working between the UK and Lebanon. His documentary work includes projects in Cuba (1999-2006), Syria (2008-11), and Lebanon (2008-). He runs Darkroom Birmingham, an analogue photography resource in Balsall Heath, South Birmingham, which is a base for socially engaged and participatory practice. Recent work includes: *Wholesale memory*, the last year of Birmingham Smithfield Wholesale Markets; *A portrait of Balsall Heath*, an archive of portraits; and a community darkroom project at Hermel Cultural Association on the Lebanon–Syria border. He has shown work in Brazil, Korea and the UK, and was highly commended for the Rebecca Vassie Memorial Award 2017.

Lisa De Propris is Professor of Regional Economic Development in the Department of Management at the University of Birmingham. Her main research interests are: small firms and clusters; competitiveness in clusters and regions; forms of clusters and governance; innovation; clusters and foreign direct investment; regional development; knowledge economy and clusters, and creative and cultural industries. In parallel, she has always been concerned with the role of the government and institutions, and she has looked at policy implications arising from her work, including cluster policy, EU regional and industrial policy.

Arshad Isakjee is a Lecturer in Social and Political Geography at the University of Liverpool. He specialises in geographies of Muslim communities and geographies of informal migration into Europe. His specific interests include exploring British Muslim identities in the policy context of policies of multiculturalism, cohesion and counter-terrorism. He gained his PhD at the University of Birmingham in 2012 and moved to the University of Liverpool in 2016. His contribution to this book was facilitated through post-doctoral fieldwork in Birmingham, as part of the *Cultural intermediation* project in 2015.

Chris Jam is a poet, radio presenter and DJ, and arts facilitator delivering poetry and radio projects in schools, communities and with arts organisations over the last 18 years. He would like to give special thanks to Phil Jones for his warmth, intellect and encouragement, and to his family for love and unending support.

Phil Jones is Senior Lecturer in Cultural Geography at the University of Birmingham. He specialises in the development of new research methods, from using innovative technologies to arts-based and participatory action approaches. He has worked in Birmingham since gaining his PhD in 2003, using the city as a major site for his empirical research. Part of the editorial work for this collection was undertaken while he was on a Universitas 21-funded scholarship in Australia and he would like to thank U21, as well as the School of Geography at the University of Melbourne for hosting him.

Saadia Kiyani is a graduate in Visual Communication (Photography) from Birmingham City University. Her style of photography is documentary. Due to health issues, she decided early on that her local communities would be her subjects. As a result, most projects show a side to her local areas that many others do not see. Selected images from this project ran for six weeks on Birmingham's buses in April 2017. The project was only possible due to the support of St Pauls Community Development Trust in Balsall Heath, Birmingham. She would like to thank: her mother, Rukhsar Ali, who has always been her support; Ian Edwards, without whom this project would have most likely stalled; and special thanks to the University of Birmingham and Phil Jones.

Paul Long is Professor of Media and Cultural History at Birmingham City University. His work is concerned with themes of cultural justice and encompasses aspects of public history centred on everyday practices of memorialisation and wider issues in the creative sector, particularly as they pertain to access, participation and identity for workers and consumers. He is currently evaluator and researcher for smARTplaces (smARTplaces.eu), a pan-European audience development project cofunded by the Creative Europe Programme of the EU, aiming to impact on the way culture and art can be perceived and consumed using digital technology and new forms of mediation. He is preparing a new book, *Memorialising popular music culture: History, heritage and the archive*, which will be published in 2020 by Rowman and Littlefield.

Dave O'Brien is the Chancellor's Fellow in Cultural and Creative Industries, based at Edinburgh College of Art. He is the author of *Cultural policy: Management, value and modernity in the creative industries* and the coeditor of *After urban regeneration: The Routledge companion to global cultural policy* and *Routledge major works collection: Cultural policy*. His next book, *Culture is bad for you*, will be published in 2019.

Beth Perry is a Professorial Fellow at the Urban Institute, University of Sheffield. Her research focuses on processes and practices of urban transformation, coproductive urban governance, citizen participation and the just city. She is the UK Director of *Realising just cities*, a four-year international programme of research and action in the Mistra Urban Futures centre, with partners in the global north and south. Currently, she leads three projects: *Whose heritage matters?* (British Academy), *Jam and justice* (ESRC Urban Transformations) and *Whose knowledge matters?* (ESRC Open Research Area). Beth is committed to critical but hopeful social science that seeks to contribute to progressive urban transformation. Beth oversees a collaborative programme of work between academics, individuals and organisations supporting progressive social, spatial and environmental change in the North of England. Across Greater Manchester and Sheffield there are over 20 action research projects on topics from spatial planning, environmental justice and food to cultural heritage and community empowerment. She has also just published two coauthored books: *Cities and the knowledge economy* and *Reflexivity: the essential guide.*

Jessica Symons is director of visioninglab.com, a startup creative digital agency focusing on immersive content including virtual and augmented reality. She is an anthropologist with a research focus on the sociological dynamics of the creative digital sector. Recent projects include exploring how to connect rural areas to the creative digital economy in Cheshire, the potential of 'future visioning' for understanding cultural contexts, learning cities and self-directed education and the development of urban strategies to support self-determination. She has coedited *Realising the urban ethnography in Manchester* with Camilla Lewis; provided papers for *Sociological Review* and *International Journal of Cultural Policy*; co-convened panels at the Royal Anthropological Institute and Association of Social Anthropology conferences and presented to policy makers in the UK and Germany on cultural self-determination.

Mark Taylor is Lecturer in Quantitative Methods (Sociology) at the Sheffield Methods Institute, University of Sheffield. His research interests are in the sociology of culture: in consumption, production, and education, and its relationship to inequality. He is currently working on AHRC-funded projects on social mobility into cultural and creative work, and on data, diversity, and inequality in the creative industries. Methodologically, he is interested in the analysis of survey data, and data visualisation.

Yvette Vaughan Jones is Chief Executive, Visiting Arts. Yvette has worked in the creative economy internationally for the past 25 years. She has worked in community arts, in policy roles and developing and running creative programmes internationally. She has worked both in the private and public sectors as well as for independent arts organisations, the Arts Council of Wales (where she set up Wales Arts International and wrote the Sector Study for the Arts and Cultural Industries for the ERDF programmes) for local and national governments. Her recent work in Europe has included chairing the OMC groups on artists' residencies in 2014 and on the impact of the digital shift on audience development across Europe in 2017. She is also an experienced moderator, most recently for the EU Presidency in June 2016 and has published a number of articles on international working. She teaches international working as part of the MA courses at King's College London and the RWCMD. She is currently the Chair of No Fit State Circus.

Saskia Warren is Lecturer in Human Geography (Assistant Professor) at University of Manchester since January 2015. She holds an Arts and Humanities Research Council Leadership Fellowship, 2017-19. The programme of research, *Geographies of Muslim women and the UK cultural and creative economy,* investigates the interplay of religious faith and gender in the sub-sectors of visual arts, fashion and digital media. It will culminate in a monograph, and groundbreaking exhibition and event programme at The Whitworth Art Gallery, Manchester (see project website: creativemuslimwomen.manchester.ac.uk/). Saskia has published widely, including in leading international journals in geography and cognate disciplines including *Transactions of the institute of cultural practices*, *Social and cultural geography*, *Cultural geographies* and the *European journal of cultural studies*. Her research and consultancy have been funded by Heritage Lottery Fund, Collections Trust, Arts Connect, the Engineering and Physical Sciences Research Council, and the Arts and Humanities Research Council.

Acknowledgements

Much of the work for this book was produced for *Cultural intermediation: Connecting communities in the creative urban economy*, a project funded by the Arts and Humanities Research Council (Ref: AH/J005320/1). Thanks are due to the AHRC and its staff for their support over the course of the project.

Many thanks for funding and support to Mistra Urban Futures, University of Salford and University of Sheffield. Thanks also to the University of Birmingham and Birmingham City University.

Thanks to colleagues who informed the project's foundation and direction: Ian Grosvenor, Tim May, Richard Clay, Kerry Wilson, Russell Beale, Antonia Layard, Natasha Macnab, Paul Haywood and Karen Smith.

A number of individuals and institutions supported the project from the outset and are deserving of our appreciation: Rachel Smithies (Arts Council England), Unity Radio (Manchester), Clayton Shaw (SAMPAD), Jane Puzey (MADE), Ruth Daniel (Un-Convention), Adam Cooper (DCMS), Mitra Memarzia (AIR- Artists' Interaction and Representation), Susan Jones (a-n The Artists' Information Company), Kaye Lowes (Brighter Sounds), Martin Halton (Seedley and Langworthy Trust), Jocelyn Cunningham (RSA – Royal Society for the Encouragement of Arts, Manufactures and Commerce), Frances Toms (Manchester City Council), Jennifer Cleary (Manchester International Festival), Brian Gambles (Birmingham Central Library), Toby Wayley (Birmingham Museums and Art Gallery), Val Birchall (Birmingham City Council), and Lakhvir Rellon (Birmingham and Solihull Mental Health NHS Foundation).

Our sincere gratitude is due to those intermediaries, local institutions and communities without whom this project would not have succeeded. Our particular thanks are extended to: Karen Shannon, Gail Skelly, Chris Doyle, Amber Sanchez, Islington Mill, Ian Edwards, Balsall Heath Women's Academy, Friction Arts, Soul City Arts, St Paul's Community Development Trust, Balsall Heath Library, Ort Gallery and the residents and workers of Balsall Heath and Ordsall. Yvette Vaughan Jones would like to thank Donna Vose for her unstinting care and integrity in carrying out difficult negotiations and relationship building throughout the *1mile²* programme.

Thanks to all at Policy Press.

Special thanks to Martha Norman-Long, who aided in the preparation of this manuscript.

Series editors' foreword

Around the globe, communities of all shapes and sizes are increasingly seeking an active role in producing knowledge about how to understand, represent and shape their world for the better. At the same time, academic research is increasingly realising the critical importance of community knowledge in producing robust insights into contemporary change in all fields. New collaborations, networks, relationships and dialogues are being formed between academic and community partners, characterised by a radical intermingling of disciplinary traditions and by creative methodological experimentation.

There is a groundswell of research practice that aims to build new knowledge, address longstanding silences and exclusions, and pluralise the forms of knowledge used to inform common sense understandings of the world.

The aim of this book series is to act as a magnet and focus for the research that emerges from this work. Originating from the UK Arts and Humanities Research Council's Connected Communities programme (www.connected-communities.org), the series showcases critical discussion of the latest methods and theoretical resources for combining academic and public knowledge via high-quality, creative, engaged research. It connects the emergent practice happening around the world with the longstanding and highly diverse traditions of engaged and collaborative practice from which that practice draws.

This series seeks to engage a wide audience of academic and community researchers, policy makers and others with an interest in how to combine academic and public expertise. The wide range of publications in the series demonstrate that this field of work is helping to reshape the knowledge landscape as a site of democratic dialogue and collaborative practice, as well as contestation and imagination. The series editors welcome approaches from academic and community researchers working in this field who have a distinctive contribution to make to these debates and practices today.

Keri Facer, Professor of Educational and Social Futures,
University of Bristol

George McKay, Professor of Media Studies,
University of East Anglia

Introduction:
Bringing communities
and culture together

Phil Jones, Beth Perry and Paul Long

Introduction

The words 'communities' and 'culture' are some of the most contested in the English language. The launch in 2010 of the *Connected communities* funding programme by the UK's Arts and Humanities Research Council (AHRC) provoked a great deal of debate among the academics and practitioners involved about precisely what these ambiguous concepts underpinning the programme meant in practice. This book, based on research funded by the *Connected communities* programme, emerges from a key theme within these initial debates, which raised questions about the ways in which ideas of culture and creativity can be positioned as mitigating social exclusion and multiple deprivation.

Underpinning this book is a need to problematise a crude assumption that people living in poverty can have their lives enriched by engaging with cultural activity of different kinds. The ambiguous meaning of culture in this context is one of the key problems with the simple formulation that 'culture is good for you', and the assumption that there is an absence in the lives of those in need of its benefits. A key element here is a well-established literature demonstrating that people from a range of socioeconomic backgrounds consume a wide variety of different cultural forms every day. We can say, therefore, that there is nothing particularly unusual about engaging with culture even if you are suffering from the effects of structural poverty and inequality (Miles and Sullivan, 2012). If people are already connecting with cultural forms, this raises questions about the *types* of culture that people are connecting with and the manner of that connection. Does watching television somehow have less of a positive impact on people's lives than visiting an art gallery? Is online video gaming more or less beneficial than going to the opera? Are communal rituals of singing, reading and recitation associated with religious observance aligned or at odds with the parameters of good culture?

Of course, choosing to engage with different cultural forms is a matter of individual taste, but that taste is mediated through socioeconomic position, cultural capital and the market mechanisms that support some manifestations of culture over others. Pierre Bourdieu (1984) talked about tastes being informed by 'cultural intermediaries', highlighting the role of journalists whose role was to notify communities about the kinds of (high) cultures they should consume. That original, rather fuzzy conception of the cultural intermediary can be broadened to encompass intermediation as a broader set of processes (Nixon and Gay, 2002). In the context of the prodigious expansion of practice and policy concerned with the cultural sector that we reference below, the ways in which intermediaries operate, their status and where they are located are equally amplified. As O'Connor (2015: 384) suggests, intermediaries are to be found in a range of institutions:

> in designated creative industries offices, usually located in economic development sections of local authorities. They come from academics and managers in higher and further education who increasingly see the vocational implications of the creative economy as prime justification for the contemporary role of arts and humanities. (O'Connor, 2015)

The reason why this book is reflecting on how communities and culture are brought together is because the existing processes of intermediation intended to do this are under threat in a variety of ways.

Cultural forms can play instrumental roles, going beyond being mere aesthetics, to playing an active role in reforming society. Of course, this instrumental role has always been present within cultural activity, but over the last 30 years, particularly in Western economies, the instrumental value of culture has been increasingly emphasised. Culture has become valued for what it *does*. Where the instrumental role of culture is discussed in relation to community, there tends to be a focus on issues around democracy and social inclusion, or, perhaps more positively, on inspiring individuals to engage with creative practice as a first step towards involvement in the creative economy (see Hadley and Belfiore, 2018). Communities that do not engage with these instrumental uses of culture are seen as somehow lacking, problematic and in need of some form of intervention.

In this book we explore the policy and social frames through which citizens and wider communities are being engaged with culture as a tool to mitigate the effects of social exclusion and deprivation. The study is based on a four-year research project investigating those individuals and organisations whose mission is to use culture, instrumentally, to help deprived communities in a variety of different ways. Our research was undertaken during a period of quite dramatic change in policy and governance within the UK's cultural sector. These changes were driven by one of the biggest experiments in refiguring the role of the public sector within the UK since 1945, as post-credit-crunch governments have responded to the challenges of a struggling global economy by employing the discourse of 'austerity'. What has emerged is a cultural intermediation sector that has refined its practices, adopting new funding models and arenas of activity. Doubtless, the changing funding landscape has done a great deal of damage, with organisations closing and activities being reduced. There are, however, examples of highly innovative practice that have emerged since the financial crisis, from which important lessons should be drawn for the future effectiveness of cultural intermediation as a sector dedicated to improving people's lives through cultural engagement (see Taylor, 2015).

Empowering communities

'Community' is a politically charged and contested concept. Individuals can belong to multiple, overlapping communities based around territorial, sociological and organisational identities. One can be involved in a community of interest around a sporting team, a community relating to ethnicity, a community of people living in a particular neighbourhood and myriad combinations of these. Some of these community identities can be adopted by individuals, but many are externally imposed, with potentially pernicious outcomes. The notion that a singular, coherent Muslim community exists, for example, would be considered laughable by many Muslims living in the UK. In the aftermath of 9/11 and the Iraq invasion of 2003, however, UK anti-terrorism policy explicitly attempted to place responsibility for turning individuals away from extremist ideologies and behaviours onto the Muslim *community* (Spalek and Lambert, 2008). Thus a very large number of ordinary citizens were put in the position of being somehow answerable for the actions of a handful of extremists because of an externally imposed discourse about the 'community' they supposedly belonged to.

Even where an identity is consciously adopted, for example in communities of interest, these communities can be deeply problematic. One does not have to look very hard on the internet to find groups all vigorously agreeing with each other while espousing the most vile racism, sexism, ageism and other despicable views (Suler, 2004). One of the effects of the fragmenting of media discourse over the last decade is that as individuals increasingly rely on social media and other filtered content for news, so they are less likely to be exposed to views with which they disagree (Barberá et al, 2015). One manifestation of this was the popular newspaper trope that appeared following the outcome of the 2016 European Referendum in the UK, in which many individuals were reported as claiming that they did not know anyone who had voted the other way to themselves (Tetlow et al, 2016).

While sociological factors driving community membership are highly significant, geographic location remains a key factor shaping community. As Frug (1996) noted, increased stratification in the housing market has meant that Americans are increasingly unlikely to ever encounter people from a different class and ethnic background in their day-to-day lives. Thus, although individuals may not strongly identify with a community of place relating to their neighbourhood, those neighbourhoods tend to concentrate individuals from similar socioeconomic and cultural backgrounds. In an age where a 'global village' mentality has supposedly reduced the importance of neighbourhood as a source of community identity, some new housing developments are explicitly designed with the intention of creating a greater sense of residential community. Yet one of the accusations made against modes of 'new urbanist' planning is that this sense of residential community can decrease the feeling of common cause with those beyond the boundaries of the immediate neighbourhood; this can be deeply problematic in a highly segmented residential sector (Hipp and Perrin, 2006).

Despite these caveats, there is a strong tendency within political discourse to construct 'community' as being something positive, as something which 'pulls together' in times of trouble, that works with the authorities to root out troublemakers, that underlies the feeling that a place 'works'. There can, however, be somewhat of an elision within these discourses between the word 'community' and groups of people living in geographic proximity who are suffering from a variety of socioeconomic problems. In turn there can be a tendency towards seeing the solution to those problems beginning at the scale of the community. Thus the solution to structural inequality is often depicted as lying in empowering communities to help themselves.

There is a seductive quality to the idea of self-sufficiency among communities, playing to discourses of sustainability, self-help and regaining control from powerful external actors. Such tropes do, however, play into the neoliberal trap that uses notions of community self-reliance as a justification for the withdrawal of state services as part of a wider attack on 'big government'. McCarthy's (2005) analysis of community forestry in the United States is instructive in this regard. He builds on the idea that neoliberalism is not homogeneous, but that it tends to coopt 'other institutional forms and political agendas' in order to create hybrid neoliberalisms (McCarthy, 2005: 998). Both community forestry and neoliberalism make claims that communities are more flexible and democratically representative actors than states, thus justifying an attack on the failure of nation-state governance.

Calls for greater community control thus fall in line with a wider neoliberal agenda of giving markets freer rein to determine how society operates. Within the UK this has been caught up in a particular discourse of localism, with power supposedly being handed down to neighbourhoods and localities to run a huge range of local services, from health visitors and elder care, through community facilities such as playing fields and even into spatial planning and local development. Alongside these new freedoms has come the opportunity for communities to bid to take over resources owned and operated by local authorities, the rub being that the right to take over such services would be in competition with private providers – effectively offering large firms (whose financial muscle means they can either outbid or undercut any community provider) carte blanche to take over community assets. Mike Raco (2013) has argued that these tendering arrangements are an example of where the forces of neoliberalism are actually very enthusiastic about 'big' government as they seek to dominate lucrative public service contracts. While the rhetoric is of local control, the effect in practice is that:

> Citizens have not been empowered to co-produce policy interventions. They have, instead, been institutionally excluded from direct oversight of the policy-making processes that affect them in the name of enhanced policy efficiency and modernisation. The very notion of democratic governance is being converted into a series of technical debates over the 'best way' to ensure that private operators meet social needs through new regulatory and contractual obligations. (Raco, 2013: 3).

Within this discourse, the community becomes a singular actor, served or not depending on how the contractual obligations have been structured with a private provider. The way in which 'community' is constructed as an actor in a set of contractual relations occludes diversity and disagreement within communities. This is far from being purely a UK problem. The UN's Convention on Intangible Cultural Heritage, for example, is intended to protect indigenous knowledges and cultures from exploitation, but presumes a singular community that owns and controls access to these (Forsyth, 2012).

Cultural industries and creative economy

'Cultural industry' was originally a somewhat pejorative term coined by Adorno and Horkenheimer in the 1950s, with 'industry' used to denote a standardisation of products and mechanised distribution systems (Blythe, 2001: 146). Like 'show business' before it, 'cultural industries' (pluralised to reflect its diversity) lost its intended irony and became a normative term for activities within the sector. By the 1990s the cultural industries were being highlighted as a key element in a post-industrial economic mix for developed economies (Hesmondhalgh, 2007). The terms cultural industries and creative economy cover a huge range of different sectors, however, with wildly differing modes of working, profitability and underlying philosophy (Markusen, 2010). Famously, the creative industries were defined in the UK government's Creative Industries Mapping Document of 2001 as 'those industries which have their origin in individual creativity, skill and talent and which have a potential for wealth and job creation through the generation and exploitation of intellectual property' (DCMS, 2001). Captured in this definition were advertising, architecture, the art and antiques market, crafts, design, designer fashion, film and video, interactive leisure software, music, the performing arts, publishing, software and computer services, television and radio. Attempting to narrow the definition, in 2011 the UK's Department for Culture, Media and Sport (DCMS) dropped software from within its classification of the creative industries. Partly this reflected the fact that software fell under the remit of a different government department (Business, Innovation and Skills), which had a greater interest in the most clearly profit-making part of the creative sector. When NESTA set out *A manifesto for the creative economy*, however, it argued that software needed to be considered alongside the wider creative economy. Including software in the definition makes the creative industries much more economically significant, thus allowing NESTA to claim that the sector employed 2.5m people in the UK and contributed 9.7% GVA (gross value added) to the economy (Bakhshi et al, 2013: 10).

Rockstar Games, a UK-based software house making 'triple-A' videogames that sell tens of millions, is part of an international gaming company with a turnover in the billions (Take Two, 2015). Clearly this kind of business, which brings together artists, designers, programmers and others with a view to producing huge profits (as well as creative products), is far removed from the solitary craft worker scraping a living working on community engagement projects or the provincial museum encouraging people to learn about the history of their area. Does this mean that software should not be included in measures of creative economic activity? In one response to this, the Warwick Commission on the Future of Cultural Value developed the idea of a 'cultural ecosystem' as a way of emphasising the connections between the different components of the cultural and creative sector (The Warwick Commission, 2015). Crudely put, the ecosystem metaphor indicates that if you remove support from one part of the creative and cultural sector then other parts will suffer in unanticipated ways. As a result, the Commission emphasised the importance of providing public funding to the wider creative and cultural economy, even those sectors which do not appear to generate financial value in and of themselves (The Warwick Commission, 2015: 20). These are interesting claims and there is clearly some very productive research to be undertaken with game designers, software engineers, film-makers, musicians and so on about precisely how their practice can be seen to be reliant on the wider, non-profit, cultural 'ecosystem'.

The idea of a cultural ecosystem has resonances with the work of Richard Florida (2002) and his claims about the existence of a 'creative class' who drive economic activity. Florida takes a similarly broad approach to what can be considered creative labour, including not just those working in the software sector, but anyone whose work involves creative thinking and problem solving, grouping together an eclectic mix of professions from artists through to lawyers. He puts these individuals at the heart of the contemporary economy. Florida's core argument, which has been somewhat controversial, is that rather than competing to attract businesses, cities now need to compete to attract creative workers who in turn attract profit-generating businesses. The nuances of Florida's ideas are interesting, although they are accompanied by an uncomfortable neoliberal undercurrent that justifies spending scarce public resources on attracting the already wealthy, rather than redistributing those resources to society's most vulnerable. There can be little doubt that Florida's work has been influential in policy circles, if sometimes indirectly and not quite true to the spirit of his ideas. If nothing else, Florida has given legitimacy to city 'boosterist' instincts seeking to invest in flagship cultural buildings in order to clean up declining industrial areas and assist place marketing (Ashworth, 2009).

The argument for the importance of the creative and cultural sector within urban policy goes far beyond simply building a shiny new museum or art gallery to feature in the Lonely Planet guide to a city. The creative and cultural sectors are claimed to offer transformative potential – not just adding economic value but also improving people's lives in a variety of ways. Many claims have been made for how creative and cultural activities can be hugely important in terms of social inclusion, wellbeing, aspiration, building confidence and skills (Matarasso, 1997; Jermyn, 2001; Karkou and Glasman, 2004; Grossi et al, 2012). Nonetheless, Kate Oakley (2006) has noted three key factors that hinder the capacity for the creative industries to drive social inclusion. At a fairly fundamental level, for the UK there is some simple geography at play, given that creative economy activity and public subsidy to the arts sector are disproportionately concentrated in London (see also De Propris, Chapter two in this volume). Bluntly, the fact that there is a thriving creative economy in London is going to do very little for social inclusion in Scunthorpe. The second factor Oakley identifies is low pay and precarity across many sectors of the creative and cultural economy, raising the barrier to entry for those from lower socioeconomic backgrounds who cannot afford to subsidise their early career. The third factor is the long established relationship between creative activity and gentrification in declining neighbourhoods (Zukin, 1982). The presence of arts and creative businesses attracts a more middle-class population which in turn reduces the deprivation of a neighbourhood, but only by displacing existing poor and vulnerable residents. Indeed, the link between creative businesses and gentrification is so well established that there have been violent incidents as communities seek to resist these visible symbols of displacement (for example, the targeting of Shoreditch's Cereal Killers café, Khomami and Halliday, 2015).

The arts and cultural sector is dominated by highly articulate individuals, often with a passionate devotion to their field, disproportionately likely to be from a middle-class background (O'Brien et al, 2016) and to possess a higher degree (DCMS, 2006). It should be little surprise then that the sector is very effective in promoting the idea that creative and cultural activities have great value beyond the aesthetic merit of a particular artwork and thus a claim to public subsidy to realise that value (Belfiore, 2006). Just because a sector is good at selling its claims, however, does not mean those claims are without merit. If one looks at the wellbeing arena, for example, there is good evidence for how arts interventions can assist with *particular* healthcare issues – for example within reminiscence therapy for dementia (Beard, 2011). As Hamilton et al (2003) point out, however, the pursuit of cast-iron evidence that engagement with arts activity promotes better health outcomes remains the 'holy grail'.

The pursuit of this holy grail within the context of evidence-based policy making became particularly important during the New Labour period in the UK, which brought with it a managerialist culture, seeking to provide metrics by which the success of particular policy initiatives could be evaluated. The emphasis on evaluation was particularly strong in relation to questions of social exclusion. Established in 1997, the Social Exclusion Unit (SEU) later found itself pushed to the policy margins during the New Labour period, being merged into other departments and rebranded before eventually being scrapped under the coalition government in 2010. During its early phase, however, the SEU influenced wider policy discourses and thus in the late 1990s a good deal of publicly funded activity – not just in the arts – found itself having to indicate how it could be seen to foster social inclusion. This created a fair amount of handwringing across the public sector, with cultural institutions such as museums looking at ways of reconfiguring their activity towards the social inclusion agenda (Sandell, 1998). By 1999 Chris Smith (Secretary of State for Culture, Media and Sport) was declaring that social inclusion had become a key outcome that was expected in return for public funding for arts and cultural activities (Belfiore, 2002). As a result, there was pressure to try to find ways to design an evaluation framework that could demonstrate the social inclusion gains of particular activities. Scholars working in the field were, however, often somewhat unconvinced by the 'evidence' that these evaluations started to produce (Belfiore, 2002).

Area-based initiatives emerged through the 1980s and 1990s as a means of targeting relatively small geographical areas for activities seeking to redress inequality (Robson et al, 1994). Although initially focused on property development, perhaps most famously at Canary Wharf, funding streams like City Challenge broadened out to look at skills and confidence building. Datasets such as the Index of Multiple Deprivation became a key mechanism by which priority areas for intervention could be identified in the context of relatively scarce public funding. A 2002 report for DCMS cast a critical eye on the claims made for the effects of engagement with cultural and sporting projects as a means of improving social inclusion within area-based initiatives. The report identified three different types of claims made by these projects for how they improved people's lives:

- empowerment – exercising own ability to act
- social exchange – interpersonal and inter-group ties
- citizenship – access to privileges, benefits and entitlements (Centre for Leisure and Sport Research, 2002: 3)

All three of these elements are quite difficult to measure and their success can only really be seen over longer timeframes than are available in the short-term evaluation of a project's success. The DCMS report's authors were scathing about the idea that simply being included in a cultural or sporting activity would somehow reduce an individual's broader social exclusion. The kinds of cultural schemes reviewed were relatively small pieces of wider programmes attempting to overcome social exclusion at the neighbourhood scale through investments in environmental infrastructure, public safety, health, education, skills and job creation. This is not to dismiss the idea that culture-led projects can have a positive impact on people's lives but – and this is a theme that recurs throughout this book – they need to be seen within a wider context of neighbourhoods blighted by structural inequality, poverty and decades of under-investment.

One has to be exceedingly cautious, therefore, about designing policy interventions around a general belief that 'culture is good for you'. To unfairly pick on one study, Sanderson's (2008) survey of 11- to 16-year-olds demonstrated that young people's attitude to dance was directly related to social class. Her conclusion was that a lack of dance within the National Curriculum was a contributory factor in the social and economic exclusion of pupils. One could equally argue, perhaps more convincingly, that it was in fact the social and economic exclusion of pupils which made them less likely to be interested in dance. The temptation, though, is to use such data to make a relatively inexpensive policy intervention around making creative and cultural activities easier to access in order to tackle social exclusion, rather than tacking the underlying structural causes of poverty and inequality.

If, however, creative activity can be assumed to have a *partial* role in reducing social exclusion, there is a question about what *kind* of engagement is necessary to have the positive effect. Does such 'engagement' work need to have any real aesthetic merit? Taking public art, for example, it has been suggested that different criteria need to be used in arts criticism when reviewing examples whose main purpose is to visibly engage a range of publics, with such work even being branded 'new genre public art'. This has led to some interesting debates about what such public art *does* and how its success can be examined (Cartiere and Zebracki, 2015: 3-4). As we indicate in later chapters, practitioners themselves disagree on whether people living in deprived communities need to be exposed to work of 'international' standard in order to get the social inclusion benefits of cultural engagement. For some, the fact that anyone on the outside is giving some kind of a damn about their community can be quite powerful, even if, ultimately, the hope for a dramatic transformation in life and livelihood is beyond the capacity of engagement with cultural activity to deliver.

Do it yourself ... with the help of cultural intermediaries

People with busy lives do not have time to read every book and see every movie. In Bourdieu's original conceptualisation of cultural intermediaries, journalists and critics played an expert role, evaluating the quality of different cultural forms and communicating that evaluation to a broadly middle-class readership. Broadening out from this, intermediaries can be seen as **guides** and **facilitators**, helping people to access and engage with culture in different ways. In attempting to give a greater theoretical weight to this conceptualisation of intermediation, Taylor (2015: 364) suggests that it comprises three modalities, 'the transactional, the regulatory and the strategic'. The **transactional** element relates to the connection between economic and social agents, the **regulatory** to the sets of social norms through which intermediation operates and the **strategic** to the social structures within which these activities are carried out. Intermediation has become a key concept within regional economics, indicating the interconnectedness of economic and social processes. Within our research we have been focusing specifically on two elements: intermediation to facilitate **consumption** of different cultural forms; and intermediation to allow individuals and communities to become **producers** of creative work. These two elements can, of course, overlap.

The great myth of the neoliberal attack on big government is that if the state gets 'out of the way', communities will be free to create local solutions to local problems. Many local problems, such as structural inequality and poverty, require regional, national and global solutions that are far beyond the capacity of local communities to implement, giving a lie to the idea of local action. Even taking the rhetoric of community control at face value, however, one of the key arguments we make in this book is that to engage with the varied benefits of the creative economy, communities are highly reliant on intermediaries and intermediation processes. Cultural engagement does not, we argue, happen spontaneously – particularly in more deprived communities.

Cultural intermediation is thus key to the way in which individuals and broader communities are able to engage with cultural activity. New cultural forms often appear to emerge spontaneously from deprived communities: one can think of Washington DC's go-go parties in the 1970s and 80s, the early noughties UK grime scene, or the *Passinho* ('little step') dance moves emerging from Brazil's *favelas* in the run up to the 2016 Olympics. These spontaneously emerging cultural forms have always relied on an infrastructure of dedicated practitioners sharing their expertise and resources with others in the community – acting, in effect, as cultural intermediaries of an organic kind. The vast majority of cultural production happening at the community level stays at that level – the highly derivative rap videos from local crews 'representing' their neighbourhoods on YouTube are only ever likely to be watched by rivals, friends and family (see Long, Chapter four in this volume). Moving beyond purely hobbyist activity means engagement with the intermediary structures of journalists, agents, publishers, promoters and so forth that help generate and monetise a mass audience. YouTube stars like Zoella may have generated their own mass followings through social media, but a web of intermediary agents have helped make them rich through sponsorship, book deals and cross-promotion.

Only a tiny number of people currently living in poverty are going to have their lives changed by creating a cultural product that breaks out into the mainstream and makes a lot of money. The forms of cultural intermediation that we concentrate on here then, whether facilitating cultural production or consumption, focus primarily on mitigating some of the effects of social exclusion. As a result, when working in these communities the role of cultural intermediaries is as much about education, skills and confidence building as it is about artistic production. One of the key lessons from our research project is this activity's reliance on a small number of particularly dedicated individuals who see working with socially excluded communities as a crucial part of their activities within the field of culture.

Given the inequalities that characterise the cultural sector and the compromises many must make in order to advance their careers in it, it is worth noting how these workers endure in remarkably difficult circumstances. Intermediation activity needs to be resourced and intermediaries have had to work in highly innovative ways to find external resourcing of different kinds to sustain their work within communities. Cuts to the public sector after the 2008 financial crisis, and particularly after the election of a coalition government in the UK in 2010, hit the cultural sector hard. The major national institutions based in London were largely protected from cuts and, by virtue of their profile, find it easier to raise funds via private sector sponsorships. Much of the burden for reducing government expenditure after 2010 was passed on to local authorities; culture, as a non-statutory service, was in the front line for nationally mandated reductions to local authority budgets. This, in turn, has meant that organisations undertaking intermediary functions within communities had to change how they operate and some, frankly, disappeared for lack of funding.

What we concentrate on in this book is how cultural intermediary processes are being managed today, offering some important empirical insights to the lived realities of workers and communities. A significant expansion in public expenditure on culture is unlikely to happen in the immediate future, which changes the working practices of individuals across the sector as they look for new ways of funding their activity. Intermediaries seeking to engage communities with cultural activity have an important role in a wider mix of measures seeking to reduce the effects of deprivation and social exclusion. This role continues to be valued within wider policy discourse, but changes to public sector funding have produced a creative response to challenging circumstances. The effectiveness of these responses and the future of the sector is our key focus throughout this book.

Case studies

As noted above, the research presented in this book was funded under the AHRC's Connected Communities scheme, as part of its £1.5m four-year project *Cultural intermediation: connecting communities in the creative urban economy*. The project sought to examine the different scales of activity involved within cultural intermediation, exploring national policy and practice but grounded within specific community-level case studies. Although a number of sites across England were examined, two field sites in particular were the subject for a deep ethnographic engagement, including active interventions. These were Birmingham, with a focus on the Balsall Heath neighbourhood, and Greater Manchester, with detailed work being undertaken in the Ordsall ward of Salford. These case studies feature throughout much of the book as a lens through which to see the impacts of wider policy trends.

Both regions lie outside the halo effect of the London conurbation and have proportionately much less activity within their creative economy than does the capital. There is some presence of TV and other media, as well as traditional cultural institutions such as orchestras, ballet, museums and galleries, some of which have national and international reputations. Beyond the outreach activities of the large cultural institutions, both cities have a number of arts and creative third sector organisations and individual artists undertaking intermediary activities in and with poorer communities.

Birmingham is a city of 1.1m people in a wider West Midlands region of around 5.6m. At the last census, Birmingham was seen to be a relatively young city, with 22.8% of its population under the age of 16 compared with an English average of 18.9%. The city is 57.9% white, with the largest non-white group being of Pakistani origins, representing around 13.5% of the population. The city's outer suburbs tend to be wealthier, whiter and older, the inner areas are poorer, younger and more diverse. The Sparkbrook ward of which Balsall Heath is part had a population in which around 61% were of Asian origins (primarily Pakistani) at the 2011 census, with 22% of households not having anyone who spoke English as their first language. Sparkbrook ward also has other markers of deprivation, with 23% of households overcrowded, nearly double the city average, while 31% of residents lack any formal qualifications, compared with a Birmingham average of 21%.

About half of Balsall Heath was subject to slum clearance after 1945 and the area became a first stopping-off point for different waves of migrants coming into the city – most recently from Somalia and Afghanistan (Jones et al, 2017). Its unsavoury reputation for drugs, gangs, prostitution and violence has largely faded since the mid-1990s, although there are still significant crime problems within the area. As Long (see Chapter four of this volume) details, the neighbourhood was historically the site of a rich cultural scene, which continues to this day, evolving into new forms. Balsall Heath sits on the corridor that links the wealthier neighbourhoods of Kings Heath and Moseley with the city's arts and creative district in Digbeth but has thus far resisted gentrification.

The population of Salford is around 233,000 and it sits within the Greater Manchester region of around 2.8m people. Salford is 90% white, with 19.3% of its population under the age of 16. Within Salford, Ordsall is 80% white and only 13% of households contain no one with English as their first language. Around 12% of Ordsall's population are students, with the University of Salford located on the edge of the neighbourhood. Large parts of the area were subject to comprehensive demolition in the 1950s and 1960s, with many of the replacement high-rise and other dwellings themselves having been demolished since the 1980s. The most famous survivor of these different phases of clearance is perhaps the Salford Lads Club, built in 1903, which appeared in the artwork for The Smiths' 1986 album, *The Queen is Dead*.

As Symons (Chapter thirteen in this volume) highlights, Ordsall has a rich cultural infrastructure of deeply rooted community organisations. These contrast starkly with the affluence of MediaCityUK, which falls within the boundaries of Ordsall and has been the subject of extensive regeneration expenditure to clean up the old docklands. MediaCityUK is home to branch offices for ITV, the BBC, SIS and Ericsson among others, as well as The Lowry, a large theatre and gallery space housed in an iconic building. This contrast between very wealthy and highly deprived parts of the ward make Ordsall a fascinating case study of the ways in which proximity to the creative industries does not translate into rapid growth for poorer neighbourhoods.

The structure of this book

This book is divided into three sections. In the first, *Changing contexts*, we examine the landscape in which cultural intermediation is operating today. Chapter one by Brook et al brings together work led by Dave O'Brien undertaking a rigorous statistical investigation alongside extensive interviewing of practitioners to produce a class-based analysis of the wider creative economy. In recent years, what was traditionally referred to as 'the arts' has effectively been unbundled from wider policy discussions of a distinct creative economy based around IT and digital. This chapter asks us to look past outliers and anecdotal evidence about individuals from different backgrounds making it to the top of the cultural sector, demonstrating instead that middle-class white men still dominate management and leadership roles. Thus, while arts and cultural policy is still fixated on older New Labour ideas of fostering social equality through increasing access, the cultural sector *itself* remains resolutely socially closed, segregated on class and gender lines. This of course raises significant questions about the extent to which the sector really can play a meaningful intermediating role in attempting to raise communities out of poverty when its doors are firmly shut for all but a lucky few.

This wider concern is also reflected in the geographical and value chain analysis undertaken by De Propris in Chapter two. By attempting to split out different elements of the value chain of cultural production, De Propris identifies three types of intermediation activity that operate at the different stages: creative, commodifying and outreach. The chapter thus begins to break down the somewhat diffuse landscape of cultural intermediation, to think through the different roles that intermediation can play. If intermediation activity is supposed to play a significant role in helping engage poorer communities with the benefits of the wider creative economy, the geographical analysis De Propris presents paints a problematic picture. Location quotients for intermediation at the creative and outreach stages of the cultural production value chain show that this activity is disproportionately concentrated in parts of London, with smaller pockets in wealthier neighbourhoods elsewhere in England.

Our Ordsall case study actually scores quite well for the presence of cultural intermediation activity because MediaCityUK is located within its boundaries. As Chapter three by Perry and Symons begins to indicate, however, geographic proximity is no guarantee of overspill effects. They argue for a policy landscape that begins to see culture as being deeply interwoven with people's lives and that this lived cultural ecology challenges ideas of the creative city and culture as something which is *done to* communities. This challenges some of the policy notions that the primary role of the cultural sector is to instrumentally drive economic activity and social justice. Reflecting on the authors' *Ideas4Ordsall* initiative, they note that communities are already understood through everyday cultural activities and do not need externally imposed notions of culture in order to drive community cohesion. The rich case studies they reflect on here give a lie to the notion that intermediaries need to come into a neighbourhood to 'save' it through culture brought from outside.

This is a theme picked up by Long in Chapter four, examining the role of amateurism or non-professional production. If individuals are already engaged in making their own cultural products, then how should this activity be regarded and valued within wider cultural policy? Given Brook et al's analysis (Chapter one, this volume), however, such productive amateurism cannot be seen as a pathway into careers within the creative economy for all but the lucky few within poorer communities. Instead, the role of intermediaries in helping to encourage amateur production falls back into discussions of enhancing wider cultural democracy, building confidence and giving people a sense of agency in an age of precarity. Indeed, connecting back to Perry and Symons in Chapter three, Long asks whether the contribution made by amateur production to the cultural ecology within a community is properly understood within policy. Given that cultural activity is already ongoing in communities, there are important questions about the role of intermediaries in bringing out those activities. Reading these two chapters together, it is clear that cultural activity is already a major part of life in deprived communities thanks to the intervention of different intermediary processes, from TV shows to community arts. This also demonstrates the much more significant point that cultural activity on its own cannot tackle entrenched poverty.

The second section of the book, *Practices of cultural intermediation*, focuses on how intermediation processes play out within communities. The opening Chapter five, by Long and Warren, takes a detailed overview of Birmingham's Balsall Heath area, examining some of its complexities and contradictions. Tracing its history of migration and transition, they highlight the rich cultural scene that has evolved with the many changes to this neighbourhood. As a predominantly Muslim neighbourhood today, the area is held up as a symbol of Birmingham's culture of diversity and tolerance. The authors explored the neighbourhood on foot with residents as a means of examining cultural activity as part of the lived experience of place. This raises fascinating issues regarding who has access to different public spaces and cultural activities (as well as who is able to participate in walking-based research), particularly given conservative attitudes to gender roles within the neighbourhood's Muslim community.

This book contains several interventions from intermediaries who were involved in the research in different ways. The first of these is Chapter six by Burwood examining his *Some cities* photography project. A fine arts photographer by background, Burwood and his collaborator Andrew Jackson set up a studio within Balsall Heath, running photographic courses for local residents and a web-based project collecting people's images of the city. Burwood's intervention is interesting because it shows how ephemeral intermediation activity can be. Despite the good work and enthusiasm they generated among their participants, *Some cities* was relatively short lived. As the initial funding for this activity wound down, both organisers involved decided to move onto other artistic endeavours rather than attempting to keep their intermediary activity going through pursuing alternative funding sources.

Of course, intermediaries are not obliged to continue being intermediaries at all stages of their career. The sector is inherently unstable, as Perry discusses in Chapter seven, reflecting on the position within urban policy of cultural intermediaries who directly work with deprived communities. In the governance of cultural activity, the work of cultural intermediaries operating in the liminal spaces between arts and community action is poorly understood and recognised within existing policy frames. With many intermediaries working on soft skills and confidence within deprived communities rather than cultural activities per se, they do not fit neatly into policy boxes around how cultural activity is *supposed* to operate. Despite, therefore, playing a vital linking role between an everyday cultural ecology within communities and wider urban policy, the role of this kind of intermediary activity is underappreciated and underfunded. Indeed, the more recent closure of two key intermediary organisations which Perry collaborated with during the research is emblematic of the lack of capacity within policy making for recognising the value of this kind of work.

In Chapter eight, Jones explores participatory budgeting for culture as a specific type of intermediation activity. Much of the work around participatory budgeting was developed as a means of bypassing corrupt local elites and creating better governance in developing countries. Nonetheless, there have been attempts to give power back to communities to set spending priorities within their neighbourhoods, with notable examples highlighted in North America and Scotland. The chapter reflects on two attempts to hand more control over cultural spend to communities in Birmingham as part of the *Cultural intermediation* project. The chapter discusses two significant issues. The first concerns how authorities are reluctant to hand full control over spending decisions to neighbourhoods, with a tendency to push communities towards the funders' spending priorities. Second, and related to this, is a lack of capacity at neighbourhood level to move beyond the ideas generation stage, towards having the confidence to design and commission cultural projects to *realise* those ideas. Again, this speaks to wider problems in deprived communities – notably education, skills and confidence – that cannot be tackled simply by adding cultural activity.

That question of confidence is directly addressed in the second intervention by one of our intermediary participants. Kiyani in Chapter nine reflects on a portrait project with community 'heroes'. As part of the project, her experience was somewhere between being a budding creative producer being helped by intermediaries and becoming an intermediary in her own right by highlighting the strengths of the community she was working with. Ultimately, by having some of her work displayed on buses passing through the neighbourhood she was using her work to cheerlead the community and help remake its image for those elsewhere in the city who see it purely as a neighbourhood struggling with poverty. It was, however, a journey for her, needing to build the confidence necessary to deliver on her artistic vision.

Ager's Chapter ten examines the production of the Bristol Radical Film Festival. Dedicated to bringing interesting and socially challenging work to their audience, the festival itself played an important intermediary role within the city's cultural ecology. More interesting, perhaps, is the detail of how the organisers put the festival together, particularly in the way that association with a university gave them a cultural legitimacy that made it easier to organise the event. This idea of borrowing institutional legitimacy gives intermediary status to the university even though the institution was ultimately not involved in producing the festival. In turn, this raises questions about whether it is possible to capture and value the impact of institutions as intermediaries when they may not even be aware that they are playing a significant role in enabling a cultural activity to take place.

In the final section, *Evaluation, impact and methodology*, we make some critical reflections on practitioner- and researcher-led intermediary practices. Isakjee in Chapter eleven examines how the aspirations that researchers bring into a project can have a significant role in shaping the intermediary activity they become involved with – not always for the better. The UK's community cohesion agenda sought to calm anxieties about 'problematic' Muslim communities, by promoting intercultural understanding and tolerance for difference. The chapter describes how the researchers themselves unconsciously attempted to 'fix' the community they were working with by pushing participants to work on projects across ethnic divides. The cultural projects undertaken can thus be read as being less directed towards addressing the aspirations of the participants and more towards addressing the liberal guilt of the researchers.

Jam's Chapter twelve takes the form of a poem, employing an artistic methodology building on a filmmaking project undertaken with residents in Balsall Heath. By collecting stories from residents about their neighbourhood, Jam was able to give space to alternative accounts about the area that rarely come through in the official record. Jam synthesises these accounts into an artistic form, with the poem giving a rhythm and lyricism that captures the diversity and dynamism of the neighbourhood. Although the final artistic product is very much that of the poet, it demonstrates a method for intermediating activity seeking to give creative voice to residents which can itself be the basis of artistic production (see also Jones and Jam (2016) and Ali, Chapter fourteen in this volume).

Building on this idea that local residents are themselves experts in understanding a neighbourhood, Symons' Chapter thirteen offers a critical account of ethnographic research in Ordsall. In reflecting on her attempt to engage the community with research on cultural activity, Symons notes that initial hostility to the project had to be broken down through careful and respectful listening to that community. Through that deep ethnographic engagement an understanding was developed of the extent to which issues of cultural activities and caring for the community were entwined. Her approach also meant that the research process could itself be adapted in response to the *actual* needs of the community, rather than a top-down assumption of what needed to be done by the research team.

But what of the artist working with and within a community and the tension between artistic vision and community need? This is one of the issues explored by Ali in Chapter fourteen, as he discusses the development of his artistic practice. The street art images he makes can be seen as a socially conscious attempt to explore identity in an age of uncertainty, as well as seeking to bring beautiful works to communities living in rundown and deprived neighbourhoods. Although a Birmingham local, with a practice rooted in the Sparkbrook district, Ali works internationally and is unafraid to make unflattering comparisons between the city's cultural scene and that of established global art hubs. Ali's practice with Soul City Arts has been a combination of working with communities, while also delivering his own artistic vision for people to engage with or dislike as they wish. His chapter, like Burwood's Chapter six, also demonstrates a restlessness, a need to move to new pursuits rather than simply being pigeonholed as the Muslim artist who works with deprived communities. Again, this highlights the idea that the types of intermediation practised by artists will evolve, coming in and out of alignment with the direction that they are taking with their creative practice at different career stages.

The final substantive chapter in the book, Chapter fifteen, is by Vaughan Jones. Sitting between the roles of artist, intermediary and researcher, she takes the long view on the evolution of more socially engaged arts practice. Frustrated by the move towards more individualised and depoliticised practices of engaged art that came to the fore in the 1990s, she relates her own artistic response to this with the formation of the *1mile²* project. Founded with a philosophy to counter the idea that artists should parachute in to *do* art in a neighbourhood, *1mile²* worked with communities to drive a process of cultural learning, with the arts organisation playing a facilitating role rather than dictating the course of action.

The book concludes with a wider reflection on the state of cultural policy, the creative economy and the position of communities suffering from socioeconomic deprivation. On the one hand, this book offers space for optimism about the existence of thriving cultural ecosystems in deprived communities which are being enhanced by different types of intermediation activities. Nonetheless, the book circles back to a core question: in the face of savage cuts to public spending that have hit the poorest communities hardest, can cultural and creative activity really make that much difference? If communities can *do* culture, both with and without intermediation, then access to culture does not seem to be a determining factor for solving economic inequality and enhancing social justice. Given the class segregation of the cultural sector and wider creative economy, getting employment in this field will only be the answer for a handful of people. This in turn raises much harder questions about the role of cultural intermediation practices as part of a suite of public spending priorities needed to overcome entrenched poverty.

References

Ashworth, G. (2009) 'The instruments of place branding: how is it done?' *European Spatial Research and Policy*, 16: 9-22.

Bakhshi, H., Hargreaves, I. and Mateos-Garcia, J. (2013) *A manifesto for the creative economy*, London: NESTA.

Barberá, P., Jost, J. T., Nagler, J. et al, (2015) 'Tweeting from left to right: is online political communication more than an echo chamber?', *Psychological Science*, 26: 1531-42.

Beard, R. L. (2011) 'Art therapies and dementia care: a systematic review', *Dementia*, 11(5): 633-56.

Belfiore, E. (2002) 'Art as a means of alleviating social exclusion: does it really work? A critique of instrumental cultural policies and social impact studies in the UK', *International Journal of Cultural Policy*, 8: 91-106.

Belfiore, E. (2006) 'The social impacts of the arts – myth or reality?' in M. Mirza (ed) *Culture vultures: is UK arts policy damaging the arts?*, London: Policy Exchange, pp. 20-37.

Blythe, M. (2001) 'The work of art in the age of digital reproduction: the significance of the creative industries', *Journal of Art & Design Education*, 20: 144-50.

Bourdieu, P. (1984) *Distinction: A social critique of the judgement of taste*, London: Routledge & Kegan Paul.

Cartiere, C. and Zebracki, M. (2015) 'Introduction', in C. Cartiere and M. Zebracki (eds) *The everyday practice of public art: Art, space and social inclusion*, Abingdon: Routledge, pp. 1-10.

Centre for Leisure and Sport Research (2002) *Count me in: The dimensions of social inclusion through culture and sport. A report for the Department for Culture, Media and Sport*, Leeds: Leeds Metropolitan University.

DCMS (2001) *Creative Industries Mapping Documents 2001*, Available at www.gov.uk/government/publications/creative-industries-mapping-documents-2001

DCMS (2006) *Developing entrepreneurship for the creative industries*, London: DCMS.

Florida, R. (2002) *The rise of the creative class and how it's transforming work, leisure, community and everyday life*, New York: Basic Books.

Forsyth, M. (2012) 'Lifting the lid on "The Community": who has the right to control access to traditional knowledge and expressions of culture?', *International Journal of Cultural Property*, 19: 1-31.

Frug, J. (1996) 'The geography of community', *Stanford Law Review*, 48: 1047-108.

Grossi, E., Tavano Blessi, G., Sacco, P. L. et al, (2012) 'The interaction between culture, health and psychological well-being: data mining from the italian culture and well-being project', *Journal of Happiness Studies*, 13: 129-48.

Hadley, S. and Belfiore, E. (2018) 'Cultural democracy and cultural policy', *Cultural Trends*, 27(3): 218-23.

Hamilton, C., Hinks, S. and Petticrew, M. (2003) 'Arts for health: still searching for the Holy Grail', *Journal of Epidemiology and Community Health*, 57: 401-02.

Hesmondhalgh, D. (2007) *The cultural industries* (2nd edn), London: Sage.

Hipp, J. R. and Perrin, A. (2006) 'Nested loyalties: local networks' effects on neighbourhood and community cohesion', *Urban Studies*, 43: 2503-23.

Jermyn, H. (2001) *The arts and social exclusion: a review prepared for the Arts Council of England*, accessed 9 August 2016: http://creativecity.smallboxcms.com/database/files/library/arts_social_exclusion_uk.pdf.

Jones, P., Isakjee, A., Jam, C. et al (2017) 'Urban landscapes and the atmosphere of place: exploring subjective experience in the study of urban form', *Urban Morphology*, 21: 29-40.

Jones, P. and Jam, C. (2016) 'Creating ambiances, co-constructing place: a poetic transect across the city', *Area*, 48: 317-24.

Karkou, V. and Glasman, J. (2004) 'Arts, education and society: the role of the arts in promoting the emotional wellbeing and social inclusion of young people', *Support for Learning*, 19: 57–65.

Khomami, N. and Halliday, J. (2015) 'Shoreditch Cereal Killer Cafe targeted in anti-gentrification protests', *The Guardian* 27 September: https://www.theguardian.com/uknews/2015/sep/2027/shoreditch-cereal-cafe-targeted-by anti-gentrification-protesters (accessed 18 June 2016).

Markusen, A. (2010) 'Organizational complexity in the regional cultural economy'. *Regional Studies*, 44: 813-28.

Matarasso, F. (1997) *Use or ornament? The social impact of participation in the arts*, London: Comedia.

McCarthy, J. (2005) 'Devolution in the woods: community forestry as hybrid neoliberalism', *Environment and Planning A*, 37: 995-1014.

Miles, A. and Sullivan, A. (2012) 'Understanding participation in culture and sport: mixing methods, reordering knowledges', *Cultural Trends*, 21: 311-24.

Nixon, S. and Gay, P. D. (2002) 'Who needs cultural intermediaries?' *Cultural Studies*, 16: 495-500.

O'Brien, D., Laurison, D., Miles, A. et al (2016) 'Are the creative industries meritocratic? An analysis of the 2014 British Labour Force Survey', *Cultural Trends*, 25: 116-31.

O'Connor, J. (2015) 'Intermediaries and imaginaries in the cultural and creative industries', *Regional Studies*, 49(3): 374-87.

Oakley, K. (2006) 'Include us out: economic development and social policy in the creative industries', *Cultural Trends*, 15: 255-73.

Raco, M. (2013) *State-led privatisation and the demise of the democratic state: Welfare reform and localism in an era of regulatory capitalism*, Farnham: Ashgate.

Robson, B., Bradford, M., Deas, I. et al (1994) *Assessing the impact of urban policy*, London: HMSO.

Sandell, R. (1998) 'Museums as agents of social inclusion', *Museum Management and Curatorship*, 17: 401-18.

Sanderson, P. (2008) 'The arts, social inclusion and social class: the case of dance', *British Educational Research Journal*, 34: 467-90.

Spalek, B. and Lambert, R. (2008) 'Muslim communities, counter-terrorism and counter-radicalisation: a critically reflective approach to engagement', *International Journal of Law, Crime and Justice*, 36: 257-70.

Suler, J. (2004) 'The online disinhibition effect', *CyberPsychology & Behavior*, 7: 321-26.

Take Two (2015) *Take Two Interactive Software Inc. Annual Report 2015*, http://ir.take2games.com/phoenix.zhtml?c=86428&p=irol-reportsannual:

Taylor, C. (2015) 'Between culture, policy and industry: modalities of intermediation in the creative economy', *Regional Studies*, 49: 362-73.

Tetlow, G., O'Connor, S. and Tighe, C. (2016) 'In Brexit Britain, the Ins and Outs are strangers to each other', *Financial Times*, 24 June.

The Warwick Commission (2015) *Enriching Britain: culture, creativity and growth. The 2015 Report by the Warwick Commission on the Future of Cultural Value*, Warwick: University of Warwick.

Zukin, S. (1982) *Loft living: Culture and capital in urban change*, Baltimore: Johns Hopkins University Press.

Part One
Changing contexts

ONE

The creative economy, the creative class and cultural intermediation

Orian Brook, Dave O'Brien and Mark Taylor*

Introduction

'*Culture is one of the things that unites us all and expresses our identity. We ignore that at our peril.*'

Tony Hall, Director General, BBC

'*In challenging times, the diverse cultural riches of the UK provide some of our most potent assets, and play a vital role in presenting the UK as an international, outwardly focused and creative nation.*'

Graham Sheffield, Director Arts, British Council

'*Arts are one of the greatest forces for openness and social mobility.*'

Matt Hancock, Minister for Culture (2016–18), UK

'*What does theatre mean? Of course it means entertainment and provocation and the power of story as a way of understanding who we are. But increasingly it is important also that theatre is the centre of debate for what's going on in the nation.*'

Rufus Norris, Artistic Director, National Theatre

How does culture relate to social inequality? The introduction to this book noted the aims of transforming individual and community lives by cultural engagement, while also showing, correctly, deep scepticism about this approach as it has been advocated and applied by policy makers. As a result, the book turns towards the role of intermediaries and intermediation; this is a focus which inevitably raises questions as to the broader structures of cultural production and cultural consumption within, or sometimes against, which intermediation takes place. This chapter aims to address these broader structures, setting the scene for the discussions that follow.

There is a relatively longstanding literature on *who* cultural intermediaries are and their position within cultural fields (Negus, 2002; Nixon and DuGay, 2002; Moor, 2008; Friedman, 2015). This set of discussions intersects with broader and more recent research exploring how the organisation of cultural production shapes, and is in turn shaped by, how consumption is patterned (Childress, 2017; Alaclovska, 2017; O'Brien et al, 2017). Within studies of cultural production and its workforce, exclusions associated with class, ethnicity and gender have come to the fore (Conor et al, 2015; O'Brien et al, 2016; Oakley et al, 2017; Saha, 2017; Gerber, 2017). Cultural work has thus become a site for understanding how cultural production, and the intermediaries and intermediation processes enabled within cultural production, function to replicate broader social inequalities (O'Brien and Oakley, 2015).

Here we address the dynamics of cultural work as a means to think about how cultural intermediation is bound up with the social reproduction of inequality. In contrast to most voices in public policy and, sadly, many prominent voices within the cultural sector such as the ones that open this chapter, the cultural production system of the UK is unlikely to deliver the sorts of social goals associated with the values of the sector.

The empirical work is focused on British examples. As a result, the chapter draws on the specificity of social organisation in Britain, which is to say the role of class as both a social scientific category and national obsession (Cannadine, 1998; Savage, 2010). In the British case, culture is organised to be productive of specific norms of the white, male, able-bodied middle class (Friedman and O'Brien 2017). Moreover, it is also ideologically productive as part of liberal cosmopolitanism, which in turn reinforces its exclusiveness.

The discussion begins with the thorny issue of class as a means to think about cultural intermediation. It then moves on to outline research findings developed as part of the *Cultural intermediation* project and follow-on research. The research findings demonstrate the characteristics of a cultural or creative 'class' within the British middle class who are dominant within the production, representation(s) and consumption of British cultural economy. The characteristics of this class, their social and economic basis, their values and tastes, along with their commitment to a socially transformative conception of culture, are theorised as important barriers to social change and crucial elements in the social reproduction of inequality. With this in mind, the chapter concludes by posing the question of the exact contribution cultural intermediation might make, specifically to challenge or perhaps transform the social settlement of an unequal creative class.

Classing the creative class?

One way of thinking about intermediaries is with reference to another category that was, for a time, dominant in both research and public policy approaches to the creative economy. This is Richard Florida's (2002) conception of the 'creative class'. This term has been subject to extensive academic critique, which it is unnecessary to rehearse here (see Markusen, 2006, and Mould, 2015). Indeed, the most notable rejection of Florida's work has been over attempts to apply 'creative' solutions to urban problems (Peck, 2005). The rejections of the idea of a 'creative class' have been bound up with the broader project of creative and cultural industries, as: a concept within cultural studies (McRobbie, 2015); a governmental agenda (Prince 2014); an economic sector, whatever the social scientific and policy work done to demarcate this sector (DCMS, 2018); and an emergent area of academic study (Ashton and Noonan, 2013).

The exact contours of the cultural and creative industries are, of course, now very well debated, both by academics (Hesmondhalgh, 2013; Oakley and O'Connor, 2016) and by policy makers and consultants aiming to draw boundaries around a sector seemingly full of 'good news' (Prince, 2014). Indeed, this latter set of research work has recently culminated in an explicit rejection of the relationship between cultural policy and creative industries (Bakhshi and Cunningham, 2016), with an attended disaggregation of economic data and measurement at policy level (DCMS, 2018). Some academics have sought to decouple specific forms of IT consultancy from activities more usually associated with 'cultural' production, such as music or visual arts (Campbell et al, 2019, in press). It would seem, in policy terms at least, we are seeing explicitly digital or computer services visions of creative industries emerging. Meanwhile, cultural occupations are relegated to the historic territory of cultural policy discussions over arts funding, social impacts or education.

This would seem, then, a strange juncture to return to Florida. However, interrogating the idea of a 'creative class' is important for two reasons: first, because of the broader, albeit much debated, changes in the middle class in the UK; and second, because of the relationship between these possible transformations and social inequality, particularly, for present purposes, with regard to the creative economy.

This first reason is grounded in the discussions over the role of class in contemporary Britain (see Bottero, 2004; Roberts, 2011; Savage, 2015; Skeggs, 2015). Within this literature there has been particular attention to transformations of the class structure in Britain, whether in terms of the emergence of new groupings at the 'top' (Savage, 2015) or 'bottom' (Standing, 2014) of the social structure, or in terms of the specific schemes used to classify social groups (Savage, 2015). This latter set of discussions, which followed the BBC's academic partnership on *The Great British class survey* (GBCS), reflected the longstanding tensions between differing class schemas (summarised in Roberts, 2011, chapter 2) concerned with occupational relationships, and the rise of an approach to class attuned to the importance of cultural or symbolic resources (summarised and usefully critiqued by Bottero, 2004).

The particulars of debates on class schemas notwithstanding, various authors have pointed to important transformations within the British middle class. For some this is directly associated with cultural and creative work, such as McRobbie's (2015) theorisation of precariousness in creative occupations foreshadowing a broader transformation of middle-class professions more generally. For others, this theme of precariousness has been important in understanding changes in the material basis of middle-class life, particularly in home ownership as a key part of middle-class identity formation, under threat from the rising exclusivity associated with the housing boom in London (Benson and Jackson, 2017). Discussions of educational routes, associated with the transformations of access to higher education, are also important (Wakeling and Savage, 2015).

Most importantly for present purposes is an argument over the changing occupational basis for the British middle class, with a bifurcation of service occupations into more technical and more socio-cultural jobs. This argument is theorised in Savage's (2010) work on the rise of a specific, technical middle class orientation following the end of World War II, and it reflects arguments based on the analysis of British and Dutch social mobility data (Guveli, 2006). Here important social cleavages are identified between socio-cultural occupations (a broad category including medicine and science, as well as 'cultural' work) and technocratic middle-class work: social and cultural specialists differ from technocrats in their social-political and economic preferences and behaviour although, when education is factored in, there are similarities in terms of cultural taste. Crucially, this new class formation of socio-cultural specialists was seen to be increasingly socially closed, an important point to note in the context of the relationship between class formations and social inequality.

In educational terms, this comparative research is extended and supported by British data identifying patterns of taste relative to educational choices (Reeves and de Vries, 2016: 550), whereby 'Compared to non-graduates, arts, humanities, and social science graduates are more likely to enjoy highbrow directors and artists, and are more likely to be cultural omnivores; while graduates from other subjects are not clearly distinct from non-graduates in their cultural preferences'. Indeed, HMRC (2016) data shows those studying arts and creative subjects were likely to have the lowest levels of earnings five years after graduation. This, again, is important in the context of specific occupational patterns within the creative economy and their effects on production, representation and consumption of culture in the UK. Culture then is bound up with new formations within the British middle class, even if these new formations do not overturn existing class schemas.

We might read this as a continuation of the longstanding belief of a dissonance between two cultures, albeit one taken from the cloisters of Snow's (1959) essay into the call centre, the coffee shop and the aerospace lab. However, as Edgerton (2005) has usefully noted, only a profoundly technocratic and technological nation could have given rise to the projection of Snow's concerns. As such, we might find a different ground upon which to scaffold the argument that there is a key division within the middle class, one with important implications for cultural intermediation.

The experience of the GBCS debates (for example, Rollock, 2014; Mills, 2014; Skeggs, 2015) suggests the need for caution when pronouncing new classes (as does, incidentally, the debate over Standing's 2014 suggestion of the 'precariat' as a new class; Scully, 2016). Thus, it is important not to read the following discussion as an intervention redefining the various class schemes used to understand contemporary and historic British life (Roberts, 2011). Instead, we are highlighting the empirical evidence suggesting that specific classed occupations have particular cultural bases. This claim should be uncontroversial, as it is present across the sociological canon (for example, Bourdieu, 1984), historical work (Thompson, 1991; Todd, 2015), and more recent sociology of British life (for example, Savage, 2015). What matters in relation to cultural or creative occupations is the relationship between the cultural basis for getting into and getting on in a given job and the impact on the wider individual, community and national representations produced by this occupational settlement.

While the exact *causal* relationship is not known, there is clearly a potential correlation between the system of cultural production, specifically its occupational basis, the representations produced by that system, and the social patterns of consumption (Oakley and O'Brien, 2015; Hesmondhalgh, 2018).

Who are the creative class?

Before turning to the creative class, it is worth noting the intersection of governmental definitions of the creative industries with the rise of a 'creative class'. In what follows, the analysis begins with the UK's Department for Culture, Media and Sport (DCMS) definitions of cultural and creative occupations and sectors of industrial activity. It uses this definition to comment on the specific contours of these occupations as constituting a distinct and separate social formation. While there may be a circularity to this approach, the discussion places the definitional decisions in the context of the bifurcation of the middle class discussed above. DCMS's well-known formation of creative industries covers nine occupational clusters: advertising and marketing; architecture; crafts; design (product, graphic and fashion design); film, TV, radio and photography; IT, software and computer services; publishing; museums, galleries and libraries; and music, performing and visual arts. These classifications correspond with around 30 groups of occupations, for example 'music, performing and visual arts' is constituted by: artists; actors, entertainers and presenters; dancers and choreographers; and musicians. Within these sectors, the core 'cultural' occupations have particular occupational characteristics, suggesting a cohesive creative or cultural class. These characteristics are outlined as we proceed.

Social closure

Within the cultural and creative part of the economy we can see that inequality – by gender, ethnicity, and social and economic status – is an important characteristic (O'Brien et al, 2016). O'Brien et al (2016) and Oakley et al (2017) have shown the exclusivity of cultural and creative work by social class. Concentrating on the 'cultural' occupations in the DCMS definition (as opposed to those more 'creative' occupations associated with IT and advertising) we can see a highly educated, socially closed, workforce. Both O'Brien et al (2016) and Oakley et al (2017) use data from the Office for National Statistics' Labour Force Survey to demonstrate the various axes of exclusion.

We can, for example, see significant underrepresentations of women in the workforce for film, TV, video, radio and photography. Women constitute only a quarter of this workforce, despite being half of the workforce in the economy overall (O'Brien et al, 2016). There are similar underrepresentations for individuals from minority ethnic groups. All the core cultural sectors are overwhelmingly white: music, performing and visual arts (93%); publishing (93%); film, TV, video, radio and photography (93%); and museums, galleries, and libraries (97.5%). This compares with the 89% of the workforce who are white. This is especially troubling in the context of the uneven geography of cultural production, which is mostly focused on London (DCMS, 2018), a city which is much more multiethnic and multicultural than the rest of the country. As Oakley et al (2017) show, although the total number of people from minority ethnic groups in the capital's creative workforce is higher than the rest of the country (representing 17%), as a proportion, this is much lower than the overall London population (around 40%).

The third axis of exclusion is socioeconomic origin. Oakley et al (2017) found just under 14% of the overall workforce are from higher managerial and professional social origins. These origins are measured by asking about parental occupation when current workers were growing up. All creative occupations, excluding craft, have overrepresentations of this social group. Over a quarter of all workers in the core creative occupations – film, museums, music and publishing – in this dataset, are 'middle class', meaning an overrepresentation of those from the most elite social origins compared with the overall population. Moreover, this overrepresentation is mirrored by an underrepresentation of those from working-class backgrounds; for example, in publishing 37% of the sector are from 'middle-class' social origins, while only just over 12.5% are from working-class starting points. This 12.5% is an underrepresentation compared with the workforce as a whole (35%) from working-class social origins.

At the same time, Labour Force Survey data suggests low rates of pay for these, currently, socially exclusive occupations. O'Brien et al (2016) calculated that, outside of film, TV, radio and photography, the core cultural sectors have the lowest rates of pay, lower than the average for similar middle-class (NS-SEC 1 and 2) occupations and lower than the average for the workforce as a whole. Alongside this, there are important pay differences within occupations according to gender and social class.

This is crucial in light of the discussion above of the emergence of a new middle class formation. We can say that work in the cultural sector is characterised by a narrow social basis underpinning those who are presently within the occupations, and that there are important barriers, such as earnings potential, which may further this narrow social basis. This is reinforced in comparison with the class basis of other occupations at the top of the class structure in Britain. Friedman et al (2017) show how journalists and the creative industries have some of the poorest levels of 'working-class' representation in their current workforces, looking more like the exclusive professions of law or medicine in terms of their class composition.

This social closure operates in other ways. In interview and survey fieldwork, Brook et al (2018) found evidence of social closure by friendship networks. The cultural workers involved in their study were least likely, on average, to know people in 'working-class' occupations, such as bus driver or postman, and most likely to know those working in other cultural occupations. This dataset resembled the similarly closed friendship networks of those working in NS-SEC 1 and 2 professions surveyed by the *Culture, class and social exclusion* project during the mid-2000s (Warde et al, 2009). Again, we have evidence for the social closure of a creative class, but here it is one, as with Friedman et al's (2017) work that points to a broader problem with elite occupations within British society.

Values

Values were one of the most important elements in Florida's (2002) claim of a new 'creative class' transforming American urban contexts. These values were: individuality and non-conformity; openness to difference and the embrace of diversity; and meritocracy, with an associated rejection of wealth as a means of judging themselves and their lives. Florida (2002) noted the contradictions and ironies of these positions: meritocracy potentially reinforced and naturalised existing, social structural, inequalities; openness and tolerance were potentially only possible in terms of a diversity of elites; and limitations were created by a creative class monopolising urban resources as they attempted to cluster together. Again, notwithstanding the coherence or otherwise of Florida's creative class, there is an important insight that applies to cultural economy in the UK. This relates to the value formations expressed by those working in cultural occupations. McAndrew et al (2017) used British Social Attitudes survey data to demonstrate that cultural occupations (such as visual arts, performance and music) were characterised by left wing, anti-authoritarian and pro-welfare clusters of values. Indeed, individuals working in cultural occupations had the most pro-welfare, left-wing, and anti-authoritarian responses to values questions of any occupational group in the UK. Not only were the individual's responses characterised by these values, the occupations themselves were important: even when controlling for a variety of demographic and social characteristics, the occupations remained as outliers compared to the rest of the population and similar 'middle-class' jobs.

Cultural consumption

Those working in cultural and creative occupations also have consumption patterns that differ from the general population, in particular differing from those in 'working-class' occupations (Campbell et al, 2018). They are most likely to consume any given art form, according to longitudinal data from the DCMS *Taking part* survey, and are, from this same data, highly omnivorous, moving across genres and art forms in their taste patterns. Again, this is an important difference to the general population, where only around 8% of the British population, according to *Taking part* data, fit the pattern of being most highly culturally engaged (Taylor, 2016).

The transformative power of culture

We can return to Brook et al's (2018) data, and to the comments which opened this chapter, to mark a final characteristic of the cultural class. Across 237 interviews with cultural workers, Brook et al found a strong commitment to the importance of culture and the intertwined social potential of engagement. For example, those working in museums and galleries had a consistent commitment to the transformative impact of engagement, participation and consumption of museum and gallery work. This transformation ranged from educational impacts, through social cohesion, to a sense of culture being able to make the world a better place and heal the wounds of a British polity fractured by a range of social divisions and social inequalities. Similar narratives were found across theatremakers and others in performing arts. This reinforces work by Durrer and O'Brien (2014) that concentrated on education officers in cultural institutions with similar commitment to the transformative potential of culture. Moreover, it suggests Bennett's conception of a 'culture complex' (2013), productive of the liberal individual capable of functioning in, and in turn allowing the functioning of, modern British society, is crucial to working in cultural occupations.

The problem of a creative class

So, to reiterate, the 'creative class' may have some important usefulness, albeit reconstituted as a 'cultural class'. This cultural class is characterised by: its social attitudes, which are the most left-wing, anti-authoritarian and liberal in British society, along with an attachment to meritocracy; its social closure, along occupational and social network lines; its specific patterns of taste and consumption; and its commitment to the social role of culture. As the analysis of characteristics noted, part of this argument can be derived from the status of cultural occupations as middle-class occupations. However, as the research surveyed demonstrates, the specific occupational differences are part of a range of consequences for the British way of cultural economy.

It may be the case that the status of cultural occupations as outliers serves a useful social function. Much like the argument for specific professions, such as the judiciary, being isolated from social, economic or cultural influences that might impede their ability to perform their social functions, perhaps the cultural economy in the UK insulates cultural production from tastes, values and commitments that would make them less successful in their work. However, this 'art for art's sake' line of thought, offering cultural workers (as cultural intermediaries) the position of philosopher kings, is limited, being fundamentally at odds with the rhetoric of individuals, institutions and policy makers within the cultural sector. This is visible in both the comments opening this chapter and the claims that cultural artefacts, engagement and participation are an important site for the creation and development of human empathy (Bazalgette, 2016).

This rhetoric of openness and social cohesion would be fatally undermined were the current settlement of the British cultural economy, with its associated social exclusions, to be justified as necessary or essential. For prominent voices within the cultural sector and in cultural policy, the sector offers a route out of a range of social and economic problems. But, as the argument for seeing a British creative or cultural 'class' makes clear, a more problematic outcome is probable.

Conclusion: creative justice and the creative class

This chapter has described the structural inequalities framing cultural intermediation in the British cultural economy. It has sought to problematise the view that cultural intermediaries have a simply benign impact within both the creative economy and beyond into wider society. While this discussion offers a starting point for much of the discussions that follow, by way of conclusion the chapter now turns to consider the idea of creative or cultural justice as it has emerged in recent academic work, and how it might be used to reformulate the role of intermediation. This is a term recently codified by Banks (2017), but a broader concern with a 'just' cultural economy can also be seen across the academic field, notably in recent work by McRobbie (2015) and Hesmondhalgh (2018).

For Banks, creative justice means: respecting cultural objects via evaluation in their own terms; allowing parity of participation in cultural occupations, through fair treatment, equal pay and an end to cultural discrimination; and reducing the physical and mental harms associated with the current organisation of creative and cultural work (Banks, 2017). These principles are enunciated, albeit from differing academic and philosophical lines of thought, by Hesmondhalgh and McRobbie's interventions in discussions of creative labour. There are obvious implications for intermediaries and intermediation here, whether in terms of what is valued or in terms of who has access.

Much of the work on intermediaries has been driven by engagements with Pierre Bourdieu's (1984) work on the sociology of culture; Bourdieu has also been an important influence on the (re)emergence of inequality as a subject for sociological research. Hesmondhalgh (2018) notes the limitations of our current understanding of cultural work as a basis for discussions of social justice, particularly the lack of formal theoretical explanation for the causal relationship between modes of production, forms of representation, and patterns of cultural consumption (see also O'Brien and Oakley, 2015). He looks to Bourdieu's work as a way of solving the problem of class and causal analysis. In his reading of Bourdieu, the role of culture as a means of domination can provide clues to better understanding the relationships between class configurations and cultural production. This might come in the form of: observations or ethnographies of how largely middle-class cultural producers conceive of working-class audiences; how these same middle-class workers 'misrecognise' working-class talents in hiring decisions; and better understandings of the transitions from education to work. These three lines of inquiry are all in the context of, in Hesmondhalgh's argument, the worsening social position of the working class in the UK. By extension we might read into Hesmondhalgh's Bourdieusian turn the possibility of applying this agenda to race, gender, sexuality or disability, with similarly associated questions of the low numbers of these social groups, the problematic and contested nature of their representations, and the uneven spread of their consumption patterns. Moreover, as the rest of the book details, the observational and ethnographic approach is crucial to connecting up intermediation with inequality.

Note

*This chapter draws on work written in collaboration with several colleagues. We'd like to thank Peter Campbell (University of Liverpool), Sam Friedman (London School of Economics), Daniel Laurison (Swarthmore College), Siobhan McAndrew (University of Bristol), Andrew Miles (University of Manchester), and Kate Oakley (University of Leeds). The chapter would also not have been possible without AHRC funding, for the follow-on project: 'Who is missing from the picture? The problem of inequality in the creative economy and what we can do about it', Project Reference AH/P013155/1.

References

Alacovska, A. (2017) 'The gendering power of genres: how female Scandinavian crime fiction writers experience professional authorship', *Organization*, 24(3): 377-96.

Ashton, D., and Noonan, C. (2013) *Cultural work and higher education*, London: Palgrave Macmillan.

Bakhshi, H., and Cunningham, S. (2016) *Cultural policy in the time of the creative industries*, London: NESTA.

Banks, M. (2017) *Creative justice: cultural industries, work and inequality*, London: Rowman & Littlefield.

Bazalgette, P. (2016) *The empathy instinct*, London: John Murray.

Bennett, T. (2013) *Making culture, changing society*, London: Routledge.

Benson, M. and Jackson, E. (2017) 'Making the middle classes on shifting ground? Residential status, performativity and middle-class subjectivities in contemporary London', *British Journal of Sociology*, 68(2): 215-33.

Bottero, W. (2004) 'Class identities and the identities of class', *Sociology*, 38(5): 985-1003.

Bourdieu, P. (1984) *Distinction: A social critique of the judgement of taste*, London: Routledge & Kegan Paul.

Brook, O., O'Brien, D. and Taylor, M. (2018) *Panic! Social class, taste and inequalities in the creative industries*, available from http://createlondon. org/wp-content/uploads/2018/04/Panic-Social-Class-Taste-and-Inequalities-in-the-Creative-Industries1.pdf

Campbell, P., O'Brien, D. and Taylor, M. (2019, in press) 'Cultural engagement and the economic performance of the cultural and creative industries: an occupational critique', *Sociology*.

Cannadine, D. (1998) *Class in Britain,* London: Penguin.

Childress, C. (2017) *Under the cover: The creation, production and reception of a novel*, Princeton: Princeton University Press.

Conor B., Gill, R. and Taylor, S. (2015) *Gender and creative labour*, London: Wiley-Blackwell.

DCMS (2018) *DCMS sector economic estimates methodology*, available from https://www.gov.uk/government/uploads/system/uploads/attachment_data/file/681217/DCMS_Sectors_Economic_Estimates_-_Methodology.pdf accessed 19/2/2018

Durrer, V. and O'Brien, D. (2014) 'Arts promotion' in J. McGuire and J. Matthews (eds) *The cultural intermediaries reader*, London: Sage, pp 100-12.

Edgerton, D. (2005) 'C. P. Snow as anti-historian of British science: revisiting the technocratic moment, 1959-1964', *History of Science*, 43(2): 187-208.

Florida, R. (2002) *The rise of the creative class*, New York: Basic Books.

Friedman, S. (2015) *Comedy and distinction*, London: Routledge.

Friedman, S., Laurison, D. and Macmillan, L. (2017) *Social mobility, the class pay gap and intergenerational worklessness: New insights from the Labour Force Survey*, London: Social Mobility Commission.

Friedman, S. and O'Brien, D. (2017) 'Resistance and resignation: responses to typecasting in British acting', *Cultural Sociology*, 11(3): 359-76.

Gerber, A. (2017) *The work of art: Value in creative careers*, Stanford: Stanford University Press.

Guveli, A. (2006) *New social classes within the service class in the Netherlands and Britain: Adjusting the EGP class schema for the technocrats and the social and cultural specialists*, Unpublished PhD thesis, available from http://repository.ubn.ru.nl/bitstream/handle/2066/56427/56427.pdf?sequence=1

Hesmondhalgh, D. (2013) *The cultural industries*, London: Sage.

Hesmondhalgh, D. (2018) 'The media's failure to represent the working class: explanations from media production and beyond' in J. Deery, and A. Press (eds), *Media and class: TV, film and digital culture*, London: Routledge.

HMRC (2016) 'Graduate outcomes: longitudinal education outcomes (LEO) data', available from https://www.gov.uk/government/statistics/graduate-outcomes-longitudinal-education-outcomes-leo-data

McAndrew, S., O'Brien, D. and Taylor, M. (2017) *Cultural values, imagined community and cultural backlash: Value divergence and social closure among British creative workers*, Working paper, available from https://osf.io/wkxs5/

McRobbie, A. (2015) *Be creative*, Cambridge: Polity Press.

Markusen, A. (2006) 'Urban development and the politics of a creative class: evidence from a study of artists', *Environment and Planning A: Economy and Space*, 38(10): 1921-40.

Mills, C. (2014) 'The Great British class fiasco: a comment on Savage et al', *Sociology*, 48(3): 437-44.

Moor, L. (2008) 'Branding consultants as cultural intermediaries', *Sociological Review*, 56(3): 408-28.

Mould, O. (2015) *Urban subversion and the creative city*, London: Routledge.

Negus, K., (2002) 'The work of cultural intermediaries and the enduring distance between production and consumption', *Cultural Studies*, 16(4): 501-15.

Nixon, S. and Du Gay, P. (2002) 'Who needs cultural intermediaries?', *Cultural Studies*, 16(4): 495-500.

O'Brien, D. and Oakley, K. (2015) *Cultural value and inequality: A critical literature review*, Swindon: AHRC.

O'Brien, D., Laurison, D., Friedman, S., and Miles, A. (2016) 'Are the creative industries meritocratic? An analysis of the 2014 British Labour Force Survey', *Cultural Trends*, 25(2): 116-31.

O'Brien, D., Allen, K., Friedman S. and Saha, A. (2017) 'Producing and consuming inequality: a cultural sociology of the cultural industries', *Cultural Sociology*, 11(3): 271-82.

Oakley K., Laurison D., O'Brien D. and Friedman, S. (2017) 'Cultural capital: arts graduates, spatial inequality, and London's impact on cultural labour markets', *American Behavioural Scientist*, 61(12): 1510-31.

Peck, J. (2005) 'Struggling with the creative class', *International Journal of Urban and Regional Research*, 29(4): 740-70.

Prince, R. (2014) 'Calculative cultural expertise? Consultants and politics in the UK cultural sector', *Sociology*, 48(4): 747-62.

Reeves, A. and de Vries, R. (2016) 'The social gradient in cultural consumption and the information-processing hypothesis', *The Sociological Review*, 64(3): 550-74.

Roberts, K. (2011) *Class in contemporary Britain*, London: Palgrave.

Rollock, N. (2014) 'Race, class and "The harmony of dispositions"', *Sociology*, 48(3): 445-51.

Saha, A. (2017) *Race and the cultural industries*, London: Polity Press.

Savage, M. (2010) *Identities and social change in Britain since 1940: The politics of method*, Oxford: Oxford University Press.

Savage, M. (2015) *Social class in the twenty first century*, London: Pelican.

Scully, B. (2016) 'Precarity North and South: a southern critique of Guy Standing', *Global Labour Journal*, 7(2): 160-73.

Skeggs, B. (2015) 'Introduction: stratification or exploitation, domination, dispossession and devaluation?', *Sociological Review*, 63(2): 205-22.

Snow, C. P. (1959) *The two cultures and the scientific revolution*, Oxford: Oxford University Press.

Standing, G. (2014) *The precariat charter*, London: Bloomsbury.

Taylor, M. (2016) 'Nonparticipation or different styles of participation? Alternative interpretations from Taking Part', *Cultural Trends*, 25(3): 169-81.

Thompson, E. P. (1991) *The making of the English working class*, London: Penguin Books.

Todd, S. (2015) *The People*, London: John Murray.

Wakeling, P. and Savage, M. (2015) 'Entry to elite positions and the stratification of higher education in Britain', *Sociological Review*, 63(2): 290-320.

Warde, A., Silva, E., Bennett, T., Savage, M., Gayo-Cal, M. and Wright, D. (2009) *Culture, class, distinction*, London: Routledge.

TWO

Mapping cultural intermediaries

Lisa De Propris

Theorising cultural intermediation

Since Bourdieu (1984) introduced the concept of cultural intermediaries, a wealth of empirical studies have deployed and refined the concept (O'Brien et al, 2011; Maguire and Matthews, 2012). Here, theory development is blighted not by the definition of culture or cultural intermediaries per se, but by the remarkable breadth of areas to which the concept has been applied. To pick on just a few of these, studies of cultural intermediaries have examined: critics and commentators of literature and other cultural products (Mee and Dowling, 2003; Doane, 2009); lifestyle advocates and consultants (Sherman, 2011; Truninger, 2011); cocktail bartenders (Ocejo, 2012); 'long-haired company freaks' (Powers, 2012); retailers of 'retro' (Baker, 2012); diplomatic missions (Giry-Deloison, 2008); children of immigrants (Aitken, 2008); medical translators and paraprofessional ethnic health workers (Fuller, 1995; Esteva et al, 2006); advertising practitioners (Soar, 2002; John and Jackson, 2011; Gee and Jackson, 2012; Kobayashi, 2012); and public relations officials (L'Etang, 2006; Schoenberger-Orgad, 2011). In all these applications, the role played by the various agents can be seen to be in line with the early usage of cultural intermediary to designate 'the ethnic diplomat' (O'Brien et al, 2011). This understanding aligns with Bourdieu's own assertion that such actors are responsible for the 'production of belief' (Kuipers, 2011: 583) and are thus able to exert 'a certain amount of cultural authority as shapers of taste and the inculcators of new consumerist dispositions' (Nixon and du Gay, 2002: 497).

Insofar as such intermediated consumption results in more efficient and culturally 'proper' consumption of the respective cultural products, then the integrity of cultural intermediation is not impaired by the breadth of its empirical application. In all these uses, however, the underlying theme appears to be that cultural intermediaries facilitate the production, distribution and/or consumption of cultural products (which includes material cultural goods and services, as well as customs, behaviours and other cultural manifestations). The object of this chapter, then, is to reconceptualise cultural intermediaries and cultural intermediation around a 'value-chain' analysis that takes account of the different stages of production and consumption in which practices of cultural intermediation are involved.

Conceptualising cultural intermediaries and cultural intermediation

Apart from intermediating various stages of production, thereby linking producers and consumers of culture, it is often argued that it is their straddling between economic and socio-cultural roles that makes cultural intermediaries unique (Woo, 2012). Still, as Kuipers (2011) finds, cultural intermediaries employ varying levels of their personal beliefs and opinions when socially constructing cultural value. Baker (2012), for example, argued that retro retailers were highly endowed with cultural capital in spite of the conventional association of small-scale retailing with unsophisticated lower classes, suggesting that 'rather than a growth in new intermediary positions, there has been a gradual change in the practices involved in existing roles' (Baker, 2012: 637).

Hesmondhalgh (2006) contends that the conceptualisation of cultural intermediaries as the professionals in the artistic industry who play a content-adding role in the production of such cultural products is a misreading of Bourdieu (1984). This raises the possibility that cultural intermediaries include 'any creative or cultural occupation or institution', indeed that 'we are all cultural intermediaries now' (Maguire and Matthews, 2012: 552). The content addition by *all* the other actors along the production chain frames how the end consumers, as well as the intervening agents, engage with the cultural goods.

Clearly, therefore, it would be useful to further refine our understanding of cultural intermediation processes. Hartley (2004) advocates for the usefulness of the 'value-chain concept' which, he observes, though 'banal' in business rhetoric, may be useful in cultural studies. Value-chain research remains rare in cultural studies, however, with Maguire and Matthews (2012: 552) suggesting that it would be helpful in allowing cultural intermediaries to be 'differentiated by their locations within commodity chains, and the actors and stages of cultural production that they negotiate with and between'.

Conceived in this way, cultural intermediation may be seen as made up of processes that increase the *accessibility and thereby consumption of a given cultural product*, by enhancing the numbers of 'cultured' consumers and their depth of knowledge. Bourdieu limited the 'cultural' to specific artistic phenomena and made cultural intermediation a one-way process. A different form of cultural intermediation emerges, however, if you relax the tacit convention that 'cultural goods' only include the 'artistic' activities (such as literature, music and the visual arts) and introduce an appreciation of interactive intermediation dynamics as a series of alternating one-way flows and effects (O'Brien et al, 2011).

This chapter therefore presents a *cultural* value chain that stretches from creative origins to the consumption of the cultural product: a value chain that begins with imagination and ends with utility (see Figure 2.1). Although presented here as a linear process, it is important to acknowledge the feedback loops that exist throughout, with the different intermediation processes influencing new rounds of creating cultural value.

The translation of imaginative and artistic activities into art forms necessitates some form of creative intermediation, which enables the form of art to be produced as a prototype or as a unique piece. In turn, commodifying the arts generates commodities (goods or services), enabled by *commodifying* intermediation. A commodity is here defined as a product available for exchange or acquisition by a (potential) consumer or user, not necessarily limited to mass-produced, standardised, fungible goods. Finally, to complete the value chain, the commodity must be transformed into consumed cultural utility. The value chain ends in earnest, not merely at the consumer, but when optimal utility is obtained. At the consumer end, it is often assumed that the consumer is fully aware of all the utility obtainable from the product and also how to properly consume the product in question; for artistic and cultural products, this might not always be the case, however. Thus there is a crucial role for *outreach* intermediation in enabling both access to and consumption of the cultural product.

Figure 2.1: A cultural value chain and the intermediating process

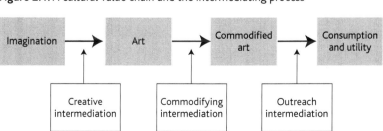

Operationalising and mapping cultural intermediaries

Drawing on a review of the published literature on cultural intermediaries, an initial summary of the key sectors of the economy involved was produced drawing on the UK's Standardised Industrial Classification of business activities. This was then augmented with the more conventional list of creative and cultural industries produced by the DCMS, Frontier Economics and the AHRC. Relying on examples of value-chain models applied to creative and cultural industries such as Frontier Economics, these were then categorised by the type of intermediary function. The result is a list of the different industrial sectors that can be classed as playing a role in one or more of **creative**, **commodifying** or **outreach** intermediation (Table 2.1).

To map creative and outreach intermediaries in the United Kingdom, 2011 data from the business register and employment survey was used; firm-level employment data was gathered at the middle-layer Super Output Areas (MSOA) level in England. To obtain the number of creative or outreach intermediaries in each locality, the employment figures of the various sectors that constitute the respective intermediary category shown in Table 2.1 were aggregated.

Location Quotients (LQs) have been computed for each MSOA by comparing the share of the pertinent jobs in a given locality with the national share of that job type. LQs indicate the density of the respective intermediation jobs in the local economy compared with the density of the same at the national level. LQs of less than 1.0 indicate that the share of that job type in a given locality is lower than the national average. LQs above 1.0 suggest that a locality has more than the national average share of jobs in that sector, with an LQ of 2.0 representing double the national average. Given the rather uniform ubiquity of commodifying intermediation industries, the analysis that follows only considers creative intermediaries and outreach intermediaries.

Findings

The density of **outreach intermediaries** in English MSOAs is spread fairly evenly across regions. Although analogous to irregular 'leopard spots', there is no obvious regional imbalance in the country. Indeed, less than 10% of English MSOAs report an LQ that is higher than 2 (only 2.3% of MSOAs have an LQ of higher than 5). However, 14% of MSOAs do not have a single outreach intermediary in their area. As expected, London shows several dark spots suggesting high

Table 2.1: Industrial sectors that can be classed as playing a role in one or more of creative, commodifying or outreach intermediation

SIC* 2007 code	SIC 2007 description	Cultural intermediation category
58210	Publishing of computer games	Creative
58290	Other software publishing	Creative
59111	Motion picture production activities	Creative
59112	Video production activities	Creative
59113	Television programme production activities	Creative
59120	Motion picture, video and television programme post-production activities	Creative
59200	Sound recording and music publishing activities	Creative
62011	Ready-made interactive leisure and entertainment software development	Creative
62012	Business and domestic software development	Creative
71111	Architectural activities	Creative
71112	Urban planning and landscape architectural activities	Creative
71121	Engineering design activities for industrial process and production	Creative
71122	Engineering related scientific and technical consulting activities	Creative
71129	Other engineering activities	Creative
72110	Research and experimental development on biotechnology	Creative
72190	Other research and experimental development on natural sciences and engineering	Creative
72200	Research and experimental development on social sciences and humanities	Creative
74100	Specialised design activities	Creative
74201	Portrait photographic activities	Creative
74202	Other specialist photography (not including portrait photography)	Creative
74209	Photographic activities not elsewhere classified (n.e.c.)	Creative
90010	Performing arts	Creative
90020	Support activities to performing arts	Creative
90030	Artistic creation	Creative
13100	Preparation and spinning of textile fibres	Commodifying
13200	Weaving of textiles	Commodifying
13300	Finishing of textiles	Commodifying
13910	Manufacture of knitted and crocheted fabrics	Commodifying
13931	Manufacture of woven or tufted carpets and rugs	Commodifying
13939	Manufacture of other carpets and rugs	Commodifying
13950	Manufacture of non-wovens and articles made from non-wovens, except apparel	Commodifying
13960	Manufacture of other technical and industrial textiles	Commodifying
13990	Manufacture of other textiles n.e.c.**	Commodifying
14110	Manufacture of leather clothes	Commodifying
14120	Manufacture of workwear	Commodifying
14131	Manufacture of other men's outerwear	Commodifying
14132	Manufacture of other women's outerwear	Commodifying

(continued)

Table 2.1: Industrial sectors that can be classed as playing a role in one or more of creative, commodifying or outreach intermediation (continued)

SIC* 2007 code	SIC 2007 description	Cultural intermediation category
14141	Manufacture of men's underwear	Commodifying
14142	Manufacture of women's underwear	Commodifying
14190	Manufacture of other wearing apparel and accessories n.e.c.	Commodifying
14200	Manufacture of articles of fur	Commodifying
14310	Manufacture of knitted and crocheted hosiery	Commodifying
14390	Manufacture of other knitted and crocheted apparel	Commodifying
15110	Tanning and dressing of leather; dressing and dyeing of fur	Commodifying
15120	Manufacture of luggage, handbags and the like, saddlery and harness	Commodifying
15200	Manufacture of footwear	Commodifying
16290	Manufacture of other products of wood; manufacture of articles of cork/straw/plaiting materials	Commodifying
17110	Manufacture of pulp	Commodifying
17120	Manufacture of paper and paperboard	Commodifying
17220	Manufacture of household and sanitary goods and of toilet requisites	Commodifying
17230	Manufacture of paper stationery	Commodifying
17290	Manufacture of other articles of paper and paperboard n.e.c.	Commodifying
18110	Printing of newspapers	Commodifying
18129	Printing n.e.c.	Commodifying
18130	Pre-press and pre-media services	Commodifying
18140	Binding and related services	Commodifying
18201	Reproduction of sound recording	Commodifying
18202	Reproduction of video recording	Commodifying
18203	Reproduction of computer media	Commodifying
20302	Manufacture of printing ink	Commodifying
20510	Manufacture of explosives	Commodifying
20590	Manufacture of other chemical products n.e.c.	Commodifying
22190	Manufacture of other rubber products	Commodifying
22230	Manufacture of builders' ware of plastic	Commodifying
22290	Manufacture of other plastic products	Commodifying
23310	Manufacture of ceramic tiles and flags	Commodifying
23410	Manufacture of ceramic household and ornamental articles	Commodifying
23490	Manufacture of other ceramic products n.e.c.	Commodifying
23700	Cutting, shaping and finishing of stone	Commodifying
23990	Manufacture of other non-metallic mineral products n.e.c.	Commodifying
24410	Precious metals production	Commodifying
24540	Casting of other non-ferrous metals	Commodifying
25710	Manufacture of cutlery	Commodifying
25720	Manufacture of locks and hinges	Commodifying
25990	Manufacture of other fabricated metal products n.e.c.	Commodifying

(continued)

Table 2.1: Industrial sectors that can be classed as playing a role in one or more of creative, commodifying or outreach intermediation (continued)

SIC* 2007 code	SIC 2007 description	Cultural intermediation category
26110	Manufacture of electronic components	Commodifying
26200	Manufacture of computers and peripheral equipment	Commodifying
26301	Manufacture of telegraph and telephone apparatus and equipment	Commodifying
26309	Manufacture of communication equipment other than telegraph, and telephone apparatus and equipment	Commodifying
26400	Manufacture of consumer electronics	Commodifying
26520	Manufacture of watches and clocks	Commodifying
26702	Manufacture of photographic and cinematographic equipment	Commodifying
26800	Manufacture of magnetic and optical media	Commodifying
28230	Manufacture of office machinery and equipment (except computers and peripheral equipment)	Commodifying
28990	Manufacture of other special-purpose machinery n.e.c.	Commodifying
30920	Manufacture of bicycles and invalid carriages	Commodifying
32120	Manufacture of jewellery and related articles	Commodifying
32130	Manufacture of imitation jewellery and related articles	Commodifying
32200	Manufacture of musical instruments	Commodifying
32401	Manufacture of professional and arcade games and toys	Commodifying
32409	Manufacture of other games and toys, n.e.c.	Commodifying
32990	Other manufacturing n.e.c.	Commodifying
33110	Repair of fabricated metal products	Commodifying
33130	Repair of electronic and optical equipment	Commodifying
33190	Repair of other equipment	Commodifying
33200	Installation of industrial machinery and equipment	Commodifying
41100	Development of building projects	Commodifying
41201	Construction of commercial buildings	Commodifying
41202	Construction of domestic buildings	Commodifying
42110	Construction of roads and motorways	Commodifying
42120	Construction of railways and underground railways	Commodifying
42130	Construction of bridges and tunnels	Commodifying
42210	Construction of utility projects for fluids	Commodifying
42220	Construction of utility projects for electricity and telecommunications	Commodifying
42910	Construction of water projects	Commodifying
42990	Construction of other civil engineering projects n.e.c.	Commodifying
43210	Electrical installation	Commodifying
43220	Plumbing, heat and air-conditioning installation	Commodifying
43290	Other construction installation	Commodifying
43310	Plastering	Commodifying
43320	Joinery installation	Commodifying
43330	Floor and wall covering	Commodifying
43341	Painting	Commodifying

(continued)

Table 2.1: Industrial sectors that can be classed as playing a role in one or more of creative, commodifying or outreach intermediation (continued)

SIC* 2007 code	SIC 2007 description	Cultural intermediation category
43342	Glazing	Commodifying
43390	Other building completion and finishing	Commodifying
43910	Roofing activities	Commodifying
43991	Scaffold erection	Commodifying
43999	Other specialised construction activities n.e.c.	Commodifying
46130	Agents involved in the sale of timber and building materials	Commodifying
46160	Agents involved in the sale of textiles, clothing, fur, footwear and leather goods	Commodifying
46240	Wholesale of hides, skins and leather	Commodifying
46410	Wholesale of textiles	Commodifying
46420	Wholesale of clothing and footwear	Commodifying
46431	Wholesale of gramophone records, audio tapes, compact discs, video tapes	Commodifying
46439	Wholesale of radios and televisions; wholesale of electrical household appliances n.e.c.	Commodifying
46440	Wholesale of china and glassware and cleaning materials	Commodifying
46470	Wholesale of furniture, carpets and lighting equipment	Commodifying
46480	Wholesale of watches and jewellery	Commodifying
46491	Wholesale of musical instruments	Commodifying
46499	Wholesale of other household goods	Commodifying
46510	Wholesale of computers, computer peripheral equipment and software	Commodifying
46520	Wholesale of electronic and telecommunications equipment and parts	Commodifying
46730	Wholesale of wood, construction materials and sanitary equipment	Commodifying
46740	Wholesale of hardware, plumbing and heating equipment and supplies	Commodifying
47110	Retail sale in non-specialised stores with food, beverages or tobacco predominating	Commodifying
47410	Retail sale of computers, peripheral units and software in specialised stores	Commodifying
47421	Retail sale of mobile telephones	Commodifying
47429	Retail sale of telecommunications equipment other than mobile telephones	Commodifying
47430	Retail sale of audio and video equipment in specialised stores	Commodifying
47530	Retail sale of carpets, rugs, wall and floor coverings in specialised stores	Commodifying
47540	Retail sale of electrical household appliances in specialised stores	Commodifying
47591	Retail sale of musical instruments and scores	Commodifying
47599	Retail sale of furniture, lighting equipment and household articles (not incl. musical instruments and scores)	Commodifying
47610	Retail sale of books in specialised stores	Commodifying
47620	Retail sale of newspapers and stationery in specialised stores	Commodifying

(continued)

Table 2.1: Industrial sectors that can be classed as playing a role in one or more of creative, commodifying or outreach intermediation (continued)

SIC* 2007 code	SIC 2007 description	Cultural intermediation category
47630	Retail sale of music and video recordings in specialised stores	Commodifying
47640	Retail sale of sports goods, fishing gear, camping goods, boats and bicycles	Commodifying
47650	Retail sale of games and toys in specialised stores	Commodifying
47710	Retail sale of clothing in specialised stores	Commodifying
47721	Retail sale of footwear in specialised stores	Commodifying
47760	Retail sale of flowers, plants, seeds, fertilizers, pet animals and pet food in specialised stores	Commodifying
47770	Retail sale of watches and jewellery in specialised stores	Commodifying
47781	Retail sale in commercial art galleries	Commodifying
47782	Retail sale by opticians	Commodifying
47789	Other retail sale of new goods in specialised stores (not incl. commercial art galleries and opticians) n.e.c.	Commodifying
47791	Retail sale of antiques, including antique books, in stores	Commodifying
47799	Retail sale of other second-hand goods in stores (not incl. antiques)	Commodifying
47910	Retail sale via mail order houses or via internet	Commodifying
47990	Other retail sale not in stores, stalls or markets	Commodifying
58110	Book publishing	Commodifying
58120	Publishing of directories and mailing lists	Commodifying
58130	Publishing of newspapers	Commodifying
58141	Publishing of learned journals	Commodifying
58142	Publishing of consumer and business journals and periodicals	Commodifying
58190	Other publishing activities	Commodifying
59131	Motion picture distribution activities	Commodifying
59132	Video distribution activities	Commodifying
59133	Television programme distribution activities	Commodifying
59140	Motion picture projection activities	Commodifying
61100	Wired telecommunications activities	Commodifying
61200	Wireless telecommunications activities	Commodifying
61300	Satellite telecommunications activities	Commodifying
61900	Other telecommunications activities	Commodifying
62020	Information technology consultancy activities	Commodifying
62090	Other information technology service activities	Commodifying
63110	Data processing, hosting and related activities	Commodifying
63120	Web portals	Commodifying
63910	News agency activities	Commodifying
63990	Other information service activities n.e.c.	Commodifying
64203	Activities of construction holding companies	Commodifying
70100	Activities of head offices	Commodifying
73120	Media representation services	Commodifying
74203	Film processing	Commodifying

(continued)

Table 2.1: Industrial sectors that can be classed as playing a role in one or more of creative, commodifying or outreach intermediation (continued)

SIC* 2007 code	SIC 2007 description	Cultural intermediation category
78101	Motion picture, television and other theatrical casting activities	Commodifying
80200	Security systems service activities	Commodifying
90040	Operation of arts facilities	Commodifying
95120	Repair of communication equipment	Commodifying
95290	Repair of personal and household goods n.e.c.	Commodifying
60100	Radio broadcasting	Outreach
60200	Television programming and broadcasting activities	Outreach
70210	Public relations and communications activities	Outreach
73110	Advertising agencies	Outreach
74300	Translation and interpretation activities	Outreach
79901	Activities of tourist guides	Outreach
79909	Other reservation service activities n.e.c.	Outreach
85510	Sports and recreation education	Outreach
85520	Cultural education	Outreach
91011	Library activities	Outreach
91012	Archives activities	Outreach
91020	Museums activities	Outreach
91030	Operation of historical sites and buildings and similar visitor attractions	Outreach
91040	Botanical and zoological gardens and nature reserves activities	Outreach
93210	Activities of amusement parks and theme parks	Outreach
93290	Other amusement and recreation activities n.e.c.	Outreach

Notes: * SIC = Standardised Industrial Classification business industries, UK; ** n.e.c. = not elsewhere classified.

Source: Author's analysis derived from Office for National Statistics

densities of outreach intermediaries relative to England as a whole (see Figure 2.2). Television broadcasting around Brent, Hammersmith and Fulham adds to the heavy presence of the same in nearby Hounslow, while radio, public relations and museums pervade the Westminster area. There is also substantial advertising activity in several localities in London, and key national landmarks, such as the national archives in Richmond and the British Library at St. Pancras, also emerge when these data are mapped.

Around Birmingham, the leading locale for outreach intermediaries appears to be near Cannon Hill Park and is characterised by significant employment in museum activities (see Figure 2.3). Other high performing areas are towards neighbouring Solihull, appearing to have

Figure 2.2: Outreach intermediaries in London

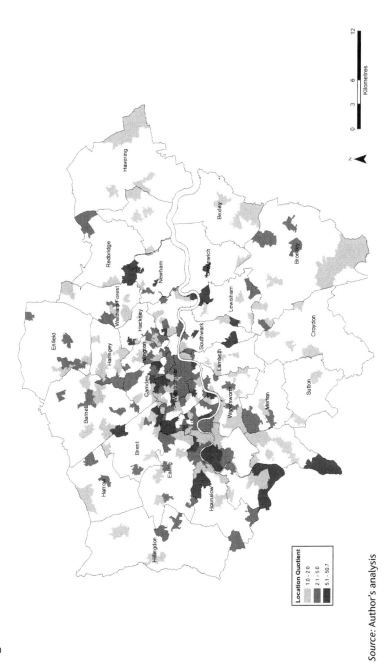

Location Quotient
1.0 – 2.0
2.1 – 5.0
5.1 – 50.7

Source: Author's analysis

Figure 2.3: Outreach intermediaries in Birmingham

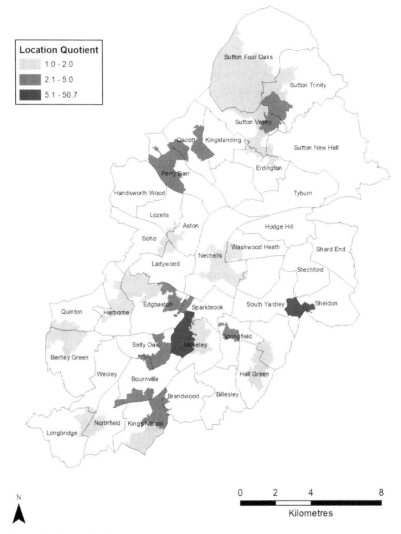

Source: Author's analysis

high employment in advertising activities. In Greater Manchester, advertising and television are dense in the Salford area with radio, public relations, amusement activities and museums also contributing significant shares of local jobs (see Figure 2.4).

Unlike the 'leopard spots' characterising the location of outreach intermediation in England, **creative intermediation** is very concentrated: about 80% of MSOAs with an LQ of above five are from the South of England, mostly the South East (see Figure 2.5 for

Figure 2.4: Outreach intermediaries in Manchester and Salford

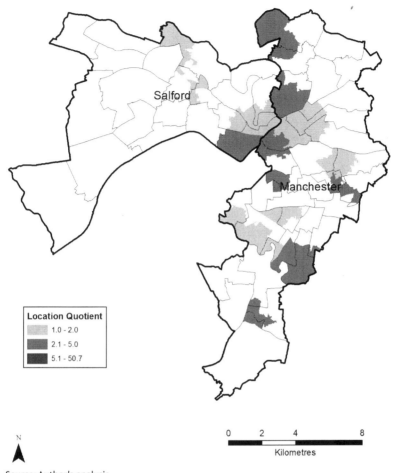

Location Quotient
1.0 - 2.0
2.1 - 5.0
5.1 - 50.7

0 2 4 8
Kilometres

N

Source: Author's analysis

London). Owing to a high density of jobs in engineering and natural sciences research, Macclesfield reports the highest LQ for creative intermediaries. In more overtly cultural sectors like performing arts and artistic creations, however, alongside London's dominance, Birmingham, Newcastle, and Salford have some representation in the top ten MSOAs by absolute numbers. Nevertheless, even within London there is significant variation, with the East End particularly underrepresented.

Taken as a whole, creative intermediation is predominantly concentrated in London and the Home Counties while Birmingham and Manchester appear to be relatively lacking in creative intermediaries. Looking at the sector-specific level, in Birmingham

Figure 2.5: Creative intermediaries in London

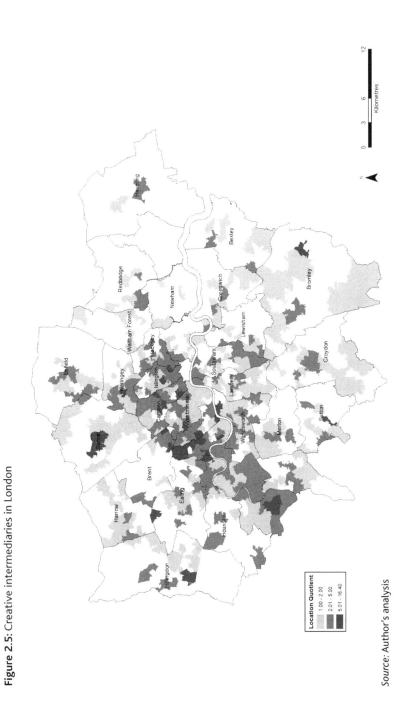

Location Quotient

1.00 - 2.00

2.01 - 5.00

5.01 - 16.40

Source: Author's analysis

there is a modestly dense representation in entertainment software, business software, engineering design and consultancy, architectural activities, engineering research, motion picture production, and performing arts. Greater Manchester has a strong presence in television-related activities. In Birmingham, creative intermediation can be seen to be concentrated in well-known spots in the city centre area, but also around neighbouring Solihull and further afield in Warwickshire (see Figure 2.6). Within the city, hotspots also appear to be well diversified with performing arts, engineering and software

Figure 2.6: Creative intermediaries in Birmingham

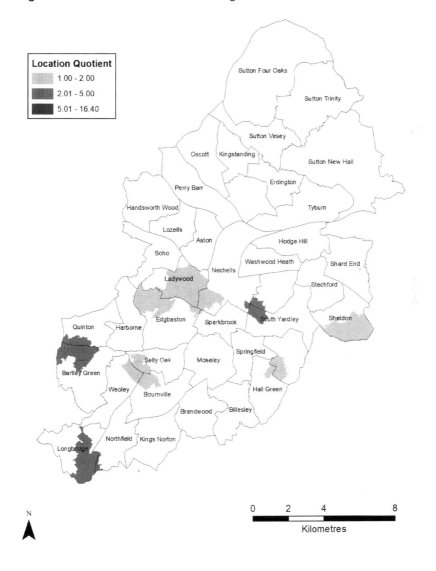

development registering a strong presence. Greater Manchester's creative hotspots are also clustered near the centre and are just as diversified, although the flagship presence of the television industry in Salford is quite distinctive (see Figure 2.7).

Figure 2.7: Creative intermediaries in Manchester and Salford

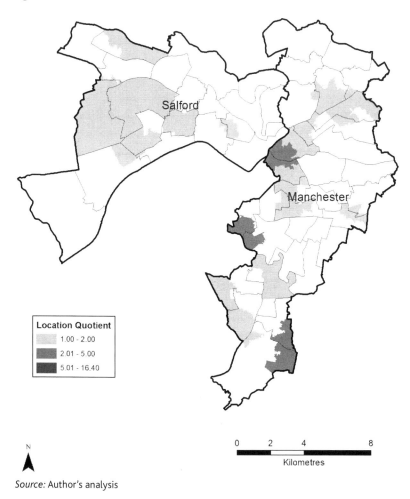

Location Quotient
1.00 - 2.00
2.01 - 5.00
5.01 - 16.40

N

0   2   4   8
Kilometres

Source: Author's analysis

Conclusion

This chapter attempts to use a value-chain analysis to reach a better understanding of what cultural intermediaries are and what contribution they make to cultural activities. Because the concept of cultural intermediation has largely developed in the fields of sociology and cultural studies, it has yet to be crystallised in a manner amenable to research from a business and economics perspective. This chapter addresses this gap by developing the cultural value-chain approach, suggesting that cultural activities can be hypothesised as a process with intervening intermediaries facilitating the creation, commodification and consumption of cultural products.

Cultural, commodifying and outreach intermediaries act as gatekeepers or facilitators along the value-chain process following creative products from their inception to consumption. Our findings suggest that, as a generic category, outreach intermediation appears to be fairly evenly distributed across England. Breaking this down to the constituent sectors, however, it becomes clear that many localities across England have overrepresentations in particular sectors. With an empirical focus here on London, Manchester and Birmingham, only London appears to have a variety of outreach intermediaries across a wide array of sectors. Nonetheless, even within London these sectors are unevenly distributed, with the eastern parts of the city in particular missing out. On the whole, in the leading English cities, London, Birmingham and Manchester, broader outreach cultural intermediation appears to be a city-centre-only phenomenon. There is perhaps then a policy debate to be had on ways in which outreach intermediation is distributed if the objective is to create more connected communities via outreach intermediation generating cultural consumption.

When it comes to the actual creation of new cultural products to be commodified and consumed by outsiders, in most parts of England there appears to be a dearth of creative intermediaries working to facilitate this. Only London and the South East of England have these sectors as important parts of their local economies; this plausibly allows this region to grow towards becoming almost exclusively responsible for new products in England.

It may be the case, however, that rather than new products needing to be created, it is the cultural catchment of existing products that may need to be expanded. Indeed, a significant number of outreach intermediaries work in advertising and the media and as such enhance the consumption of cultural products indirectly and remotely. In fact, it may yet be the case that localities with high representations of outreach intermediaries may not themselves be connected locally if the work of these intermediaries is through the mass media.

Cultural intermediation remains a complex and evolving topic. The empirically grounded value-chain analysis presented here represents an important step towards cultivating a more comprehensible and consensual approach to understanding cultural intermediation, bringing in novel perspectives from the disciplines of business studies and economics.

References

Aitken, A. (2008) 'Third culture kids and mad migrant mothers, or how to outgrow Amy Tan', *Journal of Australian Studies*, 32: 445-54.

Baker, S.E. (2012) 'Retailing retro: class, cultural capital and the material practices of the (re)valuation of style', *European Journal of Cultural Studies*, 15: 621-41.

Bourdieu, P. (1984) *Distinction: A social critique of the judgement of taste*, Cambridge, Mass.: Harvard University Press.

Childress, C.C. (2012) 'Decision-making, market logic and the rating mindset: negotiating BookScan in the field of US trade publishing', *European Journal of Cultural Studies*, 15: 604-20.

Cronin, A. (2004) 'Regimes of mediation: advertising practitioners as cultural intermediaries?' *Consumption, Markets and Culture*, 7: 349-69.

Doane, R. (2009) 'Bourdieu, cultural intermediaries and *Good Housekeeping's* George Marek: a case study of middlebrow musical taste', *Journal of Consumer Culture*, 9: 155-86.

Esteva, M., Cabrera, S., Remartinez, D., Diaz, A., and March, S. (2006) 'Perception of difficulties in family medicine in the delivery of health to economic immigrants', *Atencion primaria / Sociedad Espanola de Medicina de Familia y Comunitaria*, 37: 154-9.

Fuller, J. (1995) 'Challenging old notions of professionalism: how can nurses work with paraprofessional ethnic health-workers?', *Journal of Advanced Nursing*, 22: 465-72.

Gee, S. and Jackson, S. J. (2012) 'Leisure corporations, beer brand culture, and the crisis of masculinity: the Speight's 'Southern Man' advertising campaign', *Leisure Studies*, 31: 83-102.

Giry-Deloison, C. (2008) 'England and Spanish Low Countries, 1600-1630', *Revue Du Nord*, 90(37): 671-86.

Hartley, J. (2004) 'The 'value chain of meaning' and the new economy', *International Journal of Cultural Studies*, 7: 129-41.

Haynes, J. (2005) 'World music and the search for difference', *Ethnicities*, 5: 365-85.

Hesmondhalgh, D. (2006) 'Bourdieu, the media and cultural production', *Media, Culture & Society*, 28: 211-31.

John, A. and Jackson, S. (2011) 'Call me loyal: Globalization, corporate nationalism and the America's Cup', *International Review for the Sociology of Sport*, 46: 399-417.

Kobayashi, K. (2012), 'Corporate nationalism and glocalization of Nike advertising in "Asia": production and representation practices of cultural intermediaries', *Sociology of Sport Journal*, 29: 42-61.

Kuipers, G. (2011) 'Cultural globalization as the emergence of a transnational cultural field: transnational television and national media landscapes in four European countries', *American Behavioral Scientist*, 55: 541-57.

Kuipers, G. (2012) 'The cosmopolitan tribe of television buyers: professional ethos, personal taste and cosmopolitan capital in transnational cultural mediation', *European Journal of Cultural Studies*, 15: 581-603.

L'Etang, J. (2006) 'Public relations and sport in promotional culture', *Public Relations Review*, 32: 386-94.

Mee, K. and Dowling, R. (2003) 'Reading Idiot Box: film reviews intertwining the social and cultural', *Social & Cultural Geography*, 4: 185-99.

Nixon, S. and du Gay, P. (2002), 'Who needs cultural intermediaries?', *Cultural Studies*, 16: 495-500.

O'Brien, D., Wilson, K., and Campbell, P. (2011) 'The role of cultural intermediaries', https://tinyurl.com/ycogp25d

Ocejo, R.E. (2012) 'At your service: The meanings and practices of contemporary bartenders', *European Journal of Cultural Studies*, 15: 642-58.

Powers, D (2012), 'Long-haired, freaky people need to apply: rock music, cultural intermediation, and the rise of the "company freak"', *Journal of Consumer Culture*, 12: 3-18.

Schoenberger-Orgad, M. (2011) 'NATO's strategic communication as international public relations: The PR practitioner and the challenge of culture in the case of Kosovo', *Public Relations Review*, 37: 376-83.

Scott, M. (2012) 'Cultural entrepreneurs, cultural entrepreneurship: music producers mobilising and converting Bourdieu's alternative capitals', *Poetics*, 40: 237-55.

Sherman, R. (2011) 'The production of distinctions: class, gender, and taste work in the lifestyle management industry', *Qualitative Sociology*, 34: 201-19.

Smith Maguire, J. and Matthews, J. (2012) 'Are we all cultural intermediaries now? An introduction to cultural intermediaries in context', *European Journal of Cultural Studies*, 15: 551-62.

Soar, M. (2002) 'The first things first manifesto and the politics of culture jamming: towards a cultural economy of graphic design and advertising', *Cultural Studies*, 16: 570-92.

Strandvad, S. M. (2009) 'New Danish Screen – an organizational facilitation of creative initiatives: gatekeeping and beyond', *International Journal of Cultural Policy*, 15: 107-21.

Truninger, M. (2011) 'Cooking with Bimby in a moment of recruitment: exploring conventions and practice perspectives', *Journal of Consumer Culture*, 11: 37-59.

Woo, B. (2012) 'Alpha nerds: cultural intermediaries in a subcultural scene', *European Journal of Cultural Studies*, 15: 659-76.

Zwaan, K. and ter Bogt, T. F. M. (2009) 'Research note: breaking into the popular record industry, an insider's view on the career entry of pop musicians', *European Journal of Communication*, 24: 89-101.

THREE

Towards cultural ecologies: why urban cultural policy must embrace multiple cultural agendas

Beth Perry and Jessica Symons

Introduction

Existing understandings of culture and creativity have been framed through particular tropes which dominate global understandings of cultural practice. This is a problem because it excludes people who do not conform to stereotypes of 'cultural' or 'creative' activity and whose interests lie outside those defined by existing cultural strategies focused on arts, music or theatre. Government strategies that promote 'culture' focus primarily on 'the arts' dominated by elite middle classes. How then should we reframe culture and creativity to accommodate plural interpretations and values? This chapter draws on local ethnographic work undertaken in Ordsall (an area in Salford, UK) to argue that an ecological approach to culture can transcend binaries between formal and informal cultural activities, between the economic and expressive. While national and local policies absorb economic rationales, with investments focused on supporting engagement in legitimated, recognised forms of cultural activity, our work illustrates how local people's ideas speak back and challenge narrow framings of the creative city and what constitutes cultural activity. The chapter argues that anthropological understandings of culture as webs of significance (Geertz, 1973) and the patterns through which people accommodate their daily activities (Douglas, 1966) can help support progress towards 'cultural democracy' (Jancovich, 2017).

Cultural values, cultural economy

Current dominant framings of the cultural economy demonstrate clear hierarchies in terms of what cultural activities count, and whose culture matters. The primacy of extracting economic value from cultural activity, prioritising high art over low, the economic over the expressive and the formal over everyday understandings has come to preoccupy cultural policy. International frameworks for action narrowly define (Nurse, 2007) and instrumentalise culture as a tool for achieving wider societal goals:

> As a sector of activity, through tangible and intangible heritage, creative industries and various forms of artistic expressions, culture is a powerful contributor to economic development, social stability and environmental protection. (UNESCO, 2010: 2)

Explicit articulations of culture in the post-war period sought to acknowledge respect for difference. The 1948 UN Declaration of Human Rights stated that everyone has the right to freely participate in the cultural life of the community and to enjoy the arts. During the World Conference on Cultural Policies in Mexico City in 1982, culture was defined as not only the arts and letters, but also modes of life, the fundamental rights of the human being, value systems, traditions and beliefs. International conventions and reports, such as the 1989 UN Convention on the Rights of the Child (Article 31) and UNESCO's more recent work to promote 'cultural urban futures' have focused on fostering freedom of expression, creativity and protecting heritage (UNESCO, 2016). Such views are consistent with scholarly understandings of culture as patterns (Douglas, 1966), webs of significance (Geertz, 1973) or an entire social order (Williams, 1981). Duxbury, Cullen and Pascual (2012) have argued for more than an essentialised and instrumentalised approach to culture, rather seeing culture as a fourth pillar of sustainable development: 'culture must be seen as intangible and tangible capital; culture is a process and a way of life; culture is value-binding; and culture is creative expression' (74–5).

The subsequent capture of 'culture' into an instrumental category for enabling particular social goals brings it into the capitalist paradigm (Symons, 2017). Over the past few decades, culture as economic development has been the primary focus of national and local policies. In the UK during the 1990s, the discourse around 'a cultural economy' for stimulating growth was dominated by the notion of 'creative industries' (Garnham, 2005; Hesmondhalgh and Pratt, 2005). The UK Creative Industries Mapping Document (DCMS, 1998) signified culture's arrival at the Treasury negotiating table. This document measured the economic contribution of particular companies from music, arts, performance and film, grouping them into 'industries'. 'Creativity' was linked to the generation of wealth by packaging and selling ideas for profit, protected by intellectual property laws. In order to get funding, art and culture were 'forced to speak the language of growth, innovation and economic metrics' (O'Connor, 2016: 4). The cultural industries became a collective production system (Pratt, 1997), with culture absorbed within wider economic imaginaries which 'come to be selected and institutionalized and thereby come to co-constitute economic subjectivities, interests, activities, organizations, institutions, structural ensembles, emergent economic orders and their social embedding, and the dynamics of economic performance' (Jessop and Oosterlynck, 2008: 1156).

Cities are critical sites where tensions between expressive and economic orientations towards supporting cultural practices materialise. One of the four priorities for urban policy in the 2006 State of the English Cities report was recognition that cities are 'important as sources of identity, culture recognition and connection between communities and cultures … This points to a wider set of policy goals than simply economic ones' (Parkinson et al, 2006: 239). However, as city administrations are pressured to drive economic productivity (May and Perry, 2018), culture becomes a tool to realise urban goals. Pratt (1997, 2010) describes how creative cities rhetoric blended urban policy with arts and cultural policy. By the late 1990s, a culture-led reinvention of the post-Fordist city produced flagship arts developments, city branding, cultural quarters, enterprise support and workspaces. Charles Landry, dubbed the 'architect' of the creative city concept by Chatterton (2000: 391), urged authorities to think, plan and act creatively. By taking an economic view of cultural activities and creating cross-departmental planning regimes, local authorities were able to direct economic policy to stimulate activity in the cultural industries (Landry and Matarasso, 1996; Landry, 2000). When Florida produced his seminal 'creative city' index, administrations saw the benefits of generating income through 'cultural quarters' (Florida, 2002). At the subnational level of government, where public–private partnerships and entrepreneurial forms of arts and cultural management were brokered, different policy fields were meshed together: arts, tourism, economic development, education, youth policy, multiculturalism and social policy (Flew, 2012). However, while increased cultural consumption was a desirable outcome for city development, it was also a cooption of cultural development to the agenda of marketisation: 'a cultural zone can easily be read as a zone of affluence' (Miles, 2005: 890). As excitement about the potential for a creative economy grew, it became problematic (O'Connor, 2016). One result was a form of 'culture by the pound' (Greenwood, 1989) described as a process of cultural commodification which leads to people's disengagement from their own cultural practices, concerned they are performing their own culture rather than just living it.

The UK cultural sector has been endemically underresourced, relying on self-motivated, dedicated artists to produce work to impact on multiple areas of social cohesion, health and community building, even though their priorities were unrelated to cultural policy (Perry et al, 2015). This has led to increasing calls to 're-balance policy and academic concern to the intrinsic value of the cultural and creative field' (Pratt, 2010: 19). While instrumental and holistic views of culture can coexist, the former has come to dominate, producing concerns that 'what gets funded becomes culture' (Holden, 2008). Furthermore, creative city policies have been criticised for not delivering tangible benefits for deprived urban communities, with culture-led regeneration in specific city quarters making those areas unaffordable to local people. Drawing on Matarasso and Landry (1999), Gattinger (2011: 3) noted a persistent 'top-down elitist homogenizing approach to culture that ignored cultural expressions and practices outside of the mainstream canon'.

Tackling cultural understandings of 'culture'

To broaden understandings of culture 'we need an expanded understanding of what might constitute cultural participation, one that does not start with the presence or absence of social groups from specific forms of culture' (Crossick and Kaszynska, 2016: 32). The AHRC *Connected Communities* programme sought to tackle these tensions and funded a large £1.5m project, *Cultural intermediation in the creative urban economy*, which responded to these challenges. One aspect of the project was an initiative called '*Ideas4Ordsall*', which used an open and coproductive approach to project design and delivery in response to community views of culture (Symons, Chapter thirteen, this volume). This approach sought to avoid being the target of our own critiques, through navigating the tension between instrumentalised culture and culture as self-expression. Drawing on ethnographic insights, we decided to 'maximise what was already there' and support local people to shape the project based on their own cultural patterning (Douglas, 1966). This decision to mobilise against any top-down elitist approach that risked ignoring cultural activity outside the mainstream expectations of art, performance, theatre and music, helped us see what was important to local people, what they prioritised and where they found meaning. The *Ideas4Ordsall* project commissioned local organisations and individuals as 'cultural intermediaries' (Perry, Chapter seven, this volume) to identify 'Ideas People' to support through a schedule of activity to provide momentum, emotional and practical support, and money.

The *Ideas4Ordsall* activities comprised 25 ideas that can be analysed as representative of local 'culture' in this area of Northern England. The ideas demonstrate areas of local significance and prioritisation. People's ideas for cultural activities included dogwalking, beekeeping, photography, craft, cooking, bike workshops, a community festival, a community noticeboard and a graphic design company. They can be thematically analysed through the lenses of: connecting community; curating history; developing social enterprise; capturing a sense of place; and sharing knowledge. Alongside ethnographic field notes, we undertook semi-structured interviews and video reflections with the participants. Names are anonymised in the accounts below.

Connecting community

Four of the ideas were motivated by the desire to create contexts for community cohesion: theatre workshops, Islington Community Festival, On In Ordsall and the Ordsall Washing Line. The Ideas People focused on connecting community members, concerned that the absence of communication between individuals was affecting people's wellbeing. From accounts of people 'not going out for two years', to providing support for people coming off drugs and alcohol, to telling stories about difficult childhood experiences, to bringing warring groups of neighbours together, each idea explicitly aimed not just to facilitate communication, but to ameliorate anxiety and frustration with everyday life. Unlike formally initiated, arts-based cohesion projects, these activities reversed the idea that culture could lead to community cohesion, by showing that community already is understood and enacted in the everyday cultures of place.

Hannah's story

Hannah had struggled with mental health issues for many years before participating in this project. She would spend days at home, only going out to take her children to and from school. A local arts organisation became a lifeline for Hannah when she started volunteering on their allotment. When she encountered the *Ideas4Ordsall* project, Hannah decided to set up a Facebook group to let other residents know about what was going on in the area. She also pursued her idea of putting up a billboard, despite several drawbacks. Hannah's emphasis on communication indicated a commitment to the importance of word of mouth in letting people know what was going on in the area.

Edward's story

Edward's family had lived in the area for generations. He was known as being from one of the 'original families' who moved to Salford to work on the docks. Edward was a talented artist whose drawings of the area captured the spirit of independence and grittiness in Salford. He was self-conscious about his art and struggled to sell it, not knowing what to charge or how to approach galleries. During this project, Edward developed his art practice, from paintings to an exploration of how people felt about the area and their memories of past experiences. He ran workshops making T-shirts with local people, work which he reported significantly boosted his confidence in himself as an artist.

Keith's story

Keith had experienced significant ups and downs during his life including spending time in prison and battling addiction. His priority was to introduce people in his apartment block to a theatre practice that had helped him work through his issues and turn his life around. For Keith, it was really important to run these sessions himself, rather than people from community or theatre organisations, despite the time it took to get the sessions together.

Curating history

A common theme across several ideas related to aspects of neglected local history, focusing in particular on working class industrial revolution heritage. Two retired people focused on telling stories about the past, for instance, one researched and spoke at public events about a World War I nurse heroine who had worshipped at a local church. A third Ideas Person used project funding to buy a Victorian letterpress to show the technical prowess and social potential of hand-operated machines, while another bought foldaway tables and equipment to support a pop-up museum dedicated to celebrating the mining traditions in the area. The importance attached to local cultural identities, enshrined in preserving the spirit and ideas of the past, pointed to the need to consider intangible cultural heritage and the memories embedded in place.

Bernard's story

Bernard came from a mining family and was proud of the industrial heritage of the area. Working with his friend, he collected together memorabilia from Salford's mining history and created a 'pop-up mining museum' as well as a mining memorial in the area. In their discussions and materials, they emphasised the proud social history in the mining communities showing posters about unions and strikes. A central theme was to commemorate the coming together of the community over pit accidents and eventual closures.

Heather's story

Heather was a passionate amateur historian whose interest in family heritage came to the fore through this project. She had always wanted to write a play and flourished when matched with a theatre company. Heather carried out extensive research into the local area and developed multiple outputs including a social history play performed at a local community centre, and family histories of local people and those listed on a World War I memorial. Her play was turned into a short film and her local history into an animation by a local design company.

Developing social enterprise

The project also attracted people whose ideas had clear potential to develop into social enterprises, but who had previously struggled, either for financial support or to find time to develop their own business idea while working in full-time jobs. The ideas included nascent graphic design and print companies, an arts collective, dogwalking, and the development of a photography business. Working with cultural intermediaries gave local people the opportunity and access to trusted support where they could work their ideas through in more detail, considering potential income sources and how to develop the business. They advertised their services and developed activities to test the market and see what opportunities were available. While there were variable levels of success in an increasingly challenging economic climate, each built on their experiences to develop further work opportunities. Rather than seeking to enter the formal creative economy, such initiatives were motivated by a desire to connect necessary income-generating activities and economic survival with cultural interests and talents.

Cathy's story

Cathy was a local young woman born and raised in the area. She was passionate about becoming a photographer and wanted to explore how to set up a photographic studio. She ran several pop-up studios at a local arts organisation and at the annual community festival where she photographed people with their families.

Barrie's story

Barrie came from a family who had lived in the area for many years. He had trained as an artist but worked for 20 years in the local supermarket to support his family as they grew up. He saw an opportunity in the project for setting up a long desired art collective with a view to developing and selling work. With support, he brought together other aspirational artists who were in a similar position – working in retail while trying to develop their art – and negotiated several opportunities for people to sell their work.

Capturing a sense of place

A sense of place was the key motivation behind many of the ideas, in relation to the identity of Ordsall and the adjacent area of Islington. With ongoing regeneration and new incomers arriving in apartments that local people could not afford, many local people felt under siege. They responded to this by reaffirming and celebrating their commitment to the local area, through for instance, the development of a photo journal and exhibition by a camera club and a commemorative book celebrating 25 years of a local housing cooperative. In contrast to discourses of the creative city, such initiatives are not a means of *transforming* a place through creative intervention, but of *preserving* its essence and celebrating its distinctiveness in the face of flattening and homogenising processes of urban renewal.

Peter and Paul's story

Peter and Paul decided to take a tongue-in-cheek view of the *Ideas4Ordsall* project and created a character called 'Lord Puglington' who was initially quite snobby about the area but gradually came to like and value it after meeting people involved in the project and finding out about their work. Peter dressed as the Lord in a pug mask and cape, filmed by Paul. They brought a spirit of fun and laughter to the project and created a film that reflected the sense of connection and community that emerged from exploring the area.

Mary and Angela's story

Mary and Angela were part of a theatre company run by disabled people and they created a film that celebrated the activities in their local community centre and in the local area. Mary wanted to give a perspective from her point of view and so connected the camera to her wheelchair. They focused on the warmth and affection generated by the group and the people that worked with them.

Sharing knowledge

Passing on existing experience and knowledge in craft, cooking, music and bikes was also important. People developed ideas for workshops to support people to develop their own ability to perform or produce, rather than providing services for them. Where they did not have the experience themselves, they used the project money to buy in support from others. Culture is not the production of creative output or product, but the generation of spaces for sharing cultural practices, thereby empowering others as creative producers.

Carrie's story

Carrie was a local woman born and raised in the area who remembered going to craft workshops as a child at the local arts organisation. Now an adult, she wanted to give back to her local community and lead her own craft workshops for kids, which she did.

Steve's story

Steve was a passionate cook who had moved into the area to settle down with his partner and their child. He was well known locally as he would put on cooking workshops at the community centres in the area for children and adults. Steve was keen to set up a cooking school and used this project as an opportunity to explore this idea further. For these sessions, he developed the idea of running a cooking session and then passing the food cooked onto a homeless charity for distributing in the city.

Towards cultural ecologies

Connecting community, sharing history and expertise, celebrating place and exploring social entrepreneurship demonstrate the importance of supporting each other through the ethic of care (Gilligan, 1982).

In all cases, the Ideas People responded to the offer of funding to develop cultural activities by developing socially motivated practices that emphasised community, solidarity and knowledge exchange. Following Douglas (1966) we can see how people responded to anomalies and ambiguities in their community and so demonstrated the underlying 'patterns' that made up their culture. Social responsibility sat at the heart of their activities, indicating a culture based on care and mutual support. Through discussions with the cultural intermediaries and community members, our process revealed a rich and vibrant community in the area, running through family networks where people socialise daily with each other, increasingly through social media such as Facebook and WhatsApp. While disconnected from mainstream cultural activities, Ordsall's relative isolation from the formal cultural economy was not indicative of culture deprivation; instead, culture lay in community, in mutuality, sociality, meaning, history and place. 'Culture' in this context is understood anthropologically in terms of the relations constituted through daily life.

The focus on developing local people's own ideas was well received by community members and cultural organisations. As we have shown, these ideas clustered around five themes, which collectively represented an ethics of care and commitment to plural, holistic and anthropological understandings of culture. We do not present this insight to reinforce a banal conceptualisation of everyday culture as somehow divorced from the priorities and concerns embodied in policy. Indeed, the tapestry of ideas generated within Ordsall are not hierarchically subservient to policy priorities, but instead transcend cultural and sectoral views. The themes connect to and challenge binaries between formal and informal, expressive and instrumental. Market-making, social enterprise, heritage and sustainability were not exclusive choices, but blended into distinct cultural activities. While appearing to mirror existing cultural understandings – photos, craft, festivals, heritage – activities were motivated for different reasons, largely independent of their intrinsic or aesthetic value. However, this does not further suggest the instrumentalisation of a supposedly discrete category of 'culture' to other needs. Instead, *Ideas4Ordsall* reveals not culture *for* community cohesion, but community *as* culture; not culture *for* sustainability, but sustainability *as* culture; not social entrepreneurship *for* cultural economy; but culture *as* social entrepreneurship. Such subtle shifts are indicative of the wider need to challenge narrow and elitist understandings of culture and community development.

Cultural policy is a field of policies, with multiple and conflicting objectives (Pratt, 2010). There are different, simultaneous city-culture modalities, including heritage, creative industries, regeneration and the experience economy. *Ideas4Ordsall*'s tapestry of ideas demonstrates the intersectional approach behind culture as a fourth pillar for sustainable development. Working-class leisure is not intellectually and morally inferior (Banks, 2009) from this perspective but rather has an 'important voice in how the economy itself might be re-framed' (O'Connor, 2016: 5). Holden argues for an ecology of culture which recognises how different cultural practices relate to each other and are interdependent. We accept this proposition but also argue for *cultural ecologies* – an acknowledgement of the multiplicity of cultural contexts and a commitment not to create hierarchies between them (Holden, 2015).

The challenge for policy makers is to develop funding mechanisms that ensure equal access and support for all these different forms of self-expression. Attention should be refocused not only on the soft and hard infrastructures needed for the cultural economy (Flew, 2012), but on an ecological approach: 'a system of associative structures and social networks, connections and human interactions, that underpins and encourages the flow of ideas between individuals and institutions' (Landry, 2000: 133). We need to think differently about what the creative city means and how to support it, otherwise: 'a city's development initiatives risk counterproductively destroying the precise characteristics they are otherwise seeking to nourish, create, and, even, commodify' (Ross, 2017: 32). Culture sits in places (Escobar, 2001) and is not outside the scope of capital and modernity. City policies must acknowledge the 'subtleties of historical and locally specific practices of cultural and creative activities' (Pratt, 2010: 13). Shifts in the public use of 'culture' are a reflection on how ideologies or policies influence everyday life and provide insights into how 'subjectivity, identity, politics' may be changed through practice (Bolognani, 2012: 619). Cultural ecologies must recognise that the role of culture in economic regeneration is situated within the context of meaning-making in the everyday.

References

Banks, M. (2009) 'Fit and working again? The instrumental leisure of the "creative class"', *Environment and Planning A: Economy and Space*, 41: 668-81.

Bolognani, M. (2012) 'Good culture, bad culture...no culture! The implications of culture in urban regeneration in Bradford, UK', *Critical Social Policy*, 32: 618-35.

Chatterton, P. (2000) 'Will the real Creative City please stand up?', *City*, 4: 390-7.

Crossick, G. and Kaszynska, P. (2016) *Understanding the value of arts and culture*, Swindon: AHRC.

DCMS (1998) *Creative industries mapping document*, London: DCMS.

Douglas, M. (1966) *Purity and danger: An analysis of the concepts of pollution and taboo*, London: Routledge & Kegan Paul.

Duxbury, N., Cullen, C. and Pascual, J. (2012) 'Cities, culture and sustainable development', in H. Anheier and Y. Raj Isar (eds) *Cities, cultural policy and governance*, London: Sage, pp. 73-86.

Escobar, A. (2001) 'Culture sits in places: reflections on globalism and subaltern strategies of localization', *Political Geography*, 20: 139-74.

Flew, T. (2012) *The creative industries: Culture and policy*, London: Sage.

Florida, R. (2002) *The rise of the creative class and how it's transforming work, leisure, community and everyday life*, New York: Basic Books.

Garnham, N. (2005) 'From cultural to creative industries', *International Journal of Cultural Policy*, 11: 15-29.

Gattinger, M. (2011) *Democratization of culture, cultural democracy and governance*, Whitehorse: Canadian Public Arts Funders.

Geertz, C. (1973) 'Thick description: toward an interpretive theory of culture', in C. Geertz, (ed) *The interpretation of cultures*, New York: Basic Books, pp. 3-32.

Gilligan, C. (1982) *In a different voice: Psychological theory and women's development*, Cambridge (MA.): Harvard University Press.

Greenwood, D. (1989) 'Culture by the pound: an anthropological perspective on tourism as cultural commoditization', in V. Smith (ed) *Hosts and guests: The anthropology of tourism*, Philadelphia: University of Pennsylvania Press, pp. 171-85.

Hesmondhalgh, D. and Pratt, A. C. (2005) 'Cultural industries and cultural policy', *International Journal of Cultural Policy*, 11: 1-13.

Holden, J. (2008) *Democratic culture*, London: Demos.

Holden, J. (2015) *The ecology of culture: A report commissioned by the Arts and Humanities Research Council's Cultural Value project*, Swindon: AHRC.

Jancovich, L. (2017) 'The participation myth', *International Journal of Cultural Policy*, 23: 107-21.

Jessop, B. and Oosterlynck, S. (2008) 'Cultural political economy: On making the cultural turn without falling into soft economic sociology', *Geoforum*, 39: 1155-69.

Landry, C. (2000) *The creative city: A toolkit for urban innovators*, London: Earthscan.

Landry, C. and Matarasso, F. (1996) *The art of regeneration: Urban renewal through cultural activity. A Comedia report*, London: Comedia.

Matarasso, F. and Landry, C. (1999) *Balancing act: twenty-one strategic dilemmas in cultural policy. Cultural Policies Research and Development Unit Policy Note No. 4*, Strasbourg: Council of Europe Publishing.

May, T. and Perry, B. (2018) *Cities and the knowledge economy: Promise, politics and possibility*, London: Routledge.

Miles, M. (2005) 'Interruptions: testing the rhetoric of culturally led urban development', *Urban Studies*, 42: 889-911.

Nurse, K. (2007) 'Culture as the fourth pillar of sustainable development', in Commonwealth Secretariat (ed) *Small states: economic review and basic statistics. Annual Series: Eleventh Volume, Autumn 2006*, London: Commonwealth Secretariat, pp. 28-40.

O'Connor, J. (2016) 'After the creative industries: cultural policy in crisis', *Law, Social Justice and Global Development*, 2016: 1-18.

Parkinson, M., Champion, T., Evans, R., Simmie, J., Turok, I., Crookston, M., Katz, B., Park, A., Berube, A., Coombes, M., Dorling, D., Glass, N., Hutchins, M., Kearns, A., Martin, R. and Wood, P. (2006) *State of the English cities: A research study*, London: ODPM.

Perry, B., Smith, K. and Warren, S. (2015) 'Revealing and re-valuing cultural intermediaries in the 'real' creative city: Insights from a diary-keeping exercise', *European Journal of Cultural Studies*, 18: 724-40.

Perry, B. (2019) 'Governing the creative city: the practice, value and effectiveness of cultural intermediaries', in P. Jones, B. Perry and P. Long (eds) *Cultural intermediaries connecting community: Revisiting approaches to cultural engagement*, Bristol: Policy Press.

Pratt, A. (1997) 'The cultural industries production system: a case study of employment change in Britain, 1984–91', *Environment and Planning A: Economy and Space*, 29: 1953-74.

Pratt, A. (2010) 'Creative cities: tensions within and between social, cultural and economic development. A critical reading of the UK experience', *City, Culture and Society*, 1: 13-20.

Ross, S. G. (2017) 'Development versus preservation interests in the making of a music city: a case study of select iconic Toronto music venues and the treatment of their intangible cultural heritage value', *International Journal of Cultural Property*, 24: 31-56.

Symons, J. (2017) 'Nurturing an emergent city: parade making as a cultural trope for urban policy', in C. Lewis and J. Symons (eds) *Realising the city: Urban ethnography in Manchester*, Manchester: Manchester University Press.

Symons, J. (2018) 'Untangling creativity and art for policy purposes: ethnographic insights on Manchester International Festival and Manchester Day Parade', *International Journal of Cultural Policy*, 24: 205–19.

Symons, J. (2019) 'Strategies for overcoming research obstacles: developing the *Ordsall Method* as a process for ethnographically-informed impact in communities', in P. Jones, B. Perry and P. Long (eds) *Cultural intermediaries connecting community: Revisiting approaches to cultural engagement*, Bristol: Policy Press.

UNESCO (2010) *The power of culture for development*, Paris: UNESCO.

UNESCO (2016) *Culture: urban future. Global report on culture for sustainable urban development*, Paris: UNESCO.

Williams, R. (1981) *The sociology of culture*, New York: Schocken Books.

FOUR

State-sponsored amateurism: cultural intermediation, participation and non-professional production

Paul Long

Introduction

In the summer of 2015, in the course of the *Cultural intermediation* project, researchers came across a Salford redevelopment site surrounded by a woodchip board wall. These cheap fences are of a kind now de rigueur in urban locations, used for concealing disruptions and abject spaces: panels are often painted and laboriously repainted as they attract the unsanctioned attention and graffiti of 'taggers' (Carrington, 2009). As a consequence, or out of recognition for the alienating effect of these enclosures, those responsible for them sometimes enlist cultural intermediaries to organise a more acceptable decoration, so creating sites of officially sanctioned, if temporary, public art. For instance, in the same period at the project's other research site in Balsall Heath, Birmingham, *professional* graffiti artist Mohammed Ali of the organisation Soul City Arts decorated a similar wall that disguised derelict ground and a junkyard (see Chapter fourteen). Taking a cue from local residents, Ali produced a spectacular work that conveyed in symbolic manner the area's industrial heritage and the impact upon it of post-war migrant settlement (Long, 2014). By way of contrast, Salford's wall was 'hung' with reproductions of artworks produced by *non*-professionals drawn from the local community. This material conveyed a range of representations of the area, including ideas for its improvement, perhaps anticipating with a welcome or criticism the building to be revealed behind the wall (author's field notes).

In time, both walls came down. Although weathered and partially destroyed, parts of Ali's mural remain visible on Balsall Heath's Ladypool Road; despite its ephemerality, the art is recorded on his website as part of his portfolio, thus underwriting the value and guarantee of his name and expertise. Salford's wall reached the end of its practical usefulness with the completion of the construction it had concealed. As researchers later observed, the 'gallery' of reproductions the wall had presented was discarded with it (author's field notes). No record appears to exist of the impulse behind the Salford project, nor what became of the original contributions from the community. Nonetheless, both projects were visible examples of contemporary cultural intermediation processes, aestheticising urban space, speaking with and about the communities in which they were situated. A comparison between them and the fate of the work engendered in Salford particularly prompts reflection on the wider purposes and outcomes of participation aimed at the engagement of 'ordinary people' as creative producers.

The aim of this chapter then is to consider the underscrutinised nature and status of creative *production* by non-professionals nurtured as a result of policy processes. As Reeves puts it 'many of those studies that have documented the social gradient in cultural engagement have failed to distinguish arts participation (i.e., the personal practice of art making) from arts consumption (e.g., attending art events)' (Reeves, 2015: 625). The chapter is organised around discussion of the productive, possibly provocative, label of 'amateurism' and its associations. The chapter asks: what roles does participation as production have in cultural intermediation projects? How are individuals afforded agency in the making of cultural works and connected to the cultural ecology (Holden, 2015), between activities that are publicly funded, commercial and homemade? The chapter proceeds with an exploration of a contemporary injunction to 'be creative'. It then deals with some of the prompts for thinking with the label of amateurism in relation to an understanding of participation and processes of intermediation. Drawing on indicative examples of activity in Balsall Heath is an exploration of a form of 'sponsored amateurism'. This label describes everyday creative work among non-professionals engendered by intermediaries and cultural policy. The chapter concludes with reflections on a field of production that falls *outside* of the obvious attention of policy makers and cultural intermediation objectives. This amateur activity poses questions about where and how creative expression is manifest, of the way in which participation is understood, mapped and valued.

The contemporary injunction to create

Creativity is a contemporary buzzword the invocation of which characterises a sphere of activity beyond the bounds of cultural policy or the dimensions of a set of specialised 'industries' (Mirza, 2006; Bilton, 2010). The signal of a contemporary good, this buzzword is sounded in injunctions and invitations addressed to all and across all walks of life to be creative in some manner. By way of example, UK television abounds with material concerned with art, craft, cooking and so on, that invite one to respond beyond passive consumption through action and a concomitant commitment to create. There are those public service programmes aimed at children from an early age, expressing familiar and conventional educational aims such as the BBC's *Art ninja* (2015-) which features a figure whose 'mission is to teach you his secrets and get you creating your own art' (bbc. co.uk). Aimed at an older constituency are shows programmed by Channel 4 such as *Craft: I made this* (2016) in which 'Three craft lovers offer a guide to making cool stuff to inspire more people to get crafting' (channel4.com). *Craft it yourself* (2017) is a series that 'helps people explore the joy of craft, as the nation's growing love affair with making things by hand combines with the latest home interior trends' (channel4.com).

To this roster one might also add shows such as the BBC's *The Great British sewing bee* (2013-16) and Channel 4's *The Great British bake off* (established at the BBC from 2010-17). In these programmes, creative originality and distinctiveness act as a marker of one's character and status. Nonetheless, distinctions between expert and novice, professional and homemade outputs are clearly demarcated, emphasising how such shows are not obviously aimed at nurturing a vocational desire in participants or viewers to become professional craftmakers, designers or cooks. To some degree, these productions are extensions of the 'makeover' television that emerged in the 1990s (Moseley, 2000), in which a purposeful promotion of tastefulness has become more visibly allied with a sense of individual fulfilment to be gained through hands-on production and creative innovation.

Elsewhere, distinctions over expertise become blurred and participants get closer to the structures and contracts of the cultural industries. For instance, the cable channel Sky Arts invites entrants to compete to be *Portrait artist of the year* (2013-) or *Landscape artist of the year* (2015-) and which are 'open to all artists – amateur, professional or hobbyists' (sky.com). The winners are awarded a fee covering 'creation, completion and delivery of the Winner's Prize Artwork on dates and times and locations to be determined by the Producer at its absolute discretion' (sky.com). Furthermore, the invitation to actively participate in popular terrestrial shows such as *The X factor* (2004-), *The voice* (2010-) or *Britain's got talent* (2007-) connects more explicitly with the creative industries as a part of these formats. In each show, acts take their place amid a performance of selection, critique and reward in which individuals are elevated from among the average and woefully 'talentless' to the ranks of the professional.

The participation agenda: consumption and production

This TV landscape and the injunction to be creative connect with a wider sphere, of UK cultural policy formulated over the last two decades. By way of example, the *Culture White Paper* of 2016 makes an argument for the role of government as enabler of 'great culture' and the flourishing of creativity at large. Here, culture and creativity are framed in familiar terms for their role in the community in binding the social fabric, and for the socialisation of the individual in 'meaningful engagement with their culture and heritage' (DCMS, 2016a: 21). Here, knowledge of 'great works of art, great music, great literature and great plays' is deemed an essential part 'every child's education' (DCMS, 2016a: 21). Extending these qualities is the promotion of the inculcation of practical skills, playing a musical instrument, painting, crafting, dancing or acting. The intrinsic good of such activity is allied to the promise of an instrumental return on investment, where the cultivation of a dedication and passion for practice 'can open doors to careers in the cultural and creative sectors and elsewhere' (DCMS, 2016a: 21).

As noted by a variety of scholars, culture has been enlisted to perform a range of duties. These 'policy attachments' (Belfiore, 2006) are echoed in the *Culture White Paper* where culture is deemed to have a role in addressing health and wellbeing, social exclusion and individual self-confidence. Above all, culture is conceived as an element of contemporary citizenship where the democratic guarantee is to ensure access to it, that 'Everyone should have the chance to experience culture, participate in it, create it, and see their lives transformed by it' (DCMS, 2016a: 13). Summarising the result of the discourse encapsulated in such statements O'Brien and Oakley (2015: 10) suggest that cultural engagement has become 'a marker of a particular kind of normality'. Attendant on this condition, in tandem with the guarantee of culture by public policy, is a devotion of resources to large-scale assessments of participation such as the

DCMS's *Taking part* (2005-) survey or the *Culture and sport evidence* (CASE) (2008-) programme. Anchoring issues of social equitability to questions of cultural provision, a result of such surveys is the modeling of audience engagement and a production of typologies in which a range of anxieties emerge. These anxieties are focused in particular on those who rarely participate in the pursuits supported by cultural policy, are 'unaware' of it, or whom institutions and intermediaries have found 'hard to reach'. While it is feasible that individuals make rational choices about their preferences, the concern that many are missing out on their cultural entitlement through ignorance is accentuated by inequalities tracked across class, race and ethnicity and in allied factors such as educational attainment. Even so, Miles and Sullivan (2012) suggest that many questions about our relationship with the domain of culture are not fully illuminated by the size and scope of surveys such as *Taking part*. As they suggest, this dataset measures performance targets for arts engagement rather than answering 'questions regarding the contexts, mechanisms and consequences of participation and non-participation' (Miles and Sullivan, 2012: 321).

One complication here arises from how the cultural surveys mentioned make a broad distinction between modes of participation. At the time of writing for instance, Arts Council England (ACE), alongside Sport England, Public Health England and the Department for Transport, were engaged in the *Active lives* survey for 2015-17. This survey encompasses culture, sport and physical pursuits in capturing evidence of leisure and recreational participation. Conducted by Ipsos MORI, the survey reaches nearly 200,000 respondents aged 14 and over, indicative of the resources devoted to comprehending this aspect of social being. In terms of the relationship between consumption and production, measurement criteria include the following definitions and distinctions. 'Arts participation (doing creative, artistic, theatrical or music activity or a craft)' is contrasted with 'Arts attendance (attending an event, performance or festival involving creative, artistic, dance, theatrical or music activity)' (Arts Council England, nd). Notwithstanding important variables that might be teased out from within these definitions, productive activity is nuanced by one's familiarity with and understanding of cultural conventions, of taste and traditions in tandem with one's role as consumer. As in consumption therefore, participation in production matters for its active role in reproducing social distinctions that limit cultural orientation and access to its field. As Reeves (2015) suggests for instance, one's 'hinterland' of leisure pursuits is not a casual matter of personal satisfaction but integral to how one is valued and assessed in one's social relations.

Cultural engagement, and participation in particular, plays a role in social mobility: universities and elite firms for instance consider cultural dispositions in their recruitment processes.

For some cultural intermediaries, production as participation is enlisted as a basis for empowerment in challenging such iniquities. The discourse of those grounded in this approach evinces an overtly political tone in comparison with the *bien pensant* nature of government policy crystallised in the *Culture White Paper* (DCMS, 2016). A typical example of this ethos is expressed by Meade and Shaw (2007: 412) who posit 'a potentially crucial role for practitioners in finding ways to enhance people's potential for agency by helping to release or resource their capacity to be active and creative'. They draw upon the work of Raymond Williams in which an idea of a socially committed arts practice enables a concept of 'cultural democracy' and the recognition of the confluence of meaning-making 'through every day living and through more specialized intellectual or artistic processes' (Meade and Shaw, 2007: 417). An active engagement in producing meaning is thus framed in terms of rights and as a necessity, but reveals also a familiar anxiety about contemporary cultural lives. Meade and Shaw take a cue from American educationalist Maxine Greene in calling for a revival of a 'democratic imagination' in tandem with E. P. Thompson's notion of the need for an 'education of desire' in ordinary people. In this argument, the creative power of the majority needs nurturing in order to aid the perception of a world beyond market relations and the fulfilment of inauthentic needs, thus revealing a puritanical assumption about their cultural indolence, if not wider disengagement. In this sense, cultural policy and intermediaries of various dispositions express rather similar ideas and concerns about the potential virtues and value of creativity for ordinary people and, perforce, about the quality of those groups too. How then might the activity and status of participants as non-professional producers be assessed?

Amateurism and cultural participation

Vodanovic (2013: 170) has noted an increased scholarly interest in amateur practices, suggesting that this aids conceptualisation of 'forms of self-organization and self-production, all of which create a particular frame to address issues of participation and equality within cultural production'. While the label of non-professional is functional, the connotations of amateurism are layered with affective and economic ideas about engagement, its motivations and status. As filmmaker Maya Deren famously noted in her essay on the subject, amateur 'means one who does something for the love of the thing rather than for economic reasons or necessity' (quoted in Fox, 2004: 5). In spite of this, and perhaps accounting for its absence and general avoidance in the discourse of intermediaries, the word has an apologetic and often pejorative ring to it. As Broderick Fox suggests of the negative association of the term, amateurism is often defined in relation to what it is *not*: 'not sophisticated, not technically adept, not pretty or polished, not of popular interest, or perhaps most frequently and opaquely, "not professional"' (Fox, 2004). As Vodanovic's ideas suggest, the associations of amateurism provide a useful nuance in conceptualising the appurtenances of subjects, including the 'hard to reach', so called, when brought to bear on cultural participation in the context of intermediation and a wider landscape of creativity.

The DCMS *Taking part* survey (2005-) questions 'a nationally representative sample of adults and children' and 'Excludes people who have engaged for the purposes of paid work or academic study' (DCMS, 2016b) (latest statistics from Creative Industries Council [no date] claim that total employment in the UK creative industries is 2m). The activity captured is thus oriented to purposes of leisure, of voluntarism and the non-professional, although in their critique of the limits of such surveys, Miles and Sullivan (2012) argue that there is little to be garnered from them concerning the meaning of informal, everyday cultural practices. On this note, there is something quite suggestive about *Taking part*'s inclusions and prohibitions in terms of production: photography is defined 'as an artistic activity' but 'not family or holiday "snaps"', while film or video allows for 'making as an artistic activity (not family or holidays)' (DCMS, 2016b). Beyond the specific exclusion of family recordings, these criteria generally make no obvious allowance for a further degree of differentiation that would allow a nuanced understanding of amateur cultural production, its potential and demands.

As Reeves (2015) suggests, production requires a different set of resources from individuals when compared to consumption. These resources include forms of economic and cultural capital and the dispositions one brings to bear upon participation, as well as aspects of time and aptitude that motivate and inflect one's orientation, decisions and potential agency. Thus, to consume a drama or dance performance, view an exhibition or read a piece of writing generally involves fewer resources and certainly less time and investment than those involved in their production. Consider for instance the degree and variety of personal commitment involved in either learning to play a musical instrument or to dance in a particular style and the discipline and affective disclosure involved in acting in a drama or indeed in creative writing where the perennial advice is to 'write what you know'.

As mentioned earlier, whatever its demands, those who come to participate in culture through production do so with varying degrees of expertise and familiarity with the norms and expectations of particular practices. Reflecting on the status of 'outsider art', Vodanovic presents an idea of amateur artists as 'those cut off or disengaged from tradition'; they are thus working 'in total isolation rather than in relation to any kind of sphere or professional body' (Vodanovic, 2013: 173). While such positions are conceivable, disengagement is relational; she quotes Tom Roberts, who reflects that 'amateur work, however "personal" in its pursuit of curiosity, always exists in a relation – of aspiration, antagonism, or both – to the structures that govern the conferrance [sic] of legitimacy on practices: the school, the workplace, informal systems of judgment, the art institution, the state' (Vodanovic, 2013). There is an important aspect of reciprocity and a circuit of exchange between non-professional producer and potential consumer to consider here in terms of the competence, creativity and even conscious 'artistry' that goes into production and the degree of its recognition as such and its appreciation through consumption (after all, addressing a specified audience is not a necessary condition of non-professional practice). One might have acquired skills in musical performance, painting or other forms of production as part of one's education that are maintained through the life course as part of one's leisure activity. One might continue to pursue such expressive activity even if one's education or commitment to it was poor, or indeed if one is self-taught or simply enthusiastic about 'having a go'.

This discussion alludes to a conceptual and practical relationship: we can understand how amateur participation in cultural production might be individually motivated, informally organised or cultivated under the aegis of professional projects prompted and thus sponsored by public funds as a result of policies from national and local government or other bodies. For instance, the purview of Meade and Shaw's discussion is that of 'community arts', a term that Matarasso (2013: 214) suggests is one undergoing rehabilitation after falling out of favour in the 1990s 'to be replaced by the seemingly innocuous alternative, "participatory arts"'. Whatever label is applied to this lineage (and as Matarasso indicates, there is significance and complexity to each term), they describe a domain of public goods and values that resist the way in which 'twin forces of individualization and consumerism have come to frame our understanding of the possible' (Meade and Shaw, 2007: 415).

This practice seeks to affirm the distance described by Vodanovic, one removed from the taint of economic dictates, holding at bay an art world of markets and exchange value. Nonetheless, this is a field in which professionals do make a living directing participation in activities of cultural production by non-professional community members. The delivery of projects adds value and status to the repertoire of the intermediary – organisation or individual – within a wider cultural ecology. Furthermore, while the term 'amateur' appears to be rarely invoked in these fields in describing the subjects of intermediation projects, we might bear in mind how their established or developing skills and *their* 'repertoire' are framed in relation to this ecology. For instance, mindful of policies and cultural politics described previously, in what ways is the purpose of engagement projects conceived? Are they aimed at pleasure, enlightenment, nurturing desire, and consciousness raising and/or skills development or all of these? In relation to development, what might intermediation projects have to do, if anything, with the potential for recognising and nurturing aptitude or the 'talent' for creative expression among non-professionals?

Sponsoring amateurism

We can now turn to explore some of these issues in practice with reference to a number of intermediation activities located in or focused on the Balsall Heath area of Birmingham. The first is an example that brings together two imperatives of cultural education – offering access to expression for its own sake as well signposting a route from amateur to professional status. Originated by Birmingham-based artist Trevor Pitt, the temporary Cannon Hill Art School (CHAS), complete with 'pop-up' Chancellor, ran in the summer of 2015. It was organised and hosted in partnership with the publicly funded Midland Arts Centre (MAC), which has an explicit and familiar mission 'to make art an important part of people's lives' (Midland Arts Centre, 2019).

Pitt says of himself that: 'Although my practice is fundamentally that of an artist I work as a curator, commissioner and a researcher dependent on the nature of the "role" I take within the dynamic of the project' (Pitt, 2011). CHAS emerged from an activist role, developed as a practical intervention in response to changes in contemporary arts education. Pitt and his collaborators expressed a concern about the debt faced by students seeking cultural training in established institutions. A consequence is that this field of experience – and possible creative careers – will become increasingly the preserve of the rich. This venture built upon Pitt's democratising approach in previous initiatives of his such as *Anticurate* (2011) and *Open project* (2013), both of which sought to explore the nature of curation by challenging conventional practices and barriers to defining the status of art, artists and gallery. CHAS took its cue too from radical art schools such as Black Mountain College, USA (Palmer and Trombetta, 2017) and the 'DIY' Open School East in London (openschooleast.org; Jacobi, 2017). Supported in part by ACE, the latter offers a diverse, free, experimental and collaborative space for artistic learning, enabling creative expression whether directed towards the development of a career or for its own sake.

The Open School was also conceived as a social intervention of the kind envisaged by Pitt. Thus, CHAS sought to be open to all, 'in the belief that everyone can benefit from an art education', consciously recruiting individuals 'from any social class, educational background or age to dedicate their time and energy to a personal project'. Supporting them with small bursaries, CHAS offered 'a real opportunity for individuals, while learning the curatorial and artistic approaches needed to succeed' (Midland Arts Centre, 2015), enabling over 70 individuals from across the West Midlands to develop skills and to exhibit their work in a dedicated exhibition in the MAC's galleries.

Interesting here are expressions of individual success in this venture, where insights into its achievement come from participants, endorsing the value of CHAS and of course that of the intermediary. 'Ella' praised the opportunity for herself and others like her, that is 'people who otherwise haven't had the support and drive to develop and produce work due to jobs and other life circumstances' (Midland Arts Centre, 2015). The experience motivated her to overcome barriers to having a go at being creative, 'but not quite having the confidence and support network to do so and develop it into something I would want to show' (Midland Arts Centre, 2015). Others expressed similar sentiments: gaining confidence through collaboration, encouragement and the challenge of exhibition to a public audience. For many, this experience would not be the end of their practice, the continuation of which meant being creative for its own rewards or maybe pondering a road towards something more formalised.

Whatever the aims and prospects of CHAS's pupils, its position as champion of the value of art compares with other enterprises where participants sit in a continuum between amateur and potential professional status with a more mutually supportive role than when operating under the direction of specific intermediaries. Also based in Balsall Heath is Tindal Street Fiction Group (TSFG). Established in 1983, the group has its roots in the worker writer groups and community publishing movement of the 1970s, marked by the establishment of the Federation of Worker Writers and Community Publishers in 1976. As Woodin (2009) has documented, this was a moment with educational, political and social impact. The broad thrust of this moment sought to encourage the cultural expression of working-class and marginalised voices through literary forms: poetry, prose, autobiography and history. TSFG got its name from meeting at Tindal Street School, which was also host to lesbian and feminist activists who developed their cultural engagement through a focus on women's writing. The group organised it own imprint – Tindal Street Press – which secured funding support from local government and ACE. Over its history, TSFG published many group and individual works collecting stories from the city such as *Tindal Street fiction* (1984), Leon Blades' *Six Caribbean stories* (1985) and *The view from Tindal Street* (1986) (Beard, 2013). The imprint was developed as an independent not-for-profit publisher over two decades, and its list achieved some critical and commercial success until its decline and takeover by Profile Books in 2012. Limiting and vetting its membership now, TSFG's relationship with its engaged and culturally democratic roots is less clear. While the ethos expressed by its online presence concerns the value and dedication to writing *qua* writing, it appears oriented to the transformation, or perhaps canonisation, of its members as professionals. In so doing, this group of amateurs has the patina of those engaged in the kind of 'serious leisure' described by Stebbins (1992).

Clearly, those participating in CHAS and Tindal Street produce work that recognises and respects the stamp of their work as authors or artists. Similar in this regard is the *Some cities* project (see also Burwood, Chapter six in this volume). With a history of public funding, it is a Community Interest Company (CIC) 'that uses participatory photography to give a voice to the people and communities of Birmingham' (some-cities.org.uk). The project shares the educational remit of CHAS, where photography here serves as medium for the development of skills and the encouragement of social cohesion, 'creating opportunities for people to learn, to make considered choices about themselves and their communities and to share their thoughts and feelings with others' (some-cities.org.uk). As contributions to the project's online community attest, some of these choices are expressed in terms of how individuals develop their own creativity and orientation about the value of their work and their future. In a major feature of its work, *Some cities* invited photographers of all levels of skill and capability to contribute images of Birmingham, visually narrating a collective story about their place in the city. Across the project's online presence, employing social media sites such as Flickr and Tumblr, it makes available the many contributions it has solicited. In its various sub-projects too, *Some cities* seeks to respect participant production by recording and presenting it for others as something with which they might engage. In *A place of dreams*, for instance, with participants in the Druids Heath and Nechells areas of the city, each has produced images relevant and meaningful to them. Creating an archive, collected and curated by the groups themselves, these have been presented in a print publication and exhibition (some-cities. org.uk).

The projects discussed here are notable for how they are informed in some manner by a democratic impulse to nurture those deemed 'ordinary', non-professional, *amateur*. Each project enlists participants who may have some or no experience of creative expression, allowing for the use of different media and modes of presentation. Respecting the authorial claim of participants, each is oriented to encouraging an address to publics beyond a limited appeal to family and friends of the homemade. Compared with the project encountered in Salford discussed at the outset of this chapter, these offer some sense of durability for participants and their work. All have had their potential for creative work galvanised by intermediation projects formulated from a variety of impulses, recognisable from traditions of community engagement or policy priorities that underwrite funding allocations. Some involved in such projects might have an eye on the rewards of professionalism and indeed may develop the skills and originality that lead them to it; many involved are less ambitious and some may in turn return to a position of being deemed 'hard to reach'.

'Participation' beyond policy and intermediation?

The category of the amateur and the variety of associated practices suggests that there is a range of creative orientations and relationships that individuals have with the cultural sphere beyond those authorised by cultural intermediaries or sanctioned and sponsored by policy discourse. To recall the specific reference points of the introductory section, to explore areas like Ordsall in Salford or Balsall Heath in Birmingham is to encounter examples of everyday cultural expression produced by non-professionals. The contemporary injunction to be creative is apparent as walls and street furniture might be covered by graffiti: a great deal of it is functionally denotative and not much more than a 'tag', a signal of someone's existence or the marking out of territory. In terms of the care, attention and sometimes risk involved in their creation, other forms of graffiti exhibit an elaborated expression and expectation of attention. Mohammed Ali who, in interview, has recalled the 'mindless fun' of his creative origins articulates this quality: 'He admits, somewhat hesitantly, that he used to do illegal graffiti, spraying his first wall at the age of 14. But to him, it was adding colour to an "eyesore" as he would often seek out the ugliest walls in town that were covered in tags' (Ali quoted in Anon, no date). A site like Balsall Heath, which may or may not be typical, is home to a wide range of non-professional activity produced outside of policy support that might be equally visible or audible in the streets, on noticeboards, libraries or online. Of course, the nature of amateurism implies that much production or activity might not be intended for sharing but the material that *is* shared includes, among other things: self-published novels; group poetry writing; blogging sites and Flickr accounts; youth theatre inspired by the Islamic faith; craftwork informed by migrant traditions; and a prodigious range of music making. The last of these is worth exploring briefly in terms of its presentation, accessibility and imaginative domain.

Turning to comprehend amateur creative work available online one should recognise the complications in anchoring its origin and meaning to any physical locale. Nonetheless, online identifiers, community discussion and indeed elements of expression themselves locate individuals and their work in relation to place: Balsall Heath, neighbouring wards like Sparkbrook or Small Heath and the wider city of Birmingham. Individuals who go by names like Sparka, State, Shots, Chumbo, Lil-Smasha, Slickzz and Lz appear in performances shot on mobile phones or digital cameras. The music and imagery shared by these individuals has its roots in now global genres of rap, drum and bass, and grime. In relation to the conventions of those genres, performers evidence a variety of competencies – whether in terms of lyrical dexterity or in delivery – and indeed, some of the video presentations are ambitious and effective in their use of edits, effects and location. Sometimes these posts are based in music that has been prerecorded by the performers – perhaps using tools on a laptop computer. Music is shared freely in online platforms like Soundcloud or Mixcloud and video via YouTube, whether from the accounts of the performers or at 'channels' like *P 110* or *JDZ*.

This landscape of activity is redolent of some of the findings in the 'urban multiculture' addressed by James (2015). Concerned with similar creative activities in Inner London, James describes 'circuitries of urban culture' where technologies of the sound system, pirate radio and YouTube enabled practices and 'were constituted in, and constitutive of, urban multiculture' (James, 2015: 96). As he suggests, the 'hypermobilities' of digital connectivity manifest in these online posts and performances can, on the one hand, be thought of as a form of self-broadcasting, one which articulates 'the sovereign curating-self enshrined in neoliberal ideology' (James, 2015: 107). The performances referenced in this discussion may also be viewed as interested versions of a long-established form of self-promotion, now made visible thanks to digital technologies, aimed at the attentions of the music industries and general audiences. That said, there is an absence of any practical element of cultural enterprise in this landscape. Much of this material has the gloss of the sound and promotions produced by the commercial industries but lacks any obvious links to them in terms of a means of generating income. While the mechanism and rewards remain opaque, channels themselves may elicit advertising income from hosts like YouTube: *JDZ* boasts of its popularity, with tens of thousands of subscribers and millions of views for the videos it showcases. However, while details about individual performers might connect to social media accounts, rarely do they link to 'labels' or sites like iTunes, Spotify or to downloadable files for sale. Nor do links lead to evidence of performance before live audiences, which would suggest another mode of economic activity.

Given the finesse, expertise and presence of some of these performers and those who aid their presentation, they might be best described as the much-vaunted 'pro-am' (Leadbeater and Miller, 2004). This is a category that disturbs the ways in which cultural participation is assessed and understood but, economically speaking, these performers lie firmly at the amateur end of the cultural ecology. Either way, the significance of this activity lies in its register of a form of visible, distributed and accessible creative production, that does, by any estimation, feature a sizeable participant cohort. Given its reach, one might thus speculate about the degree to which the producers and consumers of this kind of work represent the 'hard to reach' of cultural policy and its intermediary agents. How might those seeking to develop cultural engagement understand this activity? Songs and performances from the individuals mentioned earlier reference a world of the commercial music and a symbolic economy of genres in which misogyny, homophobia and violence have currency. On the other hand, to consume even a small amount of these songs and videos is to encounter individuals acting as creative agents, who have something to say about themselves and their worlds.

Conclusion

In tandem with those who produce work encouraged by cultural intermediaries, the kind of activity signalled in the last section identifies some of the absences and challenges in conceptualising participation as production, its range, variety and meaning. Some of this has to do with the structures of the worlds of art that inform intermediation (and policy), of what counts (and what is deemed good for you) and, of course, the validation of certain types of activity and aesthetic over others. This is all supported by the distinctions between expertise of the professional and amateur and also their orientation to the economic aspects of what they do. Whatever the altruistic qualities of cultural work, its value is also one aligned with economic rationales, of what is work for some and a 'hobby' or one-off experience for others.

We can appreciate from this one snapshot of place and attendant reflections that there is a symbolic economy of some scope and nuance that raises questions for our understanding of cultural participation betwixt and between the injunctions of policy. Many people are creative in various ways that are interrelated with the cultural economy and invite us to explore what they make and how they understand their work and its purpose. If we are better to understand the value and impact of policy directives and those worlds that have sat in and outside of its reach, issues of skills development, competencies, expression and indeed aesthetics, exhibition and circulation merit further reflection.

References

Anon. (No date) 'Come and watch internationally acclaimed graffiti artist Mohammed Ali create his first London street mural on Green Street' at *Emel* (http://www.emel.com/article?id=&a_id=1510).

Arts Council England (no date) *The active lives survey* (artscouncil.org. uk/participating-and-attending/active-lives-survey).

BBC, *Art Ninja* (https://www.bbc.co.uk/cbbc/shows/art-ninja).

Beard, A. (2013) Tindall Street Fiction Group members at *Alan Beard's Site* (http://www.alanbeard.net/tsfgmembersalltime.htm)

Belfiore, E. (2006) 'The social impacts of the arts – myth or reality?', in M. Mirza (ed), *Culture vultures: Is UK arts policy damaging the arts?*, London: Policy Exchange, pp. 20–37.

Bilton, C. (2010) 'Manageable creativity', *International Journal of Cultural Policy*, 16(3): 255-69.

Carrington, V. (2009). 'I write, therefore I am: texts in the city', *Visual Communication*, 8(4): 409-25.

Channel 4, programme websites: channel4.com/programmes/craft-i-made-this/episode-guide; channel4.com/programmes/craft-it-yourself/episode-guide

Creative Industries Council. (no date) 'Creative Industries Earn UK Almost £92bn' (http://www.thecreativeindustries.co.uk/uk-creative-overview/news-and-views/news-creative-industries-earn-uk-almost-%C2%A392bn?utm_content=buffer091f8&utm_medium=social&utm_source=twitter.com&utm_campaign=buffer#).

DCMS (Department for Culture, Media and Sport) (2016a) *The Culture White Paper (Cm 9218)*. HMSO.

DCMS (Department for Culture, Media and Sport) (2016b) *Guidance: Taking Part Survey* (https://www.gov.uk/guidance/taking-part-survey)

Fox, B. (2004) 'Rethinking the amateur: editor's introduction', *Spectator: The University of Southern California Journal of Film and Television*, 24(1): 5-16.

Holden, J. (2015). 'The ecology of culture', *Arts and Humanities Research Council*, Swindon.

Jacobi, S. (2017) 'Alternative art schools in London: contested space and the emergence of new modes of learning in practice', in J. Luger and J. Ren (eds) *Art and the City: Worlding the discussion through a critical artscape*, London: Routledge, pp. 107-19.

James, M. (2015) *Urban multiculture: Youth, politics and cultural transformation in a global city*, London: Springer.

Leadbeater, C, and Miller, P. (2004) *The pro am revolution: How enthusiasts are changing our economy and society*, London: Demos.

Long, P. (2014) '"Breathing a bit of life back into the breeze blocks": cultural place making in the inner city', *Edge Condition*, 5: 123-7.

Matarasso, F. (2013) *'All in this together': The depoliticisation of community art in Britain, 1970-2011*, available from: http://parliamentofdreams.com/articles-and-papers/

Meade, R. and Shaw, M. (2007) 'Special issue: community development and the arts: reviving the democratic imagination', *Community Development Journal*, 42(4): 413-523.

Midland Arts Centre (2015) 'Art school experience for local individuals produces summer show exhibition at MAC Birmingham' (macbirmingham.co.uk/news/2015/07/16/art-school-experience-for-local-individuals-produces-summer-show-exhibition-at-mac-birmingham)

Midland Arts Centre (2019) 'About' (macbirmingham.co.uk/about)

Miles, A. and Sullivan, A. (2012) 'Understanding participation in culture and sport: mixing methods, reordering knowledges', *Cultural Trends*, 21(4): 311-24.

Mirza, M. (2006) 'The arts as painkiller' in M. Mirza (ed) *Culture vultures: Is UK arts policy damaging the arts?* London: Policy Exchange, pp. 93–110.

Moseley, R. (2000) 'Makeover takeover on British television', *Screen*, 41(3): 299-314.

O'Brien, D. and Oakley, K. (2015) *Cultural value and inequality: A critical literature review*, London: AHRC.

Palmer, J. and Trombetta, M. (2017) 'Black Mountain College: a creative art space where it was safe to fail', *World Futures*, 73(1): 16-22.

Pitt, T. (2011) 'Trevor Pitt' at *Axis Web* (axisweb.org/p/trevorpitt/#info)

Reeves, A. (2015) 'Neither class nor status: arts participation and the social strata', *Sociology*, 49(4): 624-42.

Sky TV, programme website, https://www.skyartsartistoftheyear.tv/portrait-terms

Stebbins, R. A., (1992). *Amateurs, professionals, and serious leisure*, Montreal [Que.]: McGill-Queen's University Press.

Vodanovic, L. (2013) 'The new art of being amateur: distance as participation', *Journal of Visual Art Practice*, 12(2):169-79.

Woodin, T. (2009) 'Working-class writing, alternative publishing and audience participation', *Media, Culture and Society*, 31 (1): 79-96.

Part Two
Practices of cultural intermediation

FIVE

'An area lacking cultural activity': researching cultural lives in urban space

Paul Long and Saskia Warren

Introduction

Jakob and van Heur (2015) argue that, compared with the attention afforded the cultural policies and initiatives galvanising the creative sector, less is known about the role played across this field by intermediaries. While this absence is addressed across this volume (see also Perry et al, 2015), even less understood are the *objects* of intermediaries and their activities. By way of illustration, O'Connor (2004: 40) describes intermediation as a mode of translation 'between the language of policy makers and that of the cultural producers'. How then, do individuals and communities that are earmarked for inculcation into the values of the cultural ecology understand the results of this translation? While there is a rich tradition of audience and visitor studies (see Tung Au et al, 2017; Hay, 2018), the specific ways in which individuals are situated by intermediation practices, policy imperatives, discourses and imaginaries as cultural consumers, participants and sometimes producers (see Chapter four) merits closer attention.

The *Cultural intermediation* project that impels this collection sought to investigate the connection between policies and people in terms of the variety of their roles across the cultural ecology, through explorations of sites in Salford (see Chapter thirteen) and Birmingham (here and Chapter four). Drawing on this research, this chapter investigates the relationship with the cultural ecology of people living in the Balsall Heath area of Birmingham.

Balsall Heath suggested itself as a site of investigation because of its demographic diversity, levels of deprivation, recent history of intercommunity dissonance and the relative visibility of its cultural assets. On this last note, Balsall Heath has been an object of cultural policy initiatives in which the neighbourhood saw a rise in available arts programmes which sought to engage disadvantaged and 'hard-to-reach' communities whether defined in terms of education, employment or cultural activity (for a summary, see Jancovich and Bianchini, 2013).

In proceeding, this chapter first outlines the particular socioeconomic character of this area in the context of a wider set of issues and policy impulses. It then discusses the method of walking interviews that was employed to engage with residents, of how residents guided researchers around local sites and scenes that are meaningful to them. The method was not employed in order to gather an exhaustive picture of cultural engagement; it was instead conceived as a means of 'thinking with' participants within a local landscape of social, material and religious relations that shape individual agency (see: Hopkins and Gale, 2009; Hopkins et al, 2013).

Balsall Heath amid Birmingham's cultural ecology

In conceptualising the particularities of place in which research for this chapter has been located, we draw upon a description 'from within', via the community initiative 'Balsall Heath is Our Planet' (Anon, 2018). This 'planet' comprises an inner city neighbourhood, south of Birmingham city centre, with a population of around 15,000 inhabitants. Politically, it is part of the Sparkbrook ward, 'which is one of the most ethnically diverse in England'. Since the 1950s the area has been a destination for migrants arriving in Birmingham, its population now predominantly Pakistani, Yemeni and Somali Muslim. Many recent arrivals have received few of the promises or rewards of their antecedents who experienced the post-war boom; as current statistics demonstrate: 'we have persistent problems of low income and worklessness' (Anon, 2018). The environmental focus of 'Balsall Heath is Our Planet' underlines some of the specific ways in which locals are further disadvantaged: with housing consisting mostly of economically inefficient pre-1919 terraces there is widespread fuel poverty (that is, where over 10% of household income is spent on energy bills). Nonetheless, and in spite of challenges: 'We have strong community and faith organisations, who have been major players in providing services and turning around the appearance and reputation of the area' (Anon, 2018).

The reputational burden of the area is summarised by Raja Amin, a member of the Balsall Heath Forum, who recalls prostitution, gang problems and visible street dealing in drugs. As a consequence, 'No one wanted to admit to being from Balsall Heath' (quoted in Khaleeli,

2015). In terms of how its reputation has attracted the attention of politicians and social investigators, one might describe Balsall Heath and the wider ward as 'over-determined' in its representation in policy statements and research papers. Sparkbrook more broadly was the site of John Rex and Robert Moore's *Race community and conflict* (1967), a contribution to the sociology of race and the city, with its suggestive identification of 'twilight' and 'transition' zones in describing the presence of immigrants and for understanding social tensions prompted in relation to their settlement. Others have visited Balsall Heath specifically in extending Rex and Moore's focus on migrants and housing provision (Williams, 1978; Karn, 1979), tracking demographic change (Jones, 1970), or exploring the separation of ethnic groups and migratory communities from each other and from the 'host' community (Woods, 1979).

Balsall Heath was also the location of the Dyche studio, which was favoured by many migrants in the post-war period when seeking photographic portraits of themselves and their families. Now preserved in city archives, Tina Campt (2008: 2) describes the collection of Dyche portraits (wherein the subjects are mostly anonymous), as 'a pivotal, albeit unintended, site of documentation for postwar British colonial migration during this critical phase in the creation of Black Britain'. During the period of research for this chapter, celebrations for the fiftieth anniversary of the Centre of Contemporary Cultural Studies (CCCS) at the University of Birmingham retrieved a hitherto 'hidden' history of Balsall Heath. Janet Mendelsohn, an American studying in Birmingham in the early 1970s and a keen photographic ethnographer, had compiled over 3,000 images of the area (Connell and Hilton, 2016). Mendelsohn's lens was aimed at pimps, prostitutes and a milieu of deprivation with empathy for humanity at odds with perceptions of the area and how individuals in such roles have been treated. Others have been more judgemental in their responses to these figures.

A signal figure in the history of representations of Balsall Heath is Dick Atkinson. Attached as a lecturer in sociology with the University of Birmingham in the 1960s, his position there was undermined thanks to his sympathies for student protesters and their cause. Disillusioned with academia, he responded to calls for aid made to the sociology department by Balsall Heath resident groups. Active in the area's grassroots politics from the early 1970s onwards, he later published a range of influential works on community engagement issues (for example, Atkinson, 1994a; 1994b; 1995; 2004). In each case, his insights balance local, national and global concerns, emphatically worked out amid social enterprise activity and local commitment to Balsall Heath. The application of his insights are evidenced in contributions to the establishment of a local forum, St Paul's Trust, which has run a charitable secondary school, nursery centre, urban farm, enterprise and community centre and 'acts as the village hall, village green and focal point for the surrounding neighbourhood' (1994b: 27).

In the 1990s, the prostitution that had been captured by Mendelsohn in the 1960s was protested by community demonstrations that drove away clients, pimps and sex workers (see: Sanders, 2004). As Atkinson (1994a: 27) tells it, such was the transformation that 'residents have begun to accentuate the positive. They wish to give a face-lift to their local park, employ a park keeper or sports coach, implement a traffic management scheme to slow speeding traffic and take ownership of and maintain a range of confused open spaces'. This development drew the approving attention of politicians like former Prime Minister David Cameron, for whom Balsall Heath became a totemic reference point for the neoliberal voluntarism underpinning his concept of the 'Big Society' (Hilder, 2006).

However, whatever the apparent successes of the impulse to 'clean up' Balsall Heath's streets, appreciative assessments overlook the nature of how sex workers were treated (how were they *encouraged* to cease business or to leave? Where did they *go*?). The public activities of women in the area – as well as other groups such as young men socialising on the street – have been subject to regulation in a variety of ways (see Figure 5.1). By the same degree, a flipside to the celebration of community cohesion of Balsall Heath was evinced in a suspicion of its Muslim section in the wake of Birmingham's so-called 'Trojan Horse' scandal. This concerned an alleged fundamentalist Islamist plot to take over the governance of 21 schools in Birmingham and resulted in the publication of a special investigative report. Several schools in Balsall Heath were subject to investigation (see: Holmwood and O'Toole, 2017). As a result, Michael Gove, then Education Secretary, deemed it necessary to ensure that all of England's primary and secondary schools would have to promote 'British values of tolerance and fairness' (Hope, 2014). Alongside the government's anti-terrorism strategy 'Prevent' (Awan, 2012) and reactions to it, the tenor of the moral panic surrounding the 'Trojan Horse' case is indicative of a broad field of struggle over issues of culture, social connectivity and civic virtue. While not immediately apparent, these considerations are not far removed from the more instrumental versions of culture and its commodification at work in contemporary Britain and evidenced in policy approaches to it in Birmingham.

Figure 5.1: West Midlands Police Dispersal Order

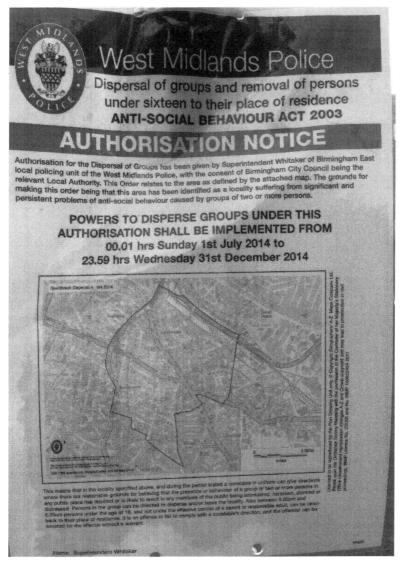

Source: Author (Long), 5 July 2014

As has been well documented, the city's industrial decline in the 1970s prompted action designed to reinvent and rebrand it as a cultural destination (Kennedy, 2004; Brookes et al, 2016). Prestige projects initiated in the 1980s – such as the construction of the International Convention Centre, National Indoor Arena, Symphony Hall, and most recently the Library of Birmingham – illustrate an investment in events and exhibition businesses and the nurturing of the service economy (Henry et al, 2002; Parker and Long, 2003, 2004). Birmingham's remaking is at one with policy discourse concerning the economic and social advantage afforded by cultural assets (Hewison, 2014) and expressed in the notion of the 'creative city' (Landry, 2000; Bianchini, 2017) and in the reception afforded Florida's concept of the creative class (2002). Thus, the developments listed above have been attended by the creation of cultural industry clusters and their role in the revival of areas such as Digbeth and the Jewellery Quarter (Chapain and Comunian, 2010).

Faith in the breadth of the virtues of the cultural ecology is evident in current policy directions. The Birmingham City Council document 'Birmingham Cultural Strategy 2016-19' (2017: 2) offers a familiar vision of cultural democracy that bestrides production and consumption, one in which 'people come together to co-create, commission, lead and participate in a wide range of locally relevant, pluralistic and community driven cultural ventures'. This policy speaks to supporting 'and enabling the growth of creative and cultural SMEs [small and medium-sized enterprises] and micro-businesses and individuals' alongside a particular focus on young people to ensure their access to and engagement with 'a diverse range of high quality arts and cultural experiences' (Birmingham City Council, 2017: 1). One can appreciate the necessity of such a broadly pitched policy as, whatever the success of Birmingham's post-industrial rebranding, it is a phenomenon very much concentrated on those assets and city centre sites listed in the previous paragraph. The city's peripheral spaces – whether inner areas such as Aston, Handsworth or Balsall Heath, as well as outer zones such as Castle Vale or Kingstanding – appear less amenable to incorporation into the narrative of the creative city. Nonetheless, aspects of what some of these areas represent has been enlisted in the promotion of the city as a space of culture and its consumption. Balsall Heath, for instance, offers a 'Balti Triangle' (see Sardar, 2008), named after a signal dish served by the many restaurants offering South Asian cuisine clustered on the Moseley Road, Ladywood Road and Stoney Lane. In turn, Balsall Heath had a role in Birmingham's (unsuccessful) 2010 bid to emulate Liverpool and Glasgow and become the UK City of Culture. Arrayed alongside the 'Balti Triangle' were Birmingham's 'Chinatown', Handsworth's Soho Road, a 'Gay Village', assets that represented a shift in the city's branding that was identified by a local BBC correspondent: 'We may no longer be the city of a thousand trades, but we clearly deserve to be the city of a thousand cultures' (Doyle, 2010).

Regional Mayor Andy Street led lobbying efforts in an ultimately failed attempt to lure the broadcaster Channel 4 to the Midlands in ways that extend this approach to culture's tradability. Local journalist Adam Yosef (2018) wryly noted how the Birmingham's multicultural character had been deployed: 'If this was an official bid, "Come and have a go if you think you're diverse enough" would probably be the campaign slogan'. Furthermore, his critical qualification identifies a significant problem in this approach, that 'while England's "second city" is a fantastic buzzing hub with a wealth of raw creative talent for C4 executives to tap into, it's also a city where decision-makers in the mainstream media industry often struggle to identify, embrace and incorporate under-represented groups' (Yosef, 2018). Certainly, the vision of the city's policy makers and agents, of a cultural offer that makes expedient use of ideas of the city's ethnic diversity, is a relatively exclusive one in which some citizens and localities are elided or have a relatively passive role (see Parker and Long, 2004). These circumstances are extended in a wider imbalance predicated on the same lines. As Brookes et al (2016: 88) observe, in spite of the urban regeneration of the city centre and local government initiatives in pursuit of social inclusion goals: 'it was acknowledged by all political parties that inequality still existed and lasting change for people living in Birmingham's most deprived neighbourhoods had not been achieved'.

In search of culture

How then does the cultural continuum sketched above frame and play out in the experiences and perspectives of local citizens? To what degree might they be conscious agents of any role they play in this landscape of positive, negative and creative ideas of culture? The approach to answering such questions with reference to residents of Balsall Heath employed here can be distinguished from the information gathering and feedback sought by cultural intermediaries. While we were respectful of the work of intermediaries with whom we were in contact, our aim was to avoid direct assessment of their projects through emulation of the various techniques employed for evaluating funding outcomes and impact for particular reasons. The scrutiny afforded publicly funded arts activity has engendered a wealth of techniques designed to measure the reach and value of particular projects. Cultural justice objectives have motivated attempts to address a perceived deficit in the quality of people's lives and to involve the 'hard to reach' in creative activities, attended by quantitative returns that evaluate the impact of arts in economic, health, community cohesion and so on (Walmsley, 2012). There is a purposefulness and potentially instrumental quality to survey techniques that sometimes involve intermediaries managing data gathering in order to satisfy policy bodies as to the 'return on investment' of their funding initiatives. By way of contrast, the *Cultural intermediation* project allowed for a critical distance in considering the basic assumptions of cultural policy and practice and the necessities of their evaluation. In organising walking methods, we sought therefore to engage residents through recruitment calls posted across the locality – via local newspaper the Balsall Heathen, resident forums, or at the St Paul's Trust. Recruits were defined by their residency in the area, inclusive of men and women of various ages, ethnicities and economic status. In each case, personal detail of a demographic kind was offered voluntarily, emerging in the course of interviews. The primary purpose was to focus on perspectives of cultural engagement from each person's experience, to gain a sense of the qualitative textures of its place in their lives and resonance for them, and their sense of this locale.

It has been argued that 'walking in the street' (when compared to say, being driven around in a car or sat in an interview room) means that both researcher and participant are exposed to the multisensory stimulation of the surrounding environment rather than cocooned in a filtered 'blandscape' (Evans and Jones, 2011: 850; see also: Laurier and Philo, 2003; Adams and Guy, 2007; Bijsterveld, 2010). As Evans and Jones suggest, it is possible therefore that walking interviews produce rich insights 'because interviewees are prompted by meanings and connections to the surrounding environment and are less likely to try and give the "right" answer. Indeed, it seems intuitively sensible for researchers to ask interviewees to talk about the places that they are interested in while they are in that place' (Evans and Jones, 2011: 849). We distinguish between guided walking interviews (Reed, 2002; Paulos and Goodman, 2004) – led by the research and focused on a previously determined question – and that of the 'go-along' (Kusenbach, 2003; Carpiano, 2009). The latter seeks to make use of a more 'natural' encounter in which the routine and purview of the participant determines a route along which the interview takes place in order to 'capture sometimes hidden or unnoticed habitual relations with place and the environment' (Evans and Jones, 2011: 850). A 'go-along' in the area in which participants are familiar seeks to position them as experts, focusing on their lived experience and knowledge while decentering that of the researcher (see Elwood and Martin, 2000). While the walking method involves an element of 'making strange' one's everyday environment, there is also a quality that highlights the role of the researcher as tourist. In this instance, the interviewee acts as guide, explaining the significance of sites, sounds, smells and experiences to the researcher.

Walking and talking 'culture'

Sardar (2008) offers a lyrical account of walking the same streets as the authors and our research participants. He reflects on feeling 'at home' among an ambience of neglect and smell of decay and yet also evinces the outsider's fascinated stare:

> From the grey façade of Karachi Fried Chicken on one side and a dilapidated garage ('Cars Wanted for Cash') on the other, I could distinguish the smell of rusting iron and the rotting leftovers of yesterday's chicken and chips. I trudged on through the all-too-familiar landscape of council flats; row upon row, street after street of uniform terraced houses with 2.4 bedrooms, a living room that allows no space for living and an impossibly small kitchen. (Sardar, 2008: 12)

As he jokes, this is hardly a 'city break' destination and yet, without denying the value of a critical perspective, as in similar accounts what is absent is recognition of the area's actual variety and validation from within. Interviewees drew our attention to the importance for them of significant green spaces in the area, to the river running through it, as well as sites of considerable personal resonance. Furthermore, Balsall Heath does boast some cultural assets of a familiar kind, although the value of their place in individual narratives can be an ambivalent one. Prime among these sites are the Edgbaston Cricket Ground, a major sporting destination, and the Midland Arts Centre (MAC). Established in 1962 and located in the sizable Cannon Hill Park, MAC claims to attract over 1,000,000 visits (*not* individual visitors) every year, 'drawing audiences from across the UK and beyond' (macbirmingham.co.uk). MAC's website attests to its purpose in offering a programme of events, theatre, dance, cinema, music, spoken word, comedy, exhibitions and classes in creative practice: 'Working both in our state-of-the-art building and out in the community, our mission is to make art an important part of people's lives' (macbirmingham.co.uk). The more recently established Ort Gallery echoes this ambition. It is 'an artist-led exhibition space [...] with the social mission to facilitate dialogue in the community' (ortgallery.co.uk). After a precarious start-up in 2011, and now a recipient of Arts Council funding, Ort Gallery seeks to explore how community can be strengthened by contemporary arts programming. It is 'concerned with bringing world-class art to an area lacking cultural activity and engaging the audiences in an organic and meaningful way' (ortgallery.co.uk).

The ambition, generalisations and assumptions in the statements of both institutions express a potentially myopic judgement of the interrelationship of people, place and the parameters of the cultural ecology in its historical and contemporary forms. In the 1930s for instance, this was the location of a surrealist collective (Warren and Forcer, 2017), it was where Tindal Street Fiction Group was founded in 1983 (see Chapter four), the same year as the theatrical venue CAVE (Community And Village Entertainment) (Cochrane, 2008). There is a rich tradition of popular music production in the area, courtesy in particular of the Oriental Star Agency (OSA). OSA nurtured Balsall Heath's innovator in bhangra music, Bally Sagoo, while its global connections have been significant in bringing to the area Qawwali singers like Nusrat Fateh Ali Khan. For Henry et al (2002: 118), OSA's cultural and economic success is significant in drawing attention to 'those groups excluded and erased from both historical and contemporary constructions of Birmingham'.

The business and reach of OSA gestures to how qualitative research into place and culture sometimes leads away from particular concepts of 'world-class' or expectations of the importance of 'art' in everyday life. Turning to consider insights drawn from walking with participants, whatever the ubiquity of culture or creativity in contemporary discourse, each evinced an individual attempt to make sense of what they meant. In each case, we explained the nature of the method and the aim of exploring what culture meant to them and where it might be found in Balsall Heath and in their lives. BA's reflection at the start of an interview was typical in working through what had been asked of her, pointing to a bustling intersection by her home as 'quite a social corner'. Perhaps prompted by the promotion of the area for its 'Balti Triangle', she noted the prodigious patronage of fast food takeaways, 'so my first thought was that there is a bit of a culture in that'. Indicating the proximity of a nearby church where she and her husband were members she suggested that 'there is tons of stuff I can tell you about that; so, like the Taekwondo and all the different cultures that are in the church'. BA's offer to list activities was a means of itemising her understanding of its domain, a checking off what might or might not count and where she might fit in. This itemisation was echoed by CH who explicitly referenced 'high culture' as something she does not engage with: 'I don't go to art galleries. If I go to the theatre, it's more likely to be a stand-up comedian than a play. I don't know anything about opera. Music-wise, I'm just kind of strictly pop'. In fact, CH suggested that TV was her main point of reference, the most everyday and democratic of cultural pursuits.

Interviews expressed historical sensibilities in which the autobiographical was narrated in relation to wider observations bequeathed by family members in their hand-me-down stories. For instance, a recurring motif reflected on the experience of change to the area and its cultural offer and textures. SB has lived in the area long enough to recall its associations with countercultural forms, notably in the post-punk era. He identified one of the former pubs in the area (the Old Coach and Horses on Edward Road) as a venue for his own and other bands: 'It was dirt cheap and they basically gave you the room and you got people to come in and they would just take money for the drinks, so it was a great place to play'. JS, a recent graduate of dual heritage, reflected on growing up in the area, noting the disappearance of the same kind of public houses and of some of the people that sustained them, that is: 'a predominantly Irish community based around Sparkbrook and Balsall Heath which doesn't seem to be here anymore. I don't know where they've moved to'. One might infer from this absence an account of the supplanting of one migrant community by another. This process might be narrativised with negative inflection or more positively, as in HF's perception of the accommodation of Commonwealth migrants. As he stated: 'When my father first came in the '60s, if you said to your employer, "Can I go to Friday prayers?" you'd be laughed at. Now, a lot of employers cater for that. Ramadan, nobody had heard of it. There wasn't a mosque in sight, now there are mosques everywhere'. For DM, these expressed a negative development, opining that 'I think that this is a place that has become less diverse culturally, not ethnically or by faith necessarily, but culturally less diverse'.

As Warren has argued elsewhere (2017), scholarly literature often foregrounds walking practice in terms of pleasure, relaxation and the liberation afforded by mobility. However, as her work attests, some of the walking interviews produced in Balsall Heath identify how movement might be circumscribed when we understand the positioning of individuals in terms of ethnicity, faith and gender. (After all, and as discussed by Warren (2017), this is a place where the public visibility of women has been subject to forms of communal regulation.) In turn, individuals might be excluded from participation in such methods, thus impacting on the knowledge that research generates. The issues alluded to here can be illustrated with reference to engagement with a women-only adult education college in the area. TF, a second-generation Pakistani Muslim teacher participated as interviewee and community researcher and was instrumental in recruiting student participants. Like many women seen in the college, most of her class wore full-length black abayas with some splashes of colour, embroidery or patterns on their sleeves and scarves. As with the wider profile of the college cohort, most were first-generation migrants from countries including Pakistan, Bangladesh, Afghanistan, Yemen, Somalia, South Sudan, the Republic of Sudan, and Algeria. Nonetheless, the ethnic and cultural variety expressed by this group undermined any sense of a homogenous group entitled 'Muslim women'. Distinctions were manifest in subcultural and friendship groups across the college, in shared language, prayer routines, styles of dress, the wearing of hijabs or uncovered hair.

College managers recommended that Saskia Warren facilitate research in order to alleviate potential anxieties about gender-mixing, building trust over time with attendance at a number of classes over the term and facilitating learning. Classes were where the idea and techniques of the walking interview were introduced. As a result, it was clear that some were uncomfortable with the idea and so a further exercise in knowledge generation was formulated. Warren developed a classroom mapping exercise that allowed women to represent their socio-spatial knowledge of Balsall Heath. It became evident from this exercise that there were distinctions among the women in terms of responsibilities or in degree of independence. Walking and talking with a 'stranger', without a practical purpose, was outside socio-spatial norms for the participants. Walking for leisure when it does occur was a recreational practice undertaken typically in an extended family context. Generally, encounters with public space were brief and children, husbands, extended family members or friends often accompanied women: they were rarely alone.

Ultimately, a number of walking interviews with college women did take place that were insightful not just about the method but also the degree to which this group might be labelled 'hard to reach' by intermediaries and about the offer of cultural assets in Balsall Heath. As JS had indicated when we walked with him, the impact of migrant cultures is apparent in local infrastructure, where road signs in the area 'reflect certain emblems of Pakistan which [...] weren't there ten years ago'. This was an important reminder of the semiotic details of culture and the ways in which interviewees were able to interpret them in situ for researchers. As TF, noted, even for women wearing full-face veils, the specific character of how eyebrows are threaded or eyelids coloured means it is possible to distinguish a woman of Pakistani or Yemini background. Similar insights emerged from walking with college women, with conversation eliciting comment and what they would otherwise see as normative: naturally, one would shop at one place and avoid another for food or clothing.

Apparent across the interviews with women from the college was a general nervousness about public space. This was prompted by the noise of the street, dangers of traffic, unwarranted attention with unfamiliar men in the street, not to mention potential judgement by the peers one might encounter there. However, many women did use Cannon Hill Park that surrounds MAC both with their children and as a space in which they could mix with other families and friends. The park is also the site of an annual *Mela* ('assembly' in Hindi) 'organised to celebrate the diversity of the South Asian Community in Birmingham through its culture, food, sport, art and entertainment' (bigjohnsbirminghammela.com). The offer of MAC however was almost invisible to them (although its washrooms were valuable when using the park). This line of discussion is not to critique MAC per se but to explore what it represents as a particular type of cultural institution. Here, TF's experience serves to speak for the majority: 'I've been coming to the park for years and I'd never been inside. ... I knew it existed but I didn't really know what it was about, what was inside there, and I didn't really take interest'. It should be noted that this was not a perspective confined to women from the college; this was space impenetrable to some other interviewees. As BA commented: 'I have been to MAC a couple of times to look at the gallery space but I found it a bit weird'. Certainly, as TF related, teachers had made an effort in the past to become familiar with MAC and to find ways of introducing their students to it. She recalled arranging to see a film there together, having vetted it in advance although even then 'it had some scenes which they found inappropriate, therefore they don't want to go again'.

Such encounters are indicative of a wider set of challenges for this group presented by culture provision in the area and more widely. As SB pointed out, a *Biennale* event (Poolman and Rowe, 2014) involved a gambling competition and had alcohol for sale, both off-limits for those abiding by Islamic stricture. On a more general note, he also commented on the cultural capital required for engagement with intermediation projects such as one designed to explore Balsall Heath's surrealist legacy. For him, many migrants would be automatically excluded even as such projects aim to engage a wide audience: 'It is such a lovely idea but really in a way you have to be educated to what surrealism/Dada is to know what the possibilities are and to open up your mind to that sort of thing'.

Such insights are not to suggest that individuals like the women from the college are ignorant or without culture. Importantly, women had attained various levels of education in their countries of origin where their social status was not defined by migration nor perceptions of them derived from residence in an area of multiple deprivations. As their teacher commented: 'They've probably done a Master's in their own country but they can't speak English. They come and they literally can't speak it. They can write English, they can read it, but they cannot have a conversation'. As many revealed, they were acquainted with canonic figures such as Shakespeare, at least through an attention to the educational experiences of their children. Furthermore, their connectivity leads them outside of the bounds of area, city and country, even if their mobility can be circumscribed. The culture of local life is one that has to account for the interactions with the global through the medium of satellite television and the internet as a medium that supports engagement, as well as the extension of community through Skype or social media apps such as Viber or WhatsApp.

Conclusion

So what might we learn from this reflection on place, people and method? What can the specificity of this place, people and culture offer for wider insights into the experience of the subjects of cultural intermediation? As Dick Atkinson has suggested, 'there is nothing unique about Balsall Heath' (1994b: 36). However, the particular conjunction of social and cultural conditions draw attention to the variables inflecting one's understanding of culture, of the potential impact (or lack of it) of cultural intermediaries and their mission. These are accentuated in a locale such as Balsall Heath at the intersection of historical knowledge, migration, class, cultural learning, gender and ethnicity for instance.

A deeper understanding of the range of ways in which culture operates indicates some of the challenges around its meaning and texture, issues developed in Chapters seven and thirteen by Perry and then Symons in their experience with the communities of Ordsall. Culture involves the maintenance of boundaries – that which counts or does not count – and how it is measured as culture. Judgements of what has value (and of what kind), what is meaningful, the nature of affective responses, and relations between consumers and communities are all qualities that make for a complex texture for the comprehension of culture as it is lived.

Ultimately, as the small sample of respondents whose voices and experiences are heard in this chapter suggests, culture is understood in relatively ordinary ways. Amid a complex hierarchy of needs, the place of culture in everyday life might be, at worst, an affront to those intermediaries with missionary zeal for its special qualities or, at best, confirmation of a need for more resources to be targeted at it in order to evidence those qualities. On the other hand, and in the context of what is at stake in policies in the city of Birmingham and other urban sites, the appeal and promise of culture may lie in its very ordinariness, an antidote to the burdens and blame placed upon it.

What is problematic for policy makers, intermediaries and indeed artists who seek to make a case for the indispensability of culture is that this is often presented in profound ways. Culture changes lives. This may be, but the moment of illumination, the mega-effect, is less apparent than a banal, everydayness. While culture may describe a way of life, and inflect dispositions, its exceptional nature is less apparent.

References

Adams, M. and Guy, S. (2007) 'Senses and the city', *The senses and society*, 2(2): 133-6.

Anon (2018) *Balsall Heath is our planet* (https://balsallheathisourplanet. wordpress.com/the-area/).

Atkinson, D. (1994a) *The common sense of community* (No. 11), London: Demos.

Atkinson, D. (1994b) *Radical urban solutions: Urban renaissance for city schools and communities*, New York: Continuum Publishing.

Atkinson, D. (1995) *Cities of pride: Rebuilding community, refocusing government*, London: Continuum Intl Pub Group.

Atkinson, D. (2004) *Civil renewal: Mending the hole in the social ozone layer*, Birmingham: Brewin Books.

Awan, I. (2012) '"I am a Muslim not an extremist": How the Prevent Strategy has constructed a "suspect" community', *Politics & Policy*, 40(6): 1158-85.

Bianchini, F. (2017) 'Reflections on the origins, interpretations and development of the creative city idea', in I. Van Damme, B. De Munck, and A. Miles (eds) *Cities and creativity from the Renaissance to the present*, London: Routledge, pp. 23-42.

Bijsterveld, K. (2010) 'Acoustic cocooning: how the car became a place to unwind', *The Senses and Society*, 5(2): 189-211.

Birmingham City Council (2017) 'Imagination, creativity and enterprise: Birmingham Cultural Strategy 2016-2019', Birmingham.

Brookes, N., Kendall, J. and Mitton, L. (2016) 'Birmingham, priority to economics, social innovation at the margins', In T. Brandsen, S. Cattacin, A. Evers and A. Zimmer (eds), *Social Innovations in the Urban Context*, Cham: Springer International Publishing, pp. 83-96.

Campt, T. (2008) 'Imaging diaspora: race, photography, and the Ernest Dyche Archive', *Letters: The Semi Annual Newsletter of the Robert Penn Watten Centre for the Humanities*, 16(2): 1-7.

Carpiano, R. M. (2009) 'Come take a walk with me: The "go-along" interview as a novel method for studying the implications of place for health and well-being', *Health & Place*, 15: 263-72.

Chapain, C. and Comunian, R. (2010) 'Enabling and inhibiting the creative economy: the role of the local and regional dimensions in England', *Regional Studies*, 44(6): 717-34.

Cochrane, C. (2008) 'A local habitation and a name': the development of black and Asian theatre in Birmingham since the 1970's' in D. Godiwala (ed), *Alternatives within the mainstream: British Black and Asian theatres*, Newcastle: Cambridge Scholars Publishing, pp. 153-74.

Connell, K and Hilton, M. (2016) 'Janet Mendelsohn, cultural studies and the social "conjuncture"' in J. Mendelsohn (ed), *Varna Road*, Birmingham: Ikon, pp. 60-5.

Doyle, L. (2010) 'Birmingham: we are a city of culture', *BBC News*, 14 July, http://news.bbc.co.uk/local/birmingham/hi/people_and_places/arts_and_culture/newsid_8806000/8806264.stm.

Elwood, S. A. and Martin, D. G. (2000) '"Placing" interviews: location and scales of power in qualitative research', *Professional Geographer*, 52: 649-57.

Evans, J., and Jones, P. (2011) 'The walking interview: methodology, mobility and place', *Applied Geography*, 31: 849-58.

Florida, R. (2002) *The rise of the creative class and how it's transforming work, leisure, community and everyday life*, New York: Basic Books.

Hay, J. (2018) *The audience and its landscape*, London and New York: Routledge.

Henry, N., McEwan, C. and Pollard, J. (2002) 'Globalization from below: Birmingham – postcolonial workshop of the world?', *Area*, 34(2): 117-27.

Hewison, R. (2014) *Cultural capital: The rise and fall of creative Britain*, London and New York: Verso Books.

Hilder, P., (2006) 'Power up, people: double devolution and beyond', *IPPR Progressive Review*, 13(4): 238-48.

Holmwood, J., and O'Toole, T. (2017) *Countering extremism in British schools?: The truth about the Birmingham Trojan Horse affair*, London: Policy Press.

Hope, C. (2014) 'Trojan Horse report: All schoolchildren to be taught British values from September, says Michael Gove Education secretary', *Daily Telegraph* 9 June. (http://www.telegraph.co.uk/education/10887329/Trojan-horse-report-All-school-children-to-be-taught-British-values-from-September-says-Michael-Gove.html). Accessed 1 June 2018.

Hopkins, P. and Gale, R. (eds) (2009) *Muslims in Britain: Race, place and identities*, Edinburgh: Edinburgh University Press.

Hopkins, P., Kong, L. and Olson, E. (eds) (2013) *Religion and place: Landscape, politics and piety*, Dordrecht: Springer Science & Business Media.

Jakob, D. and van Heur, B. (2015). 'Taking matters into third hands: intermediaries and the organization of the creative economy', *Regional Studies*, 49(3): 357-61.

Jancovich, L. and Bianchini, F. (2013) 'Problematising participation', *Cultural Trends*, 22(2): 63-66.

Jones, P. N. (1970) 'Some aspects of the changing distribution of coloured immigrants in Birmingham, 1961-66', *Transactions of the Institute of British Geographers*, 50: 199-219.

Karn, V. (1979) 'Low income owner-occupation in the inner city' in C. Jones (ed) *Urban deprivation and the inner city*, London: Routledge, pp. 160-90.

Kennedy, L. (ed) (2004/2013), *Remaking Birmingham: The visual culture of urban regeneration*, London: Routledge.

Khaleeli, H. (2015) 'How "big society" beat one Birmingham area's reputation for drugs and crime', *The Guardian*, 17 September, available at https://www.theguardian.com/cities/2015/sep/17/how-balsall-heath-big-society-drugs-crime-birmingham

Kusenbach, M. (2003) 'Street phenomenology: the go-along as ethnographic research tool', *Ethnography*, 4: 455-85.

Landry, C. (2000) *The creative city: A toolkit for urban innovators*, London: Earthscan.

Laurier, E. and Philo, C. (2003) 'The region in the boot: mobilising lone subjects and multiple objects', *Environment and Planning D: Society and Space*, 21(1): 85-106.

O'Connor, J. (2004) 'Cities, culture and "transitional economies"', in D. Power and A. J. Scott, *Cultural industries and the production of culture*, London, New York: Routledge, pp. 37-53.

Parker, D. and Long, P. (2003) 'Reimagining Birmingham: public history, selective memory and the narration of urban change', *European Journal of Cultural Studies*, 6(2): 157-78.

Parker, D. and Long, P. (2004) 'The mistakes of the past'? Visual narratives of urban decline and regeneration', *Visual Culture in Britain*, 5(1): 37-58.

Paulos, E. and Goodman, E. (2004) 'The familiar stranger: anxiety, comfort and play in public places', *Proceedings of the SIGCHI on human factors in computing systems, April 24–29*, Vienna, 6, pp. 223–30, available at http://www.paulos.net/intel/pubs/papers/Familiar%20 Stranger%20(CHI%202004).pdf.

Perry, B., Smith, K. and Warren, S. (2015) 'Revealing and re-valuing cultural intermediaries in the 'real' creative city: insights from a diary-keeping exercise', *European Journal of Cultural Studies*, 18(6): 724-40.

Poolman C. and Rowe E. (eds) (2014) *Balsall Heath Biennale*, Big Cartel, bigcartel.com.

Reed, A. (2002) 'City of details: interpreting the personality of London', *Journal of the Royal Anthropological Institute*, 8: 127-41.

Rex, J. and Moore, R. (1967) *Race community and conflict: A study of Sparkbrook*, London, New York: published for the Institute of Race Relations by OUP.

Sanders, T. (2004) 'The risks of street prostitution: punters, police and protesters', *Urban Studies*, 41(9): 1703-17.

Sardar, Z. (2008) *Balti Britain: A journey through the British Asian experience*, London: Granta UK.

Tung Au, W., Ho, G. and Wing Chuen Chan, K. (2017) 'An empirical investigation of the Arts Audience Experience Index', *Empirical Studies of the Arts*, 35(1): 27-46.

Walmsley, B. (2012) 'Towards a balanced scorecard: a critical analysis of the Culture and Sport Evidence (CASE) programme', *Cultural Trends*, 21(4): 325-34.

Warren, S. (2017) 'Pluralising the walking interview: researching (im)mobilities with Muslim women', *Social & Cultural Geography*, 18(6): 786-807.

Warren, S. and Forcer, S. (2017) 'The Birmingham Surrealist Laboratory' in M. Zebracki, and J. M. Palmer, (eds) *Public Art Encounters: Art, Space and Identity*, London: Routledge, pp. 180-97.

Williams, P. (1978) 'Building societies and the inner city', *Transactions of the Institute of British Geographers*, 3(1): 23-34.

Woods, R. (1979) 'Ethnic segregation in Birmingham in the 1960s and 1970s', *Ethnic and Racial Studies*, 2(4): 455-76.

Yosef, A. (2018) 'Should Channel 4 really move to Birmingham?' *Medium* 9 Feb. https://medium.com/@adamyosef/should-channel-4-really-move-to-birmingham-98845c3a41e8.

SIX

Intervention: *Some cities*

Dan Burwood

Some cities is a not-for-profit Community Interest Company (CIC) founded on a passion for the power that photography has to be a bridge between communities. We work with individuals and organisations to create high quality training, publications, seminars, exhibitions and inclusive participatory photographic opportunities.

The company grew out of many conversations with cofounder Andrew Jackson concerning our respective practice as photographers working in Birmingham and our desire to know the city through our lenses. We started with a simple question, emerging from the challenge of our ambition, that asked: if we, as individual photographers, can't hope to map the city in photographs in anything even approaching completeness, could we find ways to get closer to covering its territory by drawing others into collaboration?

We'd meet and develop our approach to realising this goal, over beers or coffee, often at the 'lucky table', an odd one out of those at the Edwardian Tea Rooms at Birmingham Museum and Art Gallery. We'd part and go hopeful on our separate ways when new ideas came to us or when potential partners had been identified and expressed an interest in collaboration.

One of the prompts to map the city in photographs was the recognition of its changing nature – apparent in large-scale building developments impacting in turn on demographics, culture and community. Thus, we turned to consider issues of past, present and future. We looked to who, and what, was represented in the photographic archives of the city and anticipated the changes that were likely to come to pass presently that might shift or erase communities before their moment and 'passing' could be recorded. In tandem with this archival work, we viewed the accelerating profusion of images created on camera phones and shared on social media as a daunting and exciting challenge to what we'd thought we did well as documentary photographers. We asked whether there was a way to synthesise what we considered our informed, professional practice with the perspectives and outputs of others like us: students and enthusiasts, novices and casual users of photographic technologies.

For me, the foundation of the *Some cities* approach lay in further reflections on the challenges of being a photographer and one's connection with place and the subjects one finds there. For a while, I'd found it hard to begin to make work that I believed was legitimate or that could find audiences in such a way as to make the effort meaningful. For instance, a previous project, about a festival in Syria, was shot over a day or two on consecutive years, and was a kind of direct witnessing, guided by instincts as to the shape of a story and the form of the images, in a place and through a language I understood very little. I'd since lived in Damascus and taken my time to lengthen the form of the work, almost begun to shoot coherently and then left in early 2011 and turned away from the war in the distance. Having watched just one graphic YouTube video of civilian casualties unfolding on camera phone in sunshine, dust and bloodied shouting was enough, and too much.

So *Some cities* was a way to come back and pay witness from 'inside' to the events and things that slowly become history. Reaching out to partners in order to share the project's ambition was a displacement of the responsibility of witnessing directly, and a means of building an audience for photographs among the community that was both making the work, and was, we hoped, its subject. In this way, we wanted the city to show the city to itself.

Some cities drew funding from Arts Council England, matched by Arts and Humanities Research Council (AHRC) money made available from the *Cultural intermediation* project detailed in this book. In this action, research was not a passive exercise but a proactive contributor to the environment and projects it sought to explore. As a result, we built a programme of talks by photographic artists, training, exhibitions and commissions. This activity was anchored by a web platform inviting user submissions of photographs of Birmingham, arranged in upload sequence, juxtaposing the variety of views which contributors offered of their city.

We invested in good PR and garnered a story on the project launch from the local BBC news programme *Midlands today*. That night, our Twitter-based aggregation site crashed as a lot of people sought to submit images at once. We'd already decided that as well as creating a kind of collaborative archive we were making an open source artwork. In so doing, we made it interactive by allowing users to curate their own triptych of photo translations of the city: a limited parse, a game of sequence and metonymy. The web development for such an interface was beyond the pilot budget, but the courses and talks were well attended, there was an exhibition at the Library of Birmingham of photographs made by diverse contributors to *Some cities*, many of whom had never shown their work before: amateurs, novices, enthusiasts, students, professionals.

We commissioned two photographers to make work in Balsall Heath, Stephen Burke and Attilio Fiumarella. These projects were our second show, in the Long Gallery at the Old Print Works, next to our office and darkroom. Fiumarella's work *The swimmers* (Figure 6.1) was about Moseley Road Baths and those campaigning to keep it open

Figure 6.1: Attilio Fiumarella, *The swimmers*

as its existence was under threat. This work was particularly successful, and seemed to me to be a good example of authorial, community engaged, participatory photography. The culmination of this work had over 100 swimmers in their costumes posing in the contested, disused, gala pool at the baths, patiently waiting in lines for the light to be right. A shaft of diffused sunlight sliced the space after 45 minutes or so, and two large format images were taken. This came to pass because a range of local individuals and organisations were galvanised to collaborate with the determined vision of the photographer, whose idea chimed with and depended upon the interests of a rooted community. I'd like to think that the project contributed to greater regional, national and international visibility for the campaign to save swimming at these baths, which has had some success. I was on local radio that morning talking about the project; the 100 Swimmers shoot was third on the BBC online national news site that day. Extending these principles, the project has thus far travelled to photo festivals in Georgia and the Canary Islands.

This was the apex of *Some cities'* success, although we did produce further exhibitions, a group show of documentary photography called *Some stories*, and a set of publications based on funded community projects in the Nechells and Druids Heath area of the city. Furthermore, we produced various workshops and a range of smaller projects. However, for reasons that are hard to clarify, the momentum we'd gained after our initial successes didn't carry our ambitions as far as might have been possible. Among personal factors at play, we were drawn back into working as artists again, rather than arts organisation managers and administrators – the intermediary roles explored in the projects detailed in this book.

Andrew has been working on long-term projects in the UK, Canada, Jamaica and the US, where he's a Lightworks Artist in Residence through Autograph ABP. I'm working on partnership projects between Beirut and Birmingham, running Darkroom Birmingham as an analogue and community photo resource and developing personal projects, one of which was highly commended for the Rebecca Vassie Memorial Trust Award, an ongoing work about Zambrano families in the Midlands. We still have a coffee and a beer and talk about life, the city and the work we're making, we've made, the projects still to come.

SEVEN

Governing the creative city: the practice, value and effectiveness of cultural intermediation

Beth Perry

Introduction

Creative city policies have largely failed to deliver tangible benefits for deprived urban communities, with many noting the negative impacts of culture-led regeneration on specific city quarters (Chatterton, 2000; Miles, 2005; New Economics Foundation, 2005; May and Perry, 2018). It is increasingly recognised that mainstream cultural urban policy has not worked to deliver cultural democracy (Evrard, 1997; Jancovitch, 2011, 2017). In part this can be seen as a crisis of governance, characterised by a mismatch between structures, policies, values and beliefs underpinned by a series of contrasting narratives.

On the one hand, the narrative of the creative city presumes a strong state and a cultural urban policy that invests in flagship projects aimed at harnessing professionalised 'culture', narrowly defined, for primarily economic growth objectives. A model of governance is prioritised that focuses on public-private partnerships and networks as mechanisms to steer and control cultural policy. For Peck (2005: 740-1), the contemporary spread of creativity strategies perfectly works with 'the grain of extant neoliberal development agendas, framed around interurban competition, gentrification, middle-class consumption and place-marketing'. This produces a top-down, cookie-cutter approach to the creative urban economy (Oakley, 2006) even though these approaches based on directive planning are seen as most likely to fail (Scott, 2008).

Orthodox approaches to governance have been drawn from models of urban policy which frame the creative city wholly in terms of the relationship between creative industries and economic growth, generating a highly controlled culture (Vickery, 2007). It has been widely noted both that top-down models of urban policy are unsuited for the development of the cultural urban economy and that existing initiatives and creative city policies have had little impact on deprived communities in urban areas. Florida's creative class, it is argued, reinforces the 'cult of urban creativity' (Peck, 2005: 742) comprising 'cauldrons of neoliberal gangs' (Krätke, 2009: 139), despite the fact that 'creativity is also a major survival resource for the working poor in the diverse urban worlds of contemporary capitalism' (Krätke, 2009: 139). Culture is seen as a luxury which only counts if it can be commercialised or translated into a creative industry (Pratt and Jeffcut, 2009).

This critique of the status quo and formal models of cultural urban policy leads to the conclusion that existing models have not worked (Flew, 2012: 154). A counter-narrative focuses instead on the importance of the 'everyday', highlighting the irrelevance of governance and policy frameworks to people's lives. Disrupting accepted understandings of cultural value, the emphasis is on examining vernacular cultures and arguing that the 'everyday' needs to be revalued as equal or even superior to formal cultural provision, as it resists and reevaluates the deficit model of participation (Miles and Gibson, 2016). The consequence is that the existing system of formalised agencies and professionalised delivery of culture should be set aside in favour of community-led creative activism in a 'parallel' cultural ecology.

Yet there is evidence that more '*laissez-faire*' approaches to the cultural urban economy also have unintended consequences. Existing studies conclude that neither a 'hands-off' nor 'interventionist' approach are effective in supporting the cultural ecology of the city (O'Connor, 2015). The danger is that a polarisation emerges in which the active work of governing the creative economy to meet cultural, economic, social (and increasingly environmental) benefits is dismissed as irrelevant. An over-focus on the everyday – without consideration of the systemic and structural conditions underpinning mainstream cultural economy – runs the risk of letting urban elites off the hook in terms of the effects of their decisions. By accident, rather than design, the most low-income urban communities may continue to be excluded from participating in or benefiting from mainstream cultural urban policy, with the creative city existing only as 'enclaves in an urban landscape where poverty and social deprivation still widely prevail' (Scott, 2006: 12).

Some of the early work on the creative city suggested that an emphasis on culture and creativity would offer alternative ways of doing and organising cities, in comparison with bureaucracy or non-democratic planning (Landry, 2000; Vickery, 2007). Yet this promise has not been realised. A new approach to 'governing' the cultural economy is needed which moves beyond formalised structures or networks towards understanding the practices that have developed to mediate between formal and informal cultural ecologies. For Pratt (2010: 15), 'policies therefore need to attend to the challenges of *governing the processes* that link production and reproduction. ... the field of governance of culture and creativity is critical' (emphasis added).

Responding to Pratt's call, this chapter argues that the consequence of juxtaposing a top-down with a bottom-up approach, formal with informal, professionalised with vernacular cultures, is to overlook the 'grey spaces' in the cultural urban economy. In these liminal spaces, a range of practices exist which mediate between different narratives. This chapter reappropriates the vocabulary of 'cultural intermediation' to reveal, revalue and reassess the role of cultural organisations that operate within local contexts to bridge formal and informal ways of understanding culture and creativity.

The chapter starts with a review of the literature around cultural intermediaries and a description of the study on which this paper is based (see also Perry et al, 2015). This is followed by a discussion of the role, value and effectiveness of cultural intermediation in an age of precarity and squeezed cultural resources. Finally, the chapter will discuss wider implications for how we understand the theory and practice of cultural intermediation in the context of governing the creative city.

Towards a 'third wave' of cultural intermediation

Pierre Bourdieu's notion of 'cultural intermediaries' has spawned multiple readings and reinterpretations (Hesmondhalgh, 2006; Smith Maguire and Matthews, 2012). As the main protagonists in Richard Florida's (2002) creative class, cultural intermediaries are characterised by a creative free spirit driven by the desire to make money and forge new connections between production and consumption. Drawing on Bob Jessop's notion of 'economic imaginaries', O'Connor emphasises how intermediaries work within these imaginaries to 'circumscribe a set of activities which can then become the objective correlate of policy intervention and measurement' (Jessop, 2005: 145; O'Connor, 2015: 375). This implies a particular kind of cultural worker, in pursuit of both economic and symbolic profit, 'reflecting the interplay, inherent in contemporary cultural production, between generating new styles of life and protecting established hierarchies of cultural value' (Wright, 2005: 106).

Since Bourdieu, the term 'cultural intermediaries' has been used to reflect all those cultural workers involved in mediating between production and consumption. For Hesmondhalgh (2006) this is a 'misreading' of Bourdieu's original meaning. Negus (2002), on the other hand, argues that the term directs attention to the changes brought about by the growth of workers involved in the production and circulation of symbolic forms, and encourages reflection on the reciprocal interrelationships between cultural and economic practices. Smith Maguire and Matthews (2012: 551) argue that the term is 'good to think with' as it prioritises issues of agency, negotiation and power, 'moving the everyday, contested practices of market agents to the fore for the study of the production of culture'. Much contestation of the term 'cultural intermediaries' has largely centred on its terminological muddiness and the need for more precise 'specification of the division of labour involved' (Hesmondhalgh, 2006: 227; Molloy and Larner, 2010). Yet a more serious critique relates to the singular conception of cultural intermediaries as self-interested economic actors, shaping use values and exchange values through the construction of markets (Negus, 2002).

By only seeing cultural intermediaries as those workers involved in the process of economic value-making, we reinforce and reproduce existing views of professionalised culture and cultural hierarchies. Yet, given what Taylor (2015: 5) calls the 'polyvalent elusiveness of the creative economy', we need greater nuance and sensitivity to different processes of cultural intermediation. He attests that intermediation can be located within a 'countervailing associationalist narrative' emerging within creative economy practice and discourse (Taylor, 2015: 2), noting the pluralistic discourses of values and regimes that illustrate the 'fissures' within economic imaginaries. The aspirations and dispositions of a wide diversity of actors mediating between production and consumption in different cultural and creative ecologies need to be further interrogated, including those engaged in 'the myriad creative forms and practices that saturate the dense environment of the everyday' (Edensor et al, 2010: 13). We need to reappropriate the term 'cultural intermediation' to draw attention to the otherwise invisible work undertaken by local cultural organisations in the liminal grey spaces of the creative city.

Against this background, our study sought to understand the role, value and effectiveness of a 'third wave' of cultural intermediation (Perry et al, 2015) in bridging formal and informal cultural ecologies. Local arts and cultural organisations sit at the boundaries of multiple fields, not only between culture and economy, but also culture, society and community. The current chapter draws on insights from four datasets developed as part of the Cultural Intermediation project 2012-

16: a baseline analysis of cultural governance and policy frameworks in Greater Manchester and Birmingham; 32 interviews undertaken across both cities; a diary-keeping exercise with 16 participants; and a collaborative initiative developed in Ordsall, Salford. Each method developed from what had gone before, as we moved from a more distant to a proximal perspective in terms of both the nature of the method and form of collaboration involved. As our methods increasingly enabled more granular understanding and observation of the dynamics of cultural intermediation, so too did they involve closer working relationships through an increasingly coproductive approach (see Perry and Symons, Chapter three in this volume; Symons, Chapter thirteen in this volume). This culminated in a joint process of co-analysis and development of recommendations (see Box 7.1) with three local organisations in Salford – Let's Go, Ordsall Community Arts and Chapel Street Arts.

Box 7.1: Coproduced recommendations with cultural organisations in Salford

1. Place citizens at the heart of coproducing local cultural plans.
2. Identify key individuals and organisations to motivate engagement and activity. Individuals and organisations can help animate existing and spark new creative activities.
3. Give funding for local people to access support to develop their ideas for cultural activities.
4. Enhance the cultural fabric of neighbourhoods by building on what's already there.
5. Ensure support for cultural activity is embedded in multiple strategic agendas.
6. Support people to become producers of cultural content that is meaningful in their own lives.
7. Provide pre-employment support via creative activities.
8. Develop value chains between large and smaller cultural organisations and across the country to support cultural participation in formal arts activities.
9. Undertake social infrastructure and cultural activity mapping in neighbourhoods so that people know what is going on.
10. Support physical and conceptual spaces for people to gather, share, learn and imagine.

Recommendations produced by Beth Perry, Jessica Symons, Gail Skelly, Karen Shannon and Chris Doyle (2016).

Cultural intermediation in an age of precarity

The practices of local cultural organisations in mediating between formal and informal cultural ecologies are heavily influenced by the context in which they are operating. At the time of undertaking the research, cultural governance and policy at the local level was in a state of flux and instability. Across the UK, cultural policy was a multisectoral, multi-level soup, with layers of partnerships, networks and multiple funded initiatives, as decision makers were trying to stitch together programmes of work from disparate and rapidly reducing sources of public finance. In Greater Manchester, the negotiation of new deals with central government to secure greater powers and responsibilities as part of a 'devolution deal' was leading to a fresh round of restructuring and partnership building, characterised by discussions over whether arts and cultural development should remain a local authority responsibility or be upscaled to city-regional level. With the election of the Conservative-Liberal Democrat coalition government in 2010, austerity was beginning to bite (O'Hara, 2015) with reductions in public funding for the arts, most disproportionately felt in areas outside London. Davies and Selwood highlighted the absence of a clear cultural policy from the coalition government and a hands-off approach to the Arts Council by the DCMS (Davies and Selwood, 2012). The discourse of the 'Big Society', which plagued the AHRC *Connected Communities* programme itself in the early days, was mobilised as ideological justification for attacks on local state services, under the guise of allowing communities to support each other without the 'interference' of the public sector.

Like in a bowling alley, a number of organisational pins remained standing, but on a fragile and changing base, subject to uncertainty about their sustainability. During the course of the study, local authorities were being forced to outsource cultural assets, reduce non-statutory provisions in areas such as culture and environmental sustainability, and reduce staffing. Between 2010 and 2016 local authority funding for culture was cut by 17% (Brown, 2016; Harvey, 2016). This was on top of a near 30% reduction in funding for the Arts Council England in 2010 (BBC, 2010). Salford City Council had to transfer greater responsibility for areas of culture and leisure into Salford Community Leisure, an 'independent industrial provenance society' (cooperative), established in 2003 and expanded in 2010 to include heritage, libraries, museums and arts development.

This context was the backdrop to the research undertaken alongside local cultural organisations and artists, a context increasingly difficult and frustrating to navigate. Policy was a black hole that mobilised against more strategic orientations, raising questions over who was responsible for what, how to collaborate in a context of competition for scarce resources and what support was available for local organisations to support local cultural capacity.

The practice, value and effectiveness of cultural intermediation

Although the cultural organisations in the study differed in size, type and sector, there were a number of common functions that each played, in varying ways and combinations (see Table 7.1).

First, local cultural organisations were involved in **market-making** through their intermediary functions linking production and reception. However, they performed this role in a different way from traditional cultural intermediaries. Well-meaning efforts to try to connect communities to local cultural resources and economic activity can fail to grasp the distance individuals need to travel before engagement with the creative economy is a realistic or desirable option. The cultural organisations in this study were engaged in high levels of pre-employment support and capacity building, recognising that immediate entry into a job training scheme or digital technology course would not help someone recently out of prison or with drug problems and lacking the confidence and skills to even consider entry into the creative sector. Instead, their focus was on connecting people with information, resources and skills to build competence and confidence with local people.

Second, local cultural organisations played a critical role in supporting **community-making** as part of an asset-based cultural development process. Individuals working with local cultural organisations were concerned with challenging narratives of deprivation, of poverty and

Table 7.1: Practices of cultural intermediation

Market-making	Information and resource sharing; pre-employment support; skilling up; building confidence
Community-making	Asset-based cultural development; sense of place and pride; family; addressing loneliness and isolation
Meaning-making	Valuing cultural activities; making sense of experiences
Making do	Stepping in for withdrawal of local services and reductions in public funding

Source: Author's analysis

of exclusion in order to overcome the stigmatisation of their lives, through celebrating a sense of pride in place. Grounded in a sense of palpable anger about the structural inequalities underpinning the cultural economy (and able to articulate and represent these issues on local cultural partnerships and boards), local organisations nonetheless were able to support local people in valuing what was happening within their local community. In this respect, they worked to challenge the idea that low-income places are culturally impoverished 'cold spots' (Gilmore, 2013).

A corollary function of local cultural organisations as intermediaries related to the articulation and recognition of plural cultural values. Through the collaborative initiative we developed in the study (*Ideas4Ordsall*, see Symons, Chapter thirteen in this volume), local organisations were given the opportunity to step back from the circumscribed delivery of externally funded projects and ask people what culture meant for them. This process of **meaning-making**, facilitated through our study, enabled a different practice to be supported, in which individuals were encouraged to externalise implicit cultural values and develop their own ideas, aligning with concerns about cultural justice and value (Sharp et al, 2005).

A fourth key element of the practice of cultural intermediation revealed through our study was that of **making do**. In the specific context of rescaling governance, public sector reorganisation and reductions to public funding, local cultural organisations were increasingly squeezed to step into roles traditionally performed by local government. This often involved a frontline, 24-hour service being provided to individuals – extending well beyond the stated visions and missions of the organisations.

Through these practices, local cultural organisations acted as glue, part of the cultural fabric of the local level that helps individuals and groups navigate an increasingly difficult context. They performed active work at the intersections between culture, economy and community, working across boundaries and functions and bridging amateur and professional practices, mobilising multiple meanings, competences and materials (Shove et al, 2012). While valued by those who interacted with them, they struggled to articulate and evidence this value, with their activities often 'invisible' to mainstream measures of cultural value or participation. A strong tension existed between the work these organisations were valued for within the community and the measures by which they were assessed by and for funders. This coupled with time pressures and questions over their own identity and relationship to their work, which often drained them to the point of exhaustion through cycles of 'famine and feast' in an age of precarity. Both personal and professional instability characterised the lives of many of those interviewed, 'signifying both the multiplication of precarious, unstable, insecure forms of living and, simultaneously, new forms of political struggle and solidarity that reach beyond the traditional models of the political party or trade union' (Gill and Pratt, 2008: 3).

Such challenges impacted on the ultimate effectiveness of different practices of cultural intermediation. The interviews and diaries challenged the idea that cultural intermediaries are only self-interested cultural entrepreneurs and revealed a more 'moral cultural economy' (Banks, 2006). However, the challenge of balancing organisational survival with community value and practice was ever-present. Local cultural organisations were also trapped in the liminal grey zone of the cultural economy, needing to both orient towards the needs of formal funding frameworks and build local capacity. The grey zone between formal and informal cultural ecologies is one characterised by conflicting logics and pressures, with the result that local cultural organisations may reinforce the dynamics they are otherwise seeking to challenge, through a concern with their own survival. One outcome of this was a tendency for some 'overly paternalistic' practices to emerge.

Organisational uncertainty and a set of 'ramshackle' working practices emerged, played out as well in a tension between creative and community development work. Interviewees felt that cultural intermediation was a skilled practice, but one that often remained invisible and unsupported in terms of professional development opportunities or networks. As Newsinger and Green (2016: 383) note: 'in contemporary official representations of cultural value, the discourses that correspond to cultural practitioners themselves are marginalised'.

Burnout was common, as those motivated to hold together creative/artistic aesthetic values with social/community impacts increasingly found these in tension or one dominating over the other. This was particularly the case for those organisations that worked 'deep' rather than 'wide' within communities. Those with small numbers of individualised, high quality relationships tended to have very little strategic connection with funding regimes, and policy regimes expressed difficulty in being able to navigate systems to generate income for continued survival, compared with those that worked within wider networks of influence.

Local cultural organisations are essential in building local capacity in arts and cultural development. As Stark et al (2013) note, we need a cultural ecology deep-rooted in locality, where artists and small companies are essential along with intermediate organisations. However, such organisations face a number of pressures in the face of cultural precarity, not only because of reductions in funding, but also due to the tensions and challenges involved in existing within the grey zone, balancing a more instrumental view of culture and the value of people's everyday experiences and ideas. This study supports the view of O'Connor (1999: 7) that cultural organisations could become more significant in contributing to social change in austere times, when 'the cultural hierarchies are much more fragmented and plural'. However, in the course of the study, two of three of the cultural organisations we worked with most closely were forced to close, unable to secure their organisational survival in a context of precarity and the need to demonstrate economic more than social value.

Conclusion: redefining cultural intermediation in the creative city

Cultural intermediation is a bundle of practices undertaken by local cultural organisations and artists in the grey liminal spaces between formal and informal cultural ecologies (see Figure 7.1).

These practices provide the glue between tired binaries of 'top-down' and 'bottom-up', intersecting cities, economies and

Figure 7.1: Cultural intermediation as governing practices

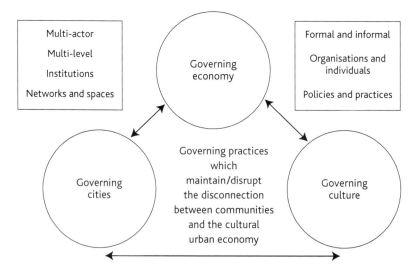

Source: Author's analysis

communities. Practices connect in multi-actor, multi-network spaces and are characterised by formality and informality, as organisations connect, broker and mediate between policies, practices and values. These governing practices of cultural intermediation simultaneously maintain and disrupt the status quo, challenging easy distinctions between formal cultural activities and everyday practices.

Such practices are not new. However, in the work of renaming lies the possibility of making visible the more morally and socially grounded cultural work of those who operate between diverse cultural, creative and social worlds. Cultural intermediation draws attention to a different kind of cultural work, which needs to be recognised and supported in professional support networks. Such a practice-based approach to governing the creative city is helpful. Governance, in this sense, is not about the steering or setting of priorities, but the practices of organising and getting things done. It emphasises new topics in the study of state including governmentality, collective identities, ideologies and resistance in governance (Bevir and Rhodes, 2010). The emphasis on 'cultural intermediation' as a new bundle of practices is characteristic of a new attempt to *do* theory 'through for example, the use of hybrid, in between figures such as the actant or cyborg, designed to connect that which has been held apart, and there reveal the diverse urban worlds that have been edited out of contention' (Amin and Thrift, 2002: 4). These appropriated vocabularies highlight emerging practices which tell a general story through aggregate concepts that refer to common meanings (Bevir and Rhodes, 2010).

Often, though not always, the practices of 'cultural intermediation' break with the narrative of neoliberalism through the articulation of alternative values – both democratic attitudes (Purcell, 2008), cultural, aesthetic and social. At the core is the creation of spaces for practices which exist *despite* entrenched traditions and narratives, rather than *because* of them. In this context, 'it is difficult and even counterproductive for public arts funders to "go it alone" or to proceed with hierarchical, centralized forms of decision-making' (Gattinger, 2011: 4). What is needed instead is a more ecological approach to the creative city, in which alternative spaces, practices and norms are made visible and valued.

References

Amin, A. H. and Thrift, N. (2002) *Cities: Re-imagining the urban*, Cambridge: Polity Press.

Banks, M. (2006) 'Moral economy and cultural work', *Sociology*, 40(3): 455-72.

BBC (2010) *Arts Council's budget cut by 30%.* https://www.bbc.co.uk/news/entertainment-arts-11582070.

Bevir, M. and Rhodes, R. A. W. (2010) *The state as cultural practice*, Oxford: Oxford University Press.

Brown, M. (2016) *Culture spending by councils 'down 17% since 2010'*, https://www.theguardian.com/culture/2016/apr/13/culture-spending-councils-arts-council-england, 13 April 2016.

Chatterton, P. (2000) 'Will the real creative city please stand up?' *City*, 4(3): 390-7.

Davies, M. and Selwood, S. (2012) 'In search of cultural policy', *Cultural Trends*, 21(3): 201-4.

Edensor, T., Leslie, D., Millington, S. and Rantisi, N. (2010) *Spaces of vernacular creativity: Rethinking the cultural economy*, London and New York: Routledge.

Evrard, Y. (1997) 'Democratizing culture or cultural democracy?', *Journal of Arts Management, Law & Society*, 27(3): 167-76.

Flew, T. (2012) (ed) *Creative industries and urban development: Creative cities in the 21st Century*, Abingdon: Routledge.

Florida, R. (2002) *The rise of the creative class*, New York: Basic Books.

Gattinger, M. (2011) *Democratization of culture, cultural democracy and governance, Canadian Public Arts Funders General Meeting presentation*, available at http://www.cpafopsac.org/en/themes/documents/CPAF_2011_AGM_Democratization_of_Culture_Cultural_Democracy_Governance_Mar082012_000.pdf.

Gill, R. and Pratt, A. (2008) 'In the social factory? Immaterial labour, precariousness and cultural work', *Theory, Culture & Society*, 25(7-8): 1-30.

Gilmore, A. (2013) 'Cold spots, crap towns and cultural deserts: the role of place and geography in cultural participation and creative place-making', *Cultural Trends*, 22(2): 86-96.

Harvey, A. (2016) *Funding arts and culture in a time of austerity*, Report for New Local Government Network and Arts Council England, available at https://www.artscouncil.org.uk/sites/default/files/download-file/Funding%20Arts%20and%20Culture%20in%20a%20time%20of%20Austerity%20%28Adrian%20Harvey%29.pdf. Accessed 03 July 2018.

Hesmondhalgh, D. (2006) 'Bourdieu, the media and cultural production', *Media, Culture and Society*, 28(2): 211-31.

Jancovich, L. (2011) 'Great art for everyone? engagement and participation policy in the arts', *Cultural Trends*, 20(3-4): 271-9.

Jancovich L (2017) 'The participation myth', *International Journal of Cultural Policy*, 23(1): 107-21.

Jessop, B. (2005) 'Cultural political economy, the knowledge-based economy and the state', in A. Barry and D. Slater (eds) *The Technological Economy*, London: Routledge, pp. 142-64.

Krätke, S. (2009) 'The new urban growth ideology of creative cities', in N. Brenner, P. Marcuse and M. Mayer (eds) *Cities for people not profit: Critical urban theory and the right to the city*, London: Routledge, pp. 138-49.

Landry, C. (2000) *The creative city: A toolkit for urban innovators*, London: Earthscan.

May, T. and Perry, B. (2018) *Cities and the knowledge economy: Promise, politics and possibility*, London: Routledge.

Miles, M. (2005) 'Interruptions: testing the rhetoric of culturally led urban development', *Urban Studies*, 42(5/6): 889-911.

Miles, A. and Gibson, L. (2016) 'Everyday participation and cultural value', *Cultural Trends*, 25(3): 151-57.

Molloy, M. and Larner, W. (2010) 'Who needs cultural intermediaries indeed?', *Journal of Cultural Economy*, 3(3): 361-77.

Negus, K. (2002) 'The work of cultural intermediaries and the enduring distance between production and consumption', *Cultural Studies*, 16(4): 501-15.

New Economics Foundation (2005) *Clone town Britain: The survey results on the bland state of the nation*, London: New Economics Foundation.

Newsinger, J. and Green, W. (2016) 'The infrapolitics of cultural value: cultural policy, evaluation and the marginalisation of practitioner perspectives', *Journal of Cultural Economy*, 9(4): 382-95.

O'Connor, J. (1999) 'Popular culture, reflexivity and urban change', in J. Verwijnen and L. Panu (eds) *Creative cities: Cultural industries, urban development and the information society*, Helsinki: University of Art and Design.

O'Connor, J. (2015) 'Intermediaries and imaginaries in the cultural and creative industries', *Regional Studies*, 49(3): 374-87.

O'Hara, M. (2015) *Austerity bites*, Bristol: Policy Press.

Oakley, K. (2006) 'Include us out – economic development and social policy in the creative industries', *Cultural Trends*, 14(4): 283-302.

Peck, J. (2005) 'Struggling with the creative class', *International Journal of Urban and Regional Research*, 29(4): 740-70.

Perry, B., Smith, K. and Warren, S. (2015) 'Revealing and re-valuing cultural intermediaries in the "real" creative city: insights from a diary-keeping exercise', *European Journal of Cultural Studies*, 18(6): 724-40.

Pratt, A. (2010) 'Creative cities: tensions within and between social, cultural and economic development. A critical reading of the UK experience', *City, Culture and Society*, 1(1): 13-20.

Pratt, A. and Jeffcut, P. (2009) 'Creativity, innovation and the cultural economy: snake oil for the 21st century?', in A. Pratt and P. Jeffcut (eds) *Creativity, innovation in the cultural economy*, London: Routledge, pp. 1-20.

Purcell, M. (2008) *Recapturing democracy: Neoliberalization and the struggle for alternative urban futures*, New York: Routledge.

Scott, A. J. (2006) 'Creative cities: conceptual issues and policy questions', *Journal of Urban Affairs*, 28(1): 1-17.

Scott, A. J. (2008) *Social economy of the metropolis: Cognitive-cultural capitalism and the global resurgence of cities*, Oxford: Oxford University Press.

Sharp, J., Pollock, V. and Paddison, R. (2005) 'Just art for a just city: public art and social inclusion in urban regeneration', *Urban Studies*, 42(5/6): 1001-23.

Shove, E., Pantzar, M. and Watson, M. (2012) *The dynamics of social practice: Everyday life and how it changes*, London: Sage.

Smith Maguire, J. and Matthews, J. (2012) 'Are we all cultural intermediaries now? An introduction to cultural intermediaries in context', *European Journal of Cultural Studies*, 15(5): 551-62.

Stark, P., Gordon, C. and Powell, D. (2013) *Rebalancing our cultural capital. A contribution to the debate on national policy for the arts and culture in England*, available at https://www.artsprofessional.co.uk/sites/artsprofessional.co.uk/files/rebalancing_our_cultural_capital.pdf.

Taylor, C. (2015) 'Between culture, policy and industry: modalities of intermediation in the creative economy', *Regional Studies*, 49(3): 362-73.

Vickery, J. (2007) 'The emergence of culture-led regeneration: a policy concept and its discontents', *Centre for Cultural Policy Studies Research Papers*, Warwick.

Wright, D. (2005) 'Mediating production and consumption: cultural capital and "cultural workers"', *The British Journal of Sociology*, 56(1): 105-21.

EIGHT

Participatory budgeting for culture: handing power to communities?

Phil Jones

Introduction

Participatory budgeting (PB) partially devolves the decision-making process over local authority spending to communities and civil society groups. In 2013 it was estimated that around 1,700 local governments in more than 40 countries were practising some form of PB (Cabannes, 2015). Nonetheless, the tremendous potential of PB to radically democratise decision-making processes has hitherto only been realised on a relatively small scale.

An instrumental approach to cultural value suggests that engaging with cultural activity can build skills, confidence and community cohesion while reducing social exclusion. There is a temptation with such an approach to adopt a deficit model, suggesting that communities need to be encouraged to engage with the *existing* cultural offer in order to derive these benefits. PB for cultural spending, by contrast, offers a real opportunity to empower communities to leverage cultural spend into their neighbourhoods and to *reshape* the existing cultural offer around their needs.

PB is, however, an inherently risky process. Communities can lack capacity – both in confidence and skills – to move from ideas and debate to actually planning and realising projects. Intermediary processes are thus key to the successful delivery of PB, from getting a diverse range of voices to engage, to building confidence to express ideas, to providing the skills necessary to deliver projects. As this chapter highlights, there is a danger that publics become mere clients in an intermediary-led PB process, particularly because of pressure to ensure delivery of 'feasible' outputs to demonstrate value-for-money when spending public money.

Origins and implementation of participatory budgeting

Examinations of PB often focus on the victory of the Brazilian Workers' Party (*Partido dos Trabalhadores*) in elections in Porto Alegre in 1989 and Belo Horizonte in 1993. In fact, some Brazilian municipalities such as Lages and Minas Gerais, had attempted to implement models of PB in the late 1970s and early 1980s, with a significant focus on providing housing for poorer workers (Souza, 2001). Indeed, in any analysis of PB it is important to bear in mind that its origins were in ensuring that basic services were provided for poorer communities. PB work in Porto Alegre and Belo Horizonte were particularly focused on street paving, sewage and housing. As this discussion will pick up, however, a process that has been shown to be effective for ensuring that the most vulnerable in society have access to very basic services does not automatically translate into an effective set of governance arrangements when considering a more complex range of public spending needs in developed nations.

One of the more unexpected outcomes of PB is that a process associated with a radically left-wing party in Brazil has been adopted globally by governments and agencies of very different political leanings, from Chávez's Venezuela, to communist China and the firmly neoliberal World Bank. The role of the World Bank – and to a lesser extent the European Union – has been crucial to the global dissemination of PB. The Bank is not a monolithic entity and different elements within the organisation promote PB as both a radical tool for empowering citizens to drive development and as a mere technical device for bypassing corrupt local elites to promote better governance (Goldfrank, 2012).

It should be highlighted, however, that PB is a very small part of the World Bank's activities; it has committed just a few hundred million dollars to PB schemes. For comparison, this scale of activity represents less than 0.1% of the amount of money loaned by the International Bank for Reconstruction and Development (Goldfrank, 2012). Similarly, while the European Union has in some cases encouraged the use of PB in the distribution of structural funds, the amounts of money involved are not large. While there are some examples of the Porto Alegre model being directly adapted within Europe – such as in Cordoba in Spain – these are very much the exception rather than the rule (Sintomer et al, 2008). Indeed, the key lesson seems to be about the importance of local adaptation and flexibility in how ideas of PB are implemented.

Because PB is a flexible concept there can be tensions in how it is deployed. Baiocchi and Ganuza (2014) identify two key strands within

PB: **communicative** and **empowering**. These elements receive a different degree of emphasis depending on the aims of those setting up PB processes. The original Porto Alegre model was about more than giving people an opportunity to feed into a budgeting process, instead seeking to radically transform society by giving people much more control over how that society functioned. The communicative strand of delivering better governance through creating greater transparency over decision making has been more commonly implemented than the empowerment strand.

Despite the enthusiasm for PB as a mechanism, there is an argument that in developed economies, it is merely an expensive way of reproducing existing democratic institutions (Baiocchi and Ganuza, 2014). Where PB has been implemented in the developed world, there has tended to be an emphasis on using it as a technique for bringing in voices that have a harder time being heard – particularly those of poorer communities, people of colour and the young. This seems to have particularly been the case in US examples of PB, which have emphasised issues of *empowerment.*

In New York City experiments with PB began in 2011 when 4 out of 55 council members offered up some or all of their discretionary budgets to a PB process. By 2016-17, some 31 council members had engaged with the process (Kasdan and Markman, 2017). New York's PB arrangements (PBNYC) throw up some interesting questions around equality. The system arises from a peculiarity of governance in some US cities, which allocate quite large sums to individual council members for discretionary spending within their wards. In part this is designed to ensure that poorer districts receive a reasonable share of public spending, rather than resources being concentrated in projects that serve the needs of the already wealthy. Given the ongoing legacy of racial inequality in the US, much of this balancing up is intended to ensure that a portion of spending is dedicated to non-white communities. Those involved with the evaluation of PBNYC explicitly argue that the process had a clear social justice goal and was attempting to involve the city's most disenfranchised groups (Kasdan and Markman, 2017).

In participating wards of New York, neighbourhood assemblies (and some online spaces) receive pitches for community projects each autumn. These are then developed by community members, with the help of city officials in undertaking feasibility studies. Detailed proposals are then put to a ballot each spring, with some wards allowing votes from participants as young as 12 (Su, 2017). Although this gives much more opportunity for individuals to feed into the process, the danger is that more articulate, better educated (and implicitly white) voices will disproportionately feed into this process, as their proposals are more likely to be seen as 'feasible' and 'reasonable' (Su, 2017: 134). The other key problem lies in the extent to which control over these projects ended up being removed from the communities from which they originated. This was particularly problematic where questions of public safety were being addressed. Public housing residents in the Bronx, for example, wanted additional surveillance cameras as part of a crime prevention strategy, but also wanted to be able to access that footage themselves as a means of offering some protection against incidents of police brutality. The video footage remained firmly in the control of the authorities, however, and was not shared with the communities who had commissioned the installation of the cameras. Thus, while PB hands over some of the decision-making power over the initial investment, it does not necessarily offer communities control over the processes which are enabled by that public spending.

In the UK, meanwhile, there are examples of meaningful PB processes, particularly in Scotland, but the sums of money involved are usually very small. Prior to 2010 there were very few PB processes operating within Scotland, though this had grown to 58 by 2016. Set against the number of wards within Scotland, this is a very small number. Neighbourhoods falling into the lowest quintile of the Scottish Index of Multiple Deprivation were the sites for 90% of these projects, indicating that PB was implicitly being used to address questions of inequality. The average spend per PB process was only £28,400 with an average of £9,300 spent on the 179 projects funded by PB in Scotland in 2010-16 (Harkins et al, 2016). When operating at this kind of scale, there is minimal potential for radically overhauling democracy and reworking social processes to favour communities who are currently excluded from these processes. As Baiocchi and Ganuza (2014) suggest:

> There is a strong attraction for Participatory Budgeting to be implemented through the path of least resistance, and thus become connected to small and discretionary budgets. This could imply community effort and organizing around issues that are less pressing from the point of view of social justice, or worse, have the agenda of movements be dictated by the administrative possibilities rather than more autonomous conversations about needs. (Baiochhi and Ganuza, 2014: 42)

While any additional spending in a severely deprived neighbourhood is generally to be welcomed, the Scottish example is typical of a type of

PB that will not lead to any significant rebalancing of power between rich and poor communities.

Creativity, the arts and social inclusion

There has long been a concern in public arts funding – which has become acute since the 1980s – that, as well as generating good art with intrinsic aesthetic value, the arts should also have instrumental value, particularly generating gains in the fields of social inclusion, health and wellbeing (Oakley, 2006, 2009). Processes of cultural intermediation have been crucial to this, seeking to connect communities with cultural activities to gain the instrumental benefits of such engagement. 'Communities' in this case are implicitly taken to mean socially excluded communities – those who supposedly have the most to gain from instrumental engagement with the arts compared to the affluent middle classes who are seen as 'voracious' cultural consumers (Katz-Gerro and Sullivan, 2010).

The assumption that it is important to get those living in 'deprived' neighbourhoods to engage in cultural activity is based on a deficit model of cultural consumption. As Miles and Sullivan (2012) have demonstrated, this deficit model is unhelpful as it fails to capture the informal and everyday cultural participation that most people engage with. Most people *do* engage with some form of cultural activity; at the same time, most people *do not* engage with what might be termed 'high' culture. Regardless, in an age where public funding is disappearing rapidly for all but the most instrumentally valuable purposes, the deficit model is useful to the cultural sector in justifying the continued existence of funding for arts and culture. This, in turn, requires that cultural activities demonstrate how they reach out to communities who have not traditionally engaged with them.

The annual *Taking part* survey run by the UK's Department for Digital, Culture, Media and Sport (DCMS) shows that engagement with the arts, broadly defined, has stayed virtually flat at around three quarters of the population since 2005 (DCMS, 2017). In a series of highly critical articles, Jancovich (2013, 2017) has highlighted the extent to which arts funding continues to be elitist and exclusionary. Despite a powerful discourse about the need for publicly funded arts to reach beyond its traditional audience, not only has participation remained flat for the last decade, Jancovich (2013: 96) points out that the vast majority of individuals engage with the arts no more than once per year and even then for profit-making commercial work rather than 'high' culture.

To date, despite the experiments with PB among UK local authorities, there has been very little use of PB as an approach to setting local arts budgets or, indeed, by Arts Council England (Jancovich, 2017). Jancovich (2013) points to a significant difference in attitude between arts administrators who have meaningfully engaged the public in decision making over the direction and type of spending and those who have not – the latter being much more concerned that less challenging and creative work of poorer artistic quality would result. For the contrasting position, the example of the *1mile²* project is instructive (Vaughan Jones, Chapter fifteen in this volume).

As local authority budgets are shrinking, there is much more enthusiasm among policy makers for engaging communities in discussions about where to reduce spending. As it concerns non-statutory services barely engaged with by the majority of citizens, arts and cultural spending at the municipal scale is often seen as being an uncontroversial source of cuts (Knell and Taylor, 2011). When PB is operationalised at a local level, however, arts spending tends to do better, with communities more likely to vote for arts outputs that are more tangible for their neighbourhoods (Jancovich, 2015: 19). What this perhaps suggests is that PB offers an opportunity to reorientate arts spending, not away from more controversial and challenging projects, but towards projects that seek to meaningfully engage communities in the process of coconstruction.

This chapter discusses the following two case studies, both based in Birmingham, UK. The *Arts champions* scheme is a confused hybrid, with some elements of control devolved to civil society organisations, but with conflict built in and with the local authority retaining a high degree of control. The second, in Balsall Heath, was a participatory action research project led by the author. This project attempted to develop beyond the communicative model of PB to a more empowering approach, through a combination of citizen meetings and collaboration with civil society organisations.

For the examination of the *Arts champions* scheme funded by Birmingham City Council, we undertook a series of semi-structured interviews and two focus groups with key organisers. We also used participant observation at two celebration events and a networking meeting as well as secondary analysis of the evaluation documents produced by the organisations involved. For the participatory action research, a community panel was established to undertake a process of cultural commissioning, spending a total of £40,000 across 2015-16 on eight different cultural activities. The research team documented this process through ethnographic field diaries, focus groups and semi-structured interviews with panel members, feedback cards given out at events, community crowdsourced video and photographic material.

Case study 1: Arts champions

Birmingham City Council's *Arts champions* scheme was established in 2005 as an innovative attempt to leverage the resources and talent of major publicly funded arts organisations based primarily in the city centre to work with communities across the city. The rationale for this approach was that these core-funded organisations (which include the City of Birmingham Symphony Orchestra, the Birmingham Rep, and Birmingham Royal Ballet) should be seen to be giving something back to the city in exchange for the large public subsidy they receive. These organisations were given a remit to engage with one of the ten districts as their 'arts champion', running local events for a period of three years before being rotated to a different district.

Birmingham City Council is notorious for its byzantine governance arrangements (Kerslake, 2014) and the *Arts champions* scheme suffers from the city council's tendencies towards bureaucratic complexity. The champions are supposed to bid for funding each year to run a set of district-level events (each district containing around 100,000 people) while simultaneously being encouraged by council officers to respond to particular themes emerging from the city's Culture Commissioning department. Each champion is also expected to collaborate with the relevant district 'local arts forum', a roundtable organisation seeking to represent arts and cultural practitioners operating within the district. The nature of this collaboration has never been clear to those involved and has been a source of considerable tension. There is also an exhaustive evaluation process to undertake at the end of each annual cycle. The funding available for all this activity is capped at just £4,000 per year per arts champion – some of which have multimillion pound turnovers in their core activities.

Despite the complexity of the governance arrangements, the *Arts champions* scheme can be seen as an attempt to devolve some of the city's cultural spend to its different districts, rather than concentrating those resources in the city centre. Although the scheme is intended to cover the whole city, in interviews with the champions it was clear that they were pushed towards targeting deprived neighbourhoods and 'hard-to-reach' groups. There is, therefore, some commonality with the 'communicative' approach to PB, attempting to address some of the inequalities in public spending by engaging with non-traditional audiences. One can also read the *Arts champions* scheme as an attempt to use intermediaries to *fix* communities through the inclusionary power of cultural engagement. Champions themselves found real difficulty, however, in reconciling competing agendas within the scheme, for example:

> They [the city council] told us that they really wanted us to work with the men because men are not engaging in the arts … – and that is why we set up the '[name removed] project' – and then they told us that they wanted to get to certain places, because it was there that there were people that were hard-to-reach. We then went there, and without all that marketing we got 4-5 [pairs of people involved]. From our experience of working across the country, we thought 'yes, this is brilliant!' – We then went to the city council and they told us that it was absolutely useless, it was rubbish and that we had done a really bad job…. (Interview with arts champion #6, January 2015)

Working with a notoriously disengaged social group in a particularly disengaged neighbourhood is unlikely to result in mass participation, but there was a clear desire within the council to see a large number of 'bums on seats' (interview with Arts champion #6, January 2015) to justify the resources spent. These contradictory agendas resulted in the champion being scolded, despite clearly working with a group that had been labelled a priority in terms of using cultural engagement to drive an instrumental social inclusion agenda.

This exchange with the local authority highlights the extent to which council officers were unwilling to relinquish control over how the funds were spent. More significant, however, was the fraught relationship with the local arts forums that meant the opportunity to use the *Arts champions* scheme to take a more PB approach to this spending was squandered. The local arts forums operate at the district level as a coordinating structure for artists and arts-based civil society organisations. In a relationship with the arts champions, the forums thus have the potential to play an intermediary PB role, leveraging spending in their district by the wealthy champions. Because the sums of money involved were so trivial, the champions were, in effect, having to cross-subsidise this activity with their existing outreach work. This gave them considerable power in the process and the relationship with the forums became at best ambiguous and, on occasion, openly hostile.

There was a risk, then, that instead of presenting an opportunity to leverage cultural spending to the neighbourhood level, the *Arts champions* scheme simply reproduced the traditional deficit model, whereby the existing cultural offer was seen as benefiting deprived communities if only they could be persuaded to engage with it. Ultimately, the opportunity for the arts champion process to drive a more locally engaged spending through a civil-society-led PB process has not been realised. More than this, for all the good intentions and the benefits of getting involved with cultural activities, schemes such as the *Arts champions* can only have a limited impact on the *material* effects of social deprivation. As one interviewee baldly stated:

> [I]t has to be skills development, health, something that means something to these poor people; the minute you say 'art' to them, they are thinking that 'we can't pay the electricity, sorry!' and 'fuck off with your arts project!' – That's the reaction that I get in [name of neighbourhood]. ... Do you think people who are in the poorest area in the country are going to care about your local fair on a Sunday afternoon when she can't give bread to her kids? Sometimes, I think that there is something wrong here! (Interview with arts champion #1, January 2015)

In the face of such intractable problems, a budget of £4,000 per year for additional arts activities in a district of 100,000 people can at best be seen merely as well-intentioned tokenism.

Case study 2: Balsall Heath community commissioning panel

Balsall Heath scores highly across many metrics of urban deprivation. As discussed by Long and Warren (Chapter five in this volume), however, there are other, considerably more positive, narratives about Balsall Heath as a neighbourhood. It has particularly strong civil society organisations. Notions of the Big Society, which animated neighbourhood policy under the UK's coalition government of 2010-15, were in part inspired by Balsall Heath (Cameron, 2011). Local civil society organisation St Paul's Trust runs multiple projects in the neighbourhood around education and social inclusion including arts activities. There is also a dynamic alternative arts scene including the Old Print Works, which rents cheap space to local creative organisations. Balsall Heath also received Pathfinder funding to pilot government proposals to help communities draw up their own neighbourhood spatial plans (Jones et al, 2015).

During the autumn and winter of 2014, through a mix of pop-up events, fliers, engagement with local arts and civil society organisations, libraries and other spaces, the research team recruited a group of around 30 community members to form a local cultural commissioning panel in Balsall Heath (Warren and Jones, 2018). Through a series of meetings from January to March 2015, panel members were encouraged to discuss their priorities for action in the neighbourhood, that is, discussing the challenges and opportunities facing the area before raising questions around how cultural activity might address some of these points. Panel members subsequently developed proposals for cultural activities, which were then commissioned in March 2015 and funded to run until the summer of 2016.

This approach to cultural commissioning – focusing on the needs of the neighbourhood rather than putting the initial emphasis on cultural activity – was partially inspired by the *1mile²* project run by Visiting Arts (Vaughan Jones, 2015). In discussions among the wider group of panel members prior to deciding which projects to commission, a number of common themes emerged that cut across ethnic and other divides. The lack of things for young men to do, particularly in the light of high youth unemployment, came up in a number of meetings and clearly reflects a fairly common concern about this demographic. The result of these discussions was the commissioning of a football tournament for 15- to 19-year-olds, an age cohort that was poorly catered to in organised sports within the neighbourhood. Other themes that cut across the panel revolved around food and day trips. Birmingham's 'Balti Triangle' of restaurants serving variations on Indian/Pakistani cuisine lies at one edge of Balsall Heath; venues serving Arabic and Kurdish food have started to open, reflecting new waves of migration to the area, and there are still some surviving places serving Jamaican dishes despite the neighbourhood's shrinking African-Caribbean community. A low-key food festival celebrating this diversity took place around Christmas 2015.

The second unifying theme, day trips, emerged from discussions about the withdrawal of city council services at a time of quite savage cuts and a retreat from any council expenditure not tied to the statutory provision of services. Older panel members talked about council-subsidised day trips that they had experienced when younger; they worried about the lack of opportunities to experience places beyond the narrow confines of the neighbourhood and parts of Birmingham. A group of Muslim women took responsibility for developing a proposal around day trips. Over the course of several meetings, two destinations were eventually settled upon: first, a day out to the large national museums in South Kensington, London; second, an overnight trip to an outward-bound centre in the Lake District (field diary entry, commissioning meeting 24 March, 2015).

This idea was not uncontroversial, however. While members of the community panel were broadly in favour of the day trips, there were some hostile voices, particularly from a group who felt that this was simply a case of people wanting to fund their own holidays, rather than driving investment in the arts (field diary entry, focus group 18 March 2015). In an attempt to keep the process relatively harmonious, separate discussions were held with the more hostile individuals, but this led to a process of the academic facilitators manipulating how different voices were heard in order to meet our own aim of getting a PB process to make some commissioning decisions in a relatively short timeframe. The researchers were playing the role that would normally be taken by the municipality in PB processes. As Su (2017) argues in relation to the New York PB:

> When community members first articulate the proposal ideas, they focus foremost on whatever they believe their families, neighbors, and neighborhoods need most. Very quickly in the process, however, the focus of budget delegates, city agencies, council staff, and voters all shift to what is eligible, 'feasible', and 'reasonable'. (Su, 2017: 134)

Much as with the New York example, for the researchers in Balsall Heath there was a temptation to prioritise delivery of 'feasible' outcomes against a bottom-up process that empowered multiple voices and which accommodated controversy and disagreement.

Conclusion: the role of intermediation in participatory cultural budgeting

PB is not an easy process but has the potential to hand real power over to communities to redirect public spending towards improving equity and social justice. PB can do more than simply operate in a communicative mode, effective though this can be for enhancing transparency and reducing corruption in developing world contexts. PB's radical potential for community *empowerment* is, however, dependent on the mechanisms through which it operates and the extent to which municipalities and funding bodies are willing to meaningfully devolve control. This is particularly sensitive in the context of arts and cultural spending, where there is a fear by some in the sector of a race to the bottom – either in choosing to reduce arts spending to offset cuts to essential services, or in simply producing low quality cultural products that do not challenge their audiences.

Intermediation is critical to how these processes work, not simply at the commissioning stage, but throughout the process in order to give communities the skills and confidence to meaningfully engage in shaping activities in their neighbourhood. Both the case studies discussed here show the weaknesses of PB but also highlight its potential for encouraging cultural intermediaries to work with communities to produce outputs and activities that meaningfully engage with local needs. There is no perfect model for PB – there will always be disagreement over priorities and marginalised voices will frequently be drowned out. What is essential, however, is that these processes are meaningful, with significant sums of money involved to avoid charges of mere tokenism. Capacity building among the communities involved is a crucial task for those intermediaries charged with facilitating the process, such that control is not merely devolved over ideas generation, but that there is a genuine diversity of individuals able to develop those ideas into projects and real power handed over to communities to oversee those projects as they are being implemented.

References

Baiocchi, G. and Ganuza, E. (2014) 'Participatory budgeting as if emancipation mattered', *Politics & Society*, 42: 29-50.

Cabannes, Y. (2015) 'The impact of participatory budgeting on basic services: municipal practices and evidence from the field', *Environment and Urbanization*, 27: 257-84.

Cameron, D. (2011) 'Comment: Have no doubt, the big society is on its way: ignore the sceptics. I have a compelling plan to engage us all in transforming Britain', *The Observer*, 13 February: 39.

DCMS (2017) *Taking Part Survey: England Adult Report, 2016/17*, London: DCMS.

Goldfrank, B. (2012) 'The World Bank and the globalization of participatory budgeting', *Journal of Public Deliberation*, 8: Article 7, 1-18.

Harkins, C., Moore, K. and Escobar, O. (2016) *Review of 1st generation participatory budgeting in Scotland*, Edinburgh: What Works Scotland.

Jancovich, L. (2013) 'Cultural policy in the public eye', *Journal of Policy Research in Tourism, Leisure and Events*, 5: 95-8.

Jancovich, L. (2015) 'Breaking down the fourth wall in arts management: the implications of engaging users in decision-making', *International Journal of Arts Management*, 18: 14-28.

Jancovich, L. (2017) 'The participation myth', *International Journal of Cultural Policy*, 23: 107-21.

Jones, P., Layard, A., Speed, C. and Lorne, C. (2015) 'MapLocal: use of smartphones for crowdsourced planning', *Planning Practice & Research*, 30: 322-36.

Kasdan, A. and Markman, E. (2017) 'Participatory budgeting and community-based research: principles, practices, and implications for impact validity', *New Political Science*, 39: 143-55.

Katz-Gerro, T. and Sullivan, O. (2010) 'Voracious cultural consumption: the intertwining of gender and social status', *Time & Society*, 19: 193-219.

Kerslake, R. (2014) *The way forward: an independent review of the governance and organisational capabilities of Birmingham City Council*, London: Department for Communities and Local Government.

Knell, J. and Taylor, M. (2011) *Arts funding, austerity and the Big Society: Remaking the case for the arts?* London: RSA.

Miles, A. and Sullivan, A. (2012) 'Understanding participation in culture and sport: mixing methods, reordering knowledges', *Cultural Trends*, 21: 311-24.

Oakley, K. (2006) 'Include us out: economic development and social policy in the creative industries', *Cultural Trends*, 15: 255-73.

Oakley, K. (2009) 'The disappearing arts: creativity and innovation after the creative industries', *International Journal of Cultural Policy*, 15: 403-13.

Sintomer, Y., Herzberg, C. and Röcke, A. (2008) 'Participatory budgeting in Europe: potentials and challenges', *International Journal of Urban and Regional Research*, 32: 164-78.

Souza, C. (2001) 'Participatory budgeting in Brazilian cities: limits and possibilities in building democratic institutions', *Environment and Urbanization*, 13: 159-84.

Su, C. (2017) 'Beyond inclusion: critical race theory and participatory budgeting', *New Political Science*, 39: 126-42.

Vaughan Jones, Y. (2015) *Artists as cultural intermediaries: a report of the Square Mile Project*. Working paper available from https://culturalintermediation.wordpress.com/outputs/

Warren, S. and Jones, P. (2018) 'Cultural policy, governance and urban diversity: resident perspectives from Birmingham, UK', *Tijdschrift voor economische en sociale geografie*, 109: 22-35.

NINE

Intervention:
Balsall Heath legends

Saadia Kiyani

One day I was invited by my contact at a local organisation to contribute towards ideas for a local project. I didn't know what was going on but I knew we would be paid for the session. This was a major draw for me as I don't work and didn't have much money. I decided to attend. During the course of the meetings I nearly stopped going but my contact pulled me back in. This was because of having to leave my children at home alone. Also a lack of confidence and feeling there was no point going. I had given up hope in any meaningful projects coming my way.

I contributed my pitch at a group session for my photography project idea. I have a degree in photography but was finding it hard to get work. Having an interest in the local area, having grown up there, I decided to do a project on people in the local area, being inspired by similar projects. However, the difference with my project would be that I would find 'regular' people from within the area. The strength of Balsall Heath being that it was as diverse an area as you could get. I wanted my project to reflect this. I wanted people who others would never think of using.

I was lucky that I had built up a modest studio set up while I was at university. Also I was lucky that the organisation that was supporting me had rooms available. I shot the photos of my 'legends' myself as well as editing and getting printed the A3 sized prints for exhibition use. This was all possible using the funds for my project.

One of my legends got a lot of attention through the project. I was told that people who previously didn't even greet her were coming up and asking what she had done to get her photo on the bus. People assume you have to do something or be worthy in some way to be on the media. All the fuss got back to people, which made her feel good that she had achieved city-wide recognition. I was able to include my mother in the project and get her some recognition too. People from far and near saw my 'legends' on the buses (see Figure 9.1). At first I had thought getting my images on the local buses was a stretch, but

Figure 9.1: *Balsall Heath legends*

Source: Saadia Kiyani

I managed it in the end. This was only through having control over what I did with the money I was given.

At the end of the day, I was enabled to make a project that helped me achieve my own personal goals on my own terms. I affected local people who normally wouldn't be given exposure in this way. Everyone all over the city saw them; even my relatives who believe women like my mom shouldn't be promoting herself like this. I gained a lot of personal and professional satisfaction by being allowed to use the money to further my project goals. Normally I would be a slave to whoever provided the funding. That is if I was able to compete for funding from an organisation. I was previously rejected just for not having a website.

The pride I felt as my images were going up the buses in my local area was priceless. The feedback and effect on the community I will probably never fully know. This is because most people in my community saw the images but couldn't give feedback for various reasons. The main reason was not being able to communicate well in English. Also not being social media users. Word of mouth conveyed to me that many saw it though and it affected them positively. I love the idea of giving arts money direct to organisations that then let the fully competent and professional local people pitch ideas. This will lead to different and unique projects, which would normally never see the light of day. Just like mine wouldn't have. Thanks to this unique arts funding project I now have an awesome project under my belt.

TEN

Screening films for social change: origins, aims and evolution of the Bristol Radical Film Festival

Laura Ager

This chapter will discuss how a mode of cognitive-cultural production, a festival, was mobilised for persuasive purposes, through a case study of a group of film scholars and researchers in Bristol, UK, who linked subject-specific knowledge with a kind of ethical praxis to reach marginalised community groups through the production of a film festival. The Bristol Radical Film Festival (BRFF) takes place annually in venues throughout the city of Bristol, in the South West of England, presenting a curated programme of 'radical' films and documentaries which are screened in non-traditional venues. The context of this work is how the changing political economy of UK higher education, along with new forms of measurement of the impacts of academic research, has led to a reevaluation of the public engagement activities of academic communities.

University festivals

Because the study described here examines the role of universities in the cultural economy (Chatterton, 2000; Hughes et al, 2011; Sapsed and Nightingale, 2013; Comunian, Smith and Taylor, 2013; Comunian and Gilmore, 2014), it needs to be acknowledged that this research coincided with a period of dramatic change in the political economy of UK higher education. Most notable was the newly elected Conservative-Liberal Democrat coalition government's Comprehensive Spending Review of October 2010 that announced deep cuts in funding for higher education for the period 2010-11 to 2014-15. The Browne Review (Browne, 2010), published at the same time, redrew the guidelines for funding academic institutions and, following this, the Higher Education Funding Council for England announced significant adaptations to the tools of measurement of academic research, specifically those that measured its impact. The arrival of the Research Excellence Framework's 'impact' agenda[1] demanded that the 'use' value of academic research to society had to be articulated more clearly than ever before.

Festivals are sites of cultural production which, through practices of curation, interpretation and presentation, connect cultural producers with the public. They were being operationalised within UK higher education for the purposes of achieving public engagement with research, and other external impacts (Buckley et al, 2011). The proliferation of university festivals between 2010 and 2014 (Ager, 2016) sparked renewed interest in practices associated with 'third mission' agendas such as widening participation and public engagement. Cultural intermediaries intuitively navigate these connective processes (a 'Swiss Army knife of soft skills', as one respondent put it). This research investigated the potential contradictions in the relationship between the mode of cultural production (a festival) and the conditions of its constitution (a university) (Peterson and Anand, 2004; May, 2005).

The Bristol Radical Film Festival (BRFF): context and place

The first three editions of the BRFF 2012-14 were produced by staff and students from the University of the West of England (UWE) in Bristol. Certain spatial and social factors are an important part of the context to the festival's evolution during this time. Bristol is a distinctive city, approximately 150 miles west of London. Historically, it was a port and merchant city, becoming prosperous through Atlantic trade when the 'New World' was discovered. Although it is hard to imagine the harbourside area as anything other than the lively cultural quarter it now is, the city's infrastructure tells a familiar story of twentieth century urban post-industrial decline and reorientation; following the closure of the port in 1975, the docks became a derelict and marginal area. The subsequent regeneration of the harbourside was spearheaded by the relocation of the Arnolfini arts centre to a derelict nineteenth century warehouse, followed by the move of the British Film Institute's first Regional Film Theatre to a building complex that is now known as the Watershed. The harbour area is now a major centre for cultural tourism and consumption, but inequalities of wealth and deprivation can be seen elsewhere in the city. Many of these areas have been changing rapidly (Boyden, 2013), as has the campus of the city's post-1992 university, the University of the West of England (UWE).

'UWE is the whole reason'

Since the first edition of the BRFF, there have been a number of changes in festival personnel, however all members of the organising team between 2012 and 2014 had a connection with the Film Studies degree course at UWE and had first met at its St Matthias campus. In fact, during 2014 out of the five BRFF coorganisers, two were lecturing in Film Studies at UWE and all of them either were or had been Film Studies students there. One of the coorganisers had lectured at UWE since 2003 and had actually taught all four of the others previously. One organiser had recently completed his PhD thesis at UWE on contemporary activist and radical film in the UK and had remained there first as a lecturer, then a research fellow.

At this time, UWE's campus was spread over three main locations. The Film Studies undergraduate and research programmes were taught at St Matthias College in Fishponds, in the north of the city. The college ceased to be independent in 1978 and its staff and students transferred to Bristol Polytechnic, which gained university status in 1992. The St Matthias campus closed in July 2014 and the site has since been sold to a housing developer. UWE's main, purpose-built Frenchay campus is located much further north, close to the city's outer ring road. UWE also has outposts for film tuition and moving-image-based research within the buildings of some of Bristol's major cultural organisations in the city centre. What is now known as the 'city campus' includes sites at creative hubs in Bower Ashton, Spike Island and in the harbourside area. The harbourside sites include Bush House, where the Arnolfini arts centre is located, and the Watershed, where the Pervasive Media Studio hosts the Digital Cultures Research Centre, one of four 'knowledge exchange hubs for the creative economy' funded between 2012 and 2016 by the Arts and Humanities Research Council.

I interviewed the festival's founding organisers for my research. Recounting the festival's origins, one of them told me:

> [name anonymised] was doing his PhD on British radical cinema and he … saw an ad for the film about Thatcher. And something in the promotion said something along the lines of 'come to see this British film' or 'this is one of the best British films' … When he came back he got in touch with me and told me 'I have this idea and we need to make it happen'. That was kind of the original embryonic idea of the whole thing. (BRFF coorganiser, in interview)

> just calls me up one day and was just like 'hey I wanna put on a film festival, it's going to be da da da' and it was like 'That's such a fucking good idea, that's exactly what we should be doing', 'do you want to get involved?', 'yes, I want to get involved' and then I was involved. (BRFF coorganiser, in interview)

Later it became clear that the festival didn't emerge as a fully formed event without any kind of precedent in practice. When asked about how the different people got involved, another organiser, a senior lecturer at UWE, mentioned that one of the younger organisers had been 'sort of' there from the beginning, because they had 'come to the screenings we were doing at uni'. This was a series of screenings called Reel World, organised by two lecturers (and BRFF cofounders) that took place on St Matthias campus on Friday nights, when the films would often be followed by a discussion in the bar. Another respondent told me that he had become involved as an undergraduate student at UWE 'through the occupation'. Going back to November 2011, before the BRFF emerged, the student union rooms and facilities at both Frenchay and St Matthias campus locations had been occupied by UWE students protesting against increased tuition fees and staff cutbacks (Killick, 2010).

> There was an occupation at (the uni) where we took over … what was the name of the place … Core 24, a café … We took all that over, we basically did an occupation against the proposed, at that time, rise in tuition fees…. Basically stayed in a café for about four weeks. (BRFF coorganiser, in interview)

During this time, this BRFF organiser had been travelling to London with other students to attend demonstrations against the raising of the tuition fee threshold, as well as handing out leaflets and talking to students back on campus. He described the sense of camaraderie he felt with other protesters as 'solidifying ourselves' as a kind of unit, and especially 'against the rest of the university'.

> That's how I met a lot of people that I hold as friends today, that's how I saw a lot of people that I didn't really know even existed on a political level before, become politicised. (BRFF coorganiser, in interview)

Meanwhile, in 2011 there were widely publicised riots happening in parts of the UK, including in parts of Bristol.

> At the same time there was a bunch of riots going on in Stokes Croft. It was a real heightened period of political awareness and activism and I think the film festival came a lot of the back of that kind of thing ... sure, the cuts had gone through, and the tuition fees cap had been raised, but it was time to you know, to take stock, and see what we actually can do ... (BRFF coorganiser, in interview)

The sense of injustice this organiser felt was the main factor in his involvement in the festival: the student protests had failed to prevent fees from rising, further violence carried risk of arrest, but screening films to raise awareness within other marginalised or oppressed communities in the city was a way he felt he could retaliate. 'They can't touch us for doing that.'

Bristol Radical Film Festival 2014

According to the inside cover of the printed programme guide in 2014, the BRFF is a festival of 'contemporary and historical works of overtly political left-wing documentary and fiction filmmaking'. The cover image of a machine gun combined with a video camera points to an association of the production of media with conflict, which is reflected in the programme content. The festival screens films that are underrepresented on other circuits, even those for documentary or specialist films. Of the thirteen feature-length films[2] that were screened at the BRFF in 2014, most were documentaries. Topics that the films engaged with ranged from the social effects of the Cambodian genocide in the 1970s and the present-day oppression of women in Iran to British coalminers' unions, representations of ageing and the plight of Palestinian children. The programme also included experimental and non-documentary feature films, video activist works, short films on a range of subjects, and a closing party with DJs (without films).

These early editions of the BRFF had a transient and fugitive model, only occasionally using cinema spaces to hold screenings. The festival in 2014 took the form of a week-long series of film events, held in different venues across Bristol each day, and ended with a packed weekend featuring films on different floors of the same building in the city's centre, the Arc, which it employed as a kind of festival hub. This

Figure 10.1: Front cover image of the BRFF 2014 programme guide

was a multi-floor, multi-use community and cultural space, managed and maintained on a not-for-profit basis by volunteer collective *Alien coconut*. It had once been a nightclub; the floors showed the remnants of glitter paint and there was a bar on the ground floor, as well as various social spaces higher up. In 2013, this building had become a temporary Palestinian Embassy in Bristol and there were signs of this around the building during the BRFF weekend, most notably the Nakba Museum[3] which was an exhibition of media and objects referring to the occupation of Palestine. Two rooms on different floors were used as screening spaces, set out with chairs in rows, and it was cold inside.

As well as introducing the films, it was apparent at 'pop-up' venues like the Arc that members of the festival team were also installing the equipment and organising the projection. Yet despite its small team and obvious lack of available finance, compared with, for example, the Open City Docs film festival based at University College London, the BRFF attracted similar-sized audiences to its screenings as those seen at better-resourced university festival events. To 'brand' the venues when a screening was taking place, BRFF posters were applied to windows and doors and event organisers wore T-shirts printed with the festival logo.

On weekday nights, screenings ran from 7.30pm until roughly 9.30pm and each day the venue was different. Site-specific, accessible film screenings are an important part of the festival's semiology; in 2014, the rationale for venue selection was written in the 'about us' section of the festival's webpage as follows:

> [The festival] aims to draw attention to a range of other progressive, community-based initiatives in the city. Previous venues include digital outreach projects, anarchist social centres, drop-in centres for sex workers, political squats, radical bookshops, community bicycle hubs, trade union halls etc. ('About us', Bristol Radical Film Festival website, 2013)

The first event of the 2014 BRFF was a screening of the documentary *Enemies of the people* (Thet Sambeth and Rob Lemkin, 2009), a disturbing look at the aftermath of a period of genocide during the Khmer Rouge regime in Cambodia between 1975 and 1979. It was shown at The Cube Microplex in Stokes Croft, an area at the north point of the city centre. A ticket for the screening cost £4 plus £1 membership fee for any non-members visiting the volunteer-run cinema. Around thirty people attended this event. The next evening the festival venue was the Single Parent Action Network Family and Study Centre at the Silai centre in Easton, about two miles from the city centre in the north eastern part of the city. The screening was of two Iranian documentaries about women's rights and the realities of women's lives in Iran. The venue was completely sold out and organisers told me that people had even been turned away due to the lack of space in the screening room.

Wednesday's screening took place at Roll for the Soul bike café, a street-level vegetarian café and bicycle repair shop, close to the pedestrian centre of the city. Leaflets and posters inside the café gave the impression of it being something of a hub for alternative lifestyle networks in the city. For the screening, four bikes had been installed inside the café. The pedal-powered screening was advertised as £4/£5 but it was not clear who was taking money and many people entered the café without paying. In the end a 'charity hat' (belonging to one of the festival organisers) was passed around the audience for donations. A short documentary about a bicycle recycling project in

Bristol that donates bikes to refugees was followed by the feature, *Man with a movie camera* (Dziga Vertov, 1929). This is a silent, avant-garde Soviet documentary film, now considered a classic. A voltage meter attached to the bikes indicated the amount of power being generated as volunteers from the audience took turns to pedal for as long as they chose. This powered the LED projector and the music being mixed live on a laptop on the bar.

The next venue was Knowle West Media Centre in a residential part of south Bristol. This was described by one of the organisers as being a riskier choice of venue, being so far out of the centre and a place where 'nobody goes'. Purpose built as a community resource, the building had a large white screening room, with projection windows set in the wall above the entrance. Wine at the back of the room was self-service, for a suggested donation of £1. The film screened was *McLibel* (Franny Armstrong, 2005), a well-known documentary that begins with the infiltration of a London activist group and ends with McDonalds suing two of the activists for libel in the longest case in English legal history.

There were three more days of film screenings and events, including the full weekend at the Arc. New works were screened by a female Iranian filmmaker, Mania Akbari, who was present for a Q&A, there was a video-activism workshop, screenings of an American labour drama *Matewan* (John Sayles, 1987) and anti-war film *Paths of glory* (Stanley Kubrick, 1957) as well as a selection of new documentaries and international short films. After the films on the Saturday, the Roll for the Soul café became the venue for an afterparty.

Why radical? The 'real' British cinema

In interviews, the BRFF organisers were unanimous on two points: that the festival has a role to present films that are left out of the main circuits of distribution, and that the screenings are for the communication of political ideas. The BRFF began as 'pretty much a showcase' for the rare British films one organiser had discovered during the research for his PhD thesis, 'The political avant-garde: oppositional documentary in Britain since 1990' (Presence, 2013).

> First and foremost it's about politics. The radicalism is political in the sense that we show films that advocate radical social change and are predominantly about democracy, sustainability, equality and social justice. (BRFF coorganiser Steve Presence, quoted in Sheppard, 2014)

Presence described the lack of attention paid to the history of radical, oppositional filmmaking and video activism in Britain as a 'missing' part of British film culture, 'I just got frustrated that there was no exhibition platform for the kind of work I was researching'. Presence clarifies his own use of and perspective on the word 'radical' in relation to particular types of political film in his thesis. Other words like 'alternative' or 'counterculture' are often used when describing films made by auteurs, independent filmmakers and activists, but the word alternative brings to mind its use in other fields, such as alternative lifestyles or alternative music and this immediately poses the question: alternatives to what? 'Alternative' suggests a personal choice within a plural culture; from a cultural studies perspective, it has been argued that the terms mainstream and alternative actually play a role in constructing each other (Thornton, 1995). Describing films as 'counter' or 'oppositional' implies an antagonistic relationship with the status quo. Both of these terms have the effect of reinforcing the mainstream as 'normal'. For the purposes of Presence's thesis and so by extension, the BRFF, which emerged while the thesis was being written, the word 'radical' is taken to mean 'from the roots'. This implies a grassroots, socially embedded form of political response that critiques the dominance of capitalism as ruling paradigm by taking a position within 'the struggle' (Presence, 2013: 17).

With respect to film culture, however, the use of the word radical is not limited solely to the kind of documentary work shown at the BRFF in 2014. Forms of aesthetic innovation in the medium of film are also frequently referred to as 'radical'. These latter works are films that 'push against the restrictive and reactionary codes and conventions of mainstream audio-visual culture' (Presence, 2013: 22). However, their predominant site of exhibition venue is the gallery space; in his opinion, this transforms what should be a public function of art into an elitist one. Presence concedes that many examples of 'aesthetic radicalism' (meaning film-based art work) also engage with political questions. Indeed, it can be argued that all representation is political. Nonetheless, confining politics to what he sees as the aesthetic realm is 'profoundly asocial' (Presence, 2013: 22) and doesn't aid the development of a revolutionary consciousness, which is necessarily part of the BRFF's intellectual project. Another founding organiser explained that Presence's research wasn't the only pedagogical perspective on the BRFF at its inception:

> We were very much in the mould of Latin American radical filmmaking, the emphasis is on non-traditional spaces. My

own research deals with something in Argentina called Cine-Piquetero which is a form of video-activism – which purposively is not screened in cinemas. They go to coffee places, to factories, to community centres. We took that as our model and that's how we kind of developed the whole thing. … We had to start thinking about which spaces and which films and it developed from there. We were learning as we were going along. (BRFF coorganiser, in interview)

In an interview with Presence, it became apparent that this approach to selecting the venues for screenings had also influenced his thinking:

The other thing we really wanted to do was map the festival onto the existing kind of countercultural, progressive activism scene in the city so that it wouldn't just be about showing the films … it was about bringing people, audiences, into progressive spaces and trying to build up that solidarity amongst wider movements for social change in the city. (Steve Presence, in interview)

The festival developed iteratively from there. Presence told me that he had wanted the festival to 'overlap onto action' by connecting with social centres around the city and bringing in local community groups. The activist or community group-based screening context offered a way for the films he discovered during his doctoral research to reclaim some of their earlier political agency.

Here's this culture, but it's absolutely part of real life activism and here are the people who are doing it now, and you should talk to them. It was very much about trying not to have this hold on these kind of cultural artefacts as ossified things that are removed from the social and political fabric. It was about saying look, this is what they're designed to do, you get impassioned and pissed off and informed about what's going on and then you can get involved in activism and debate. (Steve Presence, in interview)

Turning their research into practice, the BRFF organisers experimented with the ideas coming out of earlier periods of oppositional filmmaking, finding as they progressed that an enthusiastic audience existed in Bristol for the films that they presented. These were films that, as one organiser put it, were 'designed to catalyse action, to catalyse people doing stuff about their situation'. In this way, the content of the film programme drove the form the festival took from a pedagogical perspective.

> It was an educational tool in order to do that. And that was my main objective for having the festival and this is why we do the discussions after each film. That was the major thing for me, but I think that was the major thing for everyone. (BRFF coorganiser, in interview)

Screenings overlapping onto action and engaging with audiences in community settings are established practice in radical film culture. Films that are screened at BRFF are always introduced, then followed by a relaxed and unhurried discussion, led by festival organisers and involving the audience.

The conditions of cultural production

This chapter has explored how cultural production, individual praxis, and issues of social inclusion and intermediation have become intertwined in the production of a socially engaged film festival. The BRFF is both an act of cognitive-cultural production and a political-pedagogical mission which, in the climate of austerity and protest following the financial crash of 2008, is understood by its agents as an act of political resistance. One striking thing about the BRFF is the relationship it has with higher education (HE): while much of it has been produced 'outside' the boundaries of the HE institution that connects its organisers, and the BRFF initially seemed removed from its institutional partner, the research has revealed how much it is enabled by their respective positions to it. Where universities are involved in the production of culture, there is also a distinctive legitimating factor at work: the social influence of the academic job title or doctorate. As one of the BRFF team pointed out: 'I think the importance of being affiliated with UWE ... is that people don't just see us as a bunch of red flag waving loonies, they go "oh, ok, so your ideas came out of a book"'.

Festivals can be seen as political phenomena, tending to appear in an oppositional context at times of changing political culture (McKay, 1996; Lamond and Spracklen, 2015). Also, festival programmes are different to the types of public cultural programmes that are offered to the public on a year-round basis. Although it presents itself as a single phenomenon, the festival is actually a kind of metatext, or an assemblage of texts and discourses, polyphonic and plural. Emerging from a wider research project that critically examined universities as cultural intermediaries within the creative ecologies of their cities, the case study of the production of the BRFF in relation to its institutional context throws into sharp focus some questions surrounding the changing political economy of higher education and its effects on individuals, on departments and on disciplines. Festivals offer a spatially and temporally bounded public platform or 'pop-up third place' (Comunian and Gilmore, 2015) where university activities are externalised and made available for public exhibition and consumption. The fractured and transient form of the BRFF in some way replicates that of the academic institution from which it emerged. The risk is that the closer a festival is to the institutional centre, the greater the risk that they will become rational and goal-directed rather than communicative and discursive.

The government-incentivised alignment of interests between university and industry has become so important to the function of universities that 'knowledge transfer' leaders and their teams of staff are now a significant cohort within academic communities. Where creative arts disciplines are concerned, debates about value are also permanently inflected with economic rationality, due to the centrality of culture to the development of post-industrial economies, culture's role in the articulation of city narratives and the reordering of zones of production and consumption, and the university's role in training the future cultural workforce.

A theory-led form of film education, which takes a critical approach to the subject, and which these scholars have employed to reveal the 'gap' in contemporary film culture that they sought to fill with the BRFF, is potentially threatened by the recent agendas for teaching and research in higher education that prioritise 'measurables' like graduate career paths and the impacts of research. It is worth noting however that none of the BRFF organisers were involved in the Research Excellence Framework submission in 2014. What is interesting about the BRFF in relation to its institutional context is that a mix of disciplinary orientation, academic activism and counter-politics has positioned the festival as the 'guardian' of certain disciplinary traditions and the distinctive practices of its producers.

Notes

[1] 'Research impact' was defined in 2012 as 'any effect on, change or benefit to the economy, society, culture, public policy or services, the environment or quality of

life, beyond academia' (Higher Education Funding Council for England, 2012). It was a compulsory element introduced in the Research Excellence Framework, which replaced the earlier Research Assessment Exercise in 2014.

2   'Feature length' is not a clearly defined term. The British Film Institute (2017) suggests a feature film is any film longer than 40 minutes and a short film is no more than 40 minutes.

3   *Nakba* means 'catastrophe': the word is used by Palestinians to refer to the expulsion of Arabs from Palestine and the founding of Israel as a state in 1948.

References

Ager, L. (2016) 'Universities and festivals: cultural production in context', PhD thesis, available from University of Salford.

Boyden, P. (2013) *Culture, creativity and regeneration in Bristol: Three stories*, Bristol: Peter Boyden Consultants, available at: http://www.watershed.co.uk/sites/default/files/publications/2013-09-10/CCRB%20June2013.pdf.

Bristol Radical Film Festival (2013) 'About Us' [Website page], available at: www.bristolradicalfilmfestival.org.uk.

British Film Institute (2017) *Statistical Yearbook 2017*, London: British Film Institute.

Browne, J. (2010) *Securing a sustainable future for higher education: Report of the Independent Review of Higher Education Funding and Student Finance*, London: Department for Business, Innovation and Skills.

Buckley, N., McPhee, J. and Jensen, D. E. (2011) *University engagement in festivals: Top tips and case studies*, Bristol: National Co-ordinating Centre for Public Engagement.

Chatterton, P. (2000) 'The cultural role of universities in the community: revisiting the university-community debate', *Environment and Planning A*, 32: 165–81.

Comunian, R. and Gilmore, A. (2014) 'From knowledge sharing to co-creation: paths and spaces for engagement between higher education and the creative and cultural industries'. In A. Schramme, R. Kooyman, and G. Hagoort (eds) *Beyond frames dynamics: Between the creative industries, knowledge institutions and the urban context*, Delft: Eburon Academic Press, pp. 174–85.

Comunian, R. and Gilmore, A. (2015) 'Beyond the creative campus: reflections on the evolving relationship between higher education and the creative economy', London: King's College London.

Comunian, R., Smith, D. and Taylor, C. (2013) 'The role of universities in the regional creative economy in the UK: hidden protagonists and the challenge of knowledge transfer', *European Planning Studies*, 22(12): 2456–2476.

Higher Education Funding Council for England (2012) 'The Research Excellence Framework. A brief guide for research users', available at: http://www.ref.ac.uk/media/ref/content/researchusers/REF%20 guide.pdf.

Hughes, A., Probert, J., and Bullock A. (2011) *Hidden connections: Knowledge exchange between the arts and humanities and the private, public and third sectors. Report to the Arts and Humanities Research Council*, Cambridge: University of Cambridge Centre for Business Research.

Killick, A. (2010) 'News from occupation at University of the West of England (UWE)'. *Socialist Worker*, 27 November 2010, available at: https://socialistworker.co.uk/art/22794/News+from+occupation+ at+University+of+the+West+of+England+%28UWE%29.

Lamond, I. and Spracklen, K. (eds) (2015) *Protests as events: Politics, activism and leisure*, London: Rowman & Littlefield International.

May, T. (2005) 'Transformations in academic production: content, context and consequence', *European Journal of Social Theory*, 8(2): 193-209.

McKay, G, (1996) *Senseless acts of beauty: Cultures of resistance since the sixties*, Verso, London.

Peterson, R. and Anand, N. (2004) 'The production of culture perspective', *Annual Review of Sociology*, 30: 311-34.

Presence, S. (2013) 'The political avant-garde: oppositional documentary in Britain since 1990', PhD thesis, available from University of the West of England.

Sapsed, J., and Nightingale, P. (2013) 'The Brighton Fuse Report to Arts and Humanities Research Council' available at: http://www. brightonfuse.com/wp-content/uploads/2013/10/The-Brighton-Fuse-Final-Report.pdf.

Sheppard, A. (2014) 'Bristol Radical Film Festival returns', *Don't Panic*, 10 February 2014, available at: http://dontpaniconline.com/ magazine/arts/bristol-radical-film-festival.

Thornton, S. (1995) *Club cultures: Music, media and subcultural capital*, Cambridge: Polity Press.

Part Three
Evaluation, impact and methodology

ELEVEN

Engineering cohesion: a reflection on academic practice in a community-based setting

Arshad Isakjee

Introduction

Debates around community cohesion in the UK have been prominent since the 2001 summer of riots in northern English towns. Following unrest on the streets of Bradford, Leeds and Oldham (Ouseley, 2001), the New Labour government was provided with impetus to address what was widely seen as a 'lack of cohesion' among distinct sets of urban communities. Perhaps predictably, the concern around the cohesion of communities in the UK was concentrated in poorer areas of the UK with high minority ethnic populations. The Cantle Report, *Parallel lives* (Cantle, 2001), suggested that a crisis of ethnic community separation, or even segregation, was under way in parts of the UK; a spate of policies followed from the New Labour government to enhance community cohesion. These largely centred on the deliberate emphasis of 'shared values' as an intrinsic component of policies designed to tackle a variety of social problems manifest within poorer inner-urban neighbourhoods of the city.

Critical discourse around these policies flourished (McGhee, 2003; Robinson, 2005; Ratcliffe, 2012). Community cohesion, with its inherently integrational approach, was – with some justification – seen to be emphasising the requirements of minorities to actively attach themselves to problematically intangible British norms and cultural practices. In parallel, however, the period of relative economic prosperity prior to 2008 also coincided with increasing social liberalism, and narratives of 'diversity' were promoted as a catalyst for and signifier of an open, inclusive type of Britishness. If the Cantle Report can be characterised as a socio-urban dystopia of disengagement and conflict, then narratives of an increasingly self-confident and comfortably diverse, multicultural UK provided its utopian counterpoint. Understandably, academics and progressives have sought to emphasise the lived experiences of diversity and/or multiculturalism as a bulwark against narratives of impassable divides and divisions. This liberal imperative among academics only became stronger as the subsequent coalition and Conservative governments chipped away at positive narratives around multiculturalism and increasingly played to a hard-right, anti-immigration discourse (Lewis and Craig, 2014). Social science research has rightly been increasingly keen to operate in ways which may materially benefit the communities they research – indeed, this approach was at the heart of the AHRC's *Connected communities* scheme which funded the project I am reflecting on in this chapter.

Academics interested in issues of deprivation, diversity, race, religion and discrimination understandably work closely with residents of areas often subject to involvement in discourses and policies related to community cohesion. Balsall Heath in Birmingham is one such neighbourhood. As an area of the city with historically large numbers of black migrants from the Caribbean from the 1960s and South Asian migrants from the 1970s, this inner-city neighbourhood has long been a site of social science research. Academics in the field of policing (Sharp et al, 2008), geography (Williams, 1978; Hubbard, 1997, 1998), urban studies (Dhaya, 1974; Sanders, 2004; Gale, 2005) and public health (Beal, 1973) have all contributed significant case studies of the area. Politicians too have variously problematised the neighbourhood for its history as a zone of prostitution, drug consumption and gay sex (Chan, 2006).

In researching community cohesion, while academic interrogations have tended towards policy-based critiques, much less reflection has centred on the research practices of academics themselves. It is within this lacuna that this chapter makes a contribution. Here I seek to give a narrative account my involvement with the *Cultural intermediation* project. Beyond achieving the key aims of the research project (to explore how community budgeting of cultural and arts programmes could work in a diverse, relatively disadvantaged urban area), I draw out how, with the project's primary investigator and without much preliminary self-reflection, we instinctively worked towards a secondary goal of community cohesion. At the time, we saw this secondary goal of 'bringing people together' as unproblematic, but alongside a self-reflection on our positionality, here we apply a more critical analysis of our own research practice.

The 'community' we constructed

The research into the potential for community budgeting began with various assumptions, as all projects must. As our project was looking to engage those who might be conceived 'hard to reach', we assumed that cultural intermediaries would have to play a role in recruiting and training our community commissioners. More fundamentally, however, we also implicitly anticipated that, if we were to engage the 'hard to reach', that would naturally be a challenging process. On reflection, this difficulty existed for two key reasons.

The first of these is rather obvious: the very act of setting out to engage the 'unengaged' or reach the 'hard to reach' implies a problem of social or institutional disconnectedness. It would then become necessary to find creative solutions which would reach the 'hard to reach', and perseverance to sustain that engagement (Benoit et al, 2005). Furthermore, being 'hard to reach' we would expect participants to be more likely to be socially excluded, or for them to be lacking in traditional conceptualisations of social capital. Second, we were conscious of one of the chief problems with notions of community representation: how can we meaningfully find a group of people who we could consider *representative* of the 'community' in the neighbourhood?

The notion of community is, of course, deeply problematic. In any neighbourhood the idea that there exists a single, coherent community is plainly nonsense, with people living their lives within a number of communities cutting across demographic characteristics, interests and geographies. As Worley (2005) noted, the very notion of community cohesion was a deliberate slippage to deracialise policy language. Yet an area like Balsall Heath is deeply fractured across ethnic divides, despite having exceedingly strong and well-organised 'community' groups that deploy a powerful narrative around inclusion. Indeed, as a neighbourhood with a high turnover of population, this fracturing is periodically reinvigorated by new waves of incomers – most recently from Somali and Syria – as longer established populations rub shoulders with new arrivals to the area.

The idea of trying to gather a group of people who represent the neighbourhood was flawed from the outset therefore, but it was done with an unreflexive, unexpressed belief that it was important to 'get' people from different ethnic groups and 'bring them together'. On one level, this can be seen as symbolic of white, liberal guilt from the research team. The two lead researchers (including the overall project leader) are both white middle-class men, with another member of the field team a white, middle-class woman. Although I am from a working-class, Muslim background, like my other colleagues I was coming at this project as a middle-class professional, living in a leafy suburb geographically close to Balsall Heath but culturally very different. In common with the rest of the research team, my patterns of cultural consumption are decidedly middle-class, possessing a familiarity and comfort with high cultural venues and 'edgy' spaces for more experimental arts practice. This meant that, in helping to set up a cultural budgeting process, I was bringing conscious and unconscious assumptions about valid forms of cultural activity.

I came into this project having already studied the wider south and east Birmingham area as part of my PhD. That research examined how discourses of inclusion and diversity were being written onto the bodies of young Muslim men, particularly through policing strategies focused on preventing violent extremism (Isakjee and Allen, 2013; Isakjee, 2016). There was some relief on the part of the *Cultural intermediation* project leader that, in joining the team, I would bring specific expertise by virtue of not only my research but also my ethnic and class background; it was hoped this would facilitate the bringing together of different ethnic groups in a predominantly Muslim neighbourhood. This was nuanced, however, by an understanding that my class, gender and professional status would simultaneously erect barriers and shape my own assumptions about projects around culture and creativity.

There was also an important social context to consider. At the time that the research was being undertaken, a strong anti-immigrant, anti-multiculturalism discourse had emerged in UK media and politics (Lentin, 2014), that would reach a peak, a few years later, during the Brexit vote. There was no question a project that successfully brought a multiethnic community together around culture and creativity would have provided a 'feel-good' moment for the socially liberal research team and a success story to sell as academic 'impact' on wider society.

Creating a budget for culture

When I joined the project much of the initial work to recruit a community cultural budgeting panel had already been undertaken. For the most part this recruitment had taken place through existing community gatekeepers in the neighbourhood, with a presumption that those already working there would have much deeper links into communities that would otherwise be hard for the researchers to access. This not only created a distance between the panel members and the research team, since the point of contact was the gatekeeper, it also created what was sometimes a difficult power dynamic between those gatekeepers and the researchers.

The first panel meeting was set up as a roundtable discussion with around 30 people present. In creating breakout discussion groups, we had been keen to create ethnically mixed conversations – again this was largely driven by an implicit desire to 'do' multiculturalism with the project. Very quickly, however, the discussion groups settled into divisions based on the gatekeepers who had recruited them. On one level this was unsurprising: a rather nervous group of people, unsure what the meeting was about, gravitated towards familiar faces. This division broke down almost entirely on ethnic lines and in brainstorming ideas for projects, some were overtly built around ethnic and class interests, notably the plan to set up an African Caribbean debating society.

Ironically, an idea that cut across ethnic divides was one of the first that we intervened to remove from the discussion. Illegal car racing had, until recently, been a significant feature of the neighbourhood with surprisingly large, multiethnic, crowds gathering to watch the action. Although the police had stepped in to stop the racing, it remained a symbol of different ethnic groups coming together, particularly among younger members of the panel. Older residents, meanwhile, reflected fondly on the Birmingham Superprix Formula 3000 race which had taken place on streets adjacent to Balsall Heath in the mid- to late-1980s (Collins and Page, 2010). Despite the fact that the idea of a Balsall Heath *grand prix* received a relatively warm reception across the different panel members, the project leader quickly moved the discussion to other topics, using his inherent authority as the person from 'the university'. In part this was simply because he had no idea how it could be realised, but also because he was nervous about how organising something themed around motor-racing would be perceived by our institution and funder as part of a supposedly 'cultural' project.

After the initial brainstorming session, we established a series of separate subpanels which met to develop the initial project ideas. Again, these fell almost exclusively along ethnic lines. I'm going to focus on just two of those subpanels here: a group of African Caribbean men in their 40s and 50s who wanted to set up a debating society; and a group of Muslim women in their 20s to 40s who were keen to establish a series of day trips. In both groups, the position of the academic team both in relation to the gatekeepers and in attempting to negotiate a more multicultural and inclusive set of activities was crucial. In neither case can this agenda be said to have succeeded.

The African Caribbean debating society

Balsall Heath's African Caribbean population has been declining for many years while the proportion of the population with Muslim origins has grown rapidly. The sense of being pushed out of the neighbourhood was palpable among the debating society subpanel – indeed, some members no longer lived in the area. As I organised the various subpanel meetings, there was a distinct sense of distrust towards the project, and to a certain extent some nervousness towards me – partly because of my academic and professional position but also implicitly because of my own status as Muslim. In my field diary from the time, I recorded how I'd emphasised that I was Muslim by background rather than religious practice:

> But I feel guilty that I emphasise my non-Muslim-ness, in order to fit in. I'm effectively saying 'don't worry about me, I'm not really Muslim!' – but should I also be saying 'and if I were, then so what?' (Field diary, March 2015)

Again, this instinct that I should have been more challenging of ethnic divisions reflects my own desire to use the project as a vehicle for 'doing' inclusion. But the strategy of de-emphasising was important, not least because the gatekeeper who had helped recruit this group of people insisted on sitting in on the first few meetings and at times sought to exclude me from conversations, suggesting that the group needed time to form and develop trust with each other away from my influence.

In the ongoing conversations about setting up the debating society, I found myself lobbying the subpanel to include events that would explicitly engage with a wider – explicitly multiethnic – audience. As with the other subpanel groups, I helped write the pitch that was brought back to the main panel to request funding for these activities. This pitch included a series of events; some of these were seen as being private to the African Caribbean community, but with others there was an explicit intent to reach out to other ethnic groups living in the area. Some group members were keen to run these events to counter their own perception that the Muslim population saw black people as inherently threatening or problematic. The hope was that by showcasing African Caribbean culture and creativity, some of these negative perceptions could be broken down.

Of course, this idea resonated strongly with the research team's desire to bring different communities together, and I made sure that this was highlighted in the pitch for funding that this subpanel subsequently made to the full community budgeting panel. In common with the other subpanels, I helped the debating society group put a budget together for their events – very much with an eye on the expenditures being planned by the other subpanels to make sure that all the groups were able to secure some funding out of the total pot. Running a series of small events in local venues with some catering and hiring local artists to perform was relatively inexpensive compared with some of the more ambitious ideas planned by the other subpanels. From the point of view of the research team, this was helpful as it meant that more projects could be funded from the limited commissioning budget. It did, however, cause a certain amount of resentment once it became clear that some of the other subpanels ended up receiving significantly larger sums – the day trips subpanel ending up with three times as much to spend as the debating society subpanel.

The subpanel's work progressed slowly from this point. The gatekeeper, a cultural intermediary working with a local arts organisation, withdrew from the project and so the group were left reliant on me to help them actually deliver the programme of events that the pitch document had contained. There were significant issues of confidence here among the subpanel members, particularly in making sure that they had the maximum impact with the money they had received and being afraid of wasting it. In the end, only one event was actually organised, but the member of the group who was tasked with publicising it did not do so very effectively. Thus, while it was a well-run event with live music and food, very few people actually attended. More than this, however, the ambition to create a diverse and inclusive event was always going to be limited by the realities of tensions between the different ethnic groups in the neighbourhood. Within the wider group of panel members, for example, the group of Muslim women who formed one of its major constituencies were never going to be allowed by their parents or husbands to attend an evening event run by a group of black men.

The group would have struggled to deliver on their original idea for creating a forum to exchange ideas within the African Caribbean community even without the additional layer of promoting inclusion and diversity that myself and the project lead nudged them towards. That ambition was, frankly, beyond the capacity of the group, even with the limited assistance they received from the research team in terms of helping them to deliver the planned events. This raises uncomfortable questions about whether in our desire to use this research project as a vehicle for 'doing' multiculturalism, we worked against the project's avowed aim of giving socially excluded communities an opportunity to realise their creative vision.

The Balsall Heath 'travel agency'

The second of the subpanels that I discuss here was formed primarily around a community gatekeeper who taught English at a local college. Comprised exclusively of Muslim women, primarily of South Asian origins, in the first full panel meeting this group landed quickly on the idea of organising day trips beyond Birmingham. The wider panel was generally quite enthusiastic about this idea and was happy for the gatekeeper and one of her teaching colleagues to lead a subpanel developing ideas in this area.

As the discussions developed among the day trips subpanel, one member pushed the idea of doing something more adventurous than just another 'shopping trip' to a different city. The Lake District is a well-known tourist destination in the UK: none of the panel members had ever visited or engaged with the area but, after an offhand comment by the project leader, momentum suddenly gathered around making it a location for a potential overnight trip.

Adding an overnight component immediately changed the dynamic of the discussion. In my field notes I recorded one key moment that challenged the assumption I had made up until that point that any trips should be fully inclusive of all community members:

> Then [name of subpanel member] states the following: Do you think these girls' parents will let their girls go to the Lake District with a bunch of ka'le? Ka'le is the Urdu/Punjabi word for 'black', at best it's very impolite. I'm being charitable – I find it racially offensive if I'm honest.
>
> And yet I see what [name of subpanel member] is getting at – as a researcher of Muslim communities I should have known that the young women might have parents disapproving of such a trip – but it is always difficult to gauge the conservative-ness of a person, yet alone that of their parents, without really knowing them. (Field diary, March 2015)

Here my insider status as a Muslim meant that the subpanellist was willing to share a key concern that she would almost certainly not have expressed to the (white) project leader, or at least not in these terms. I was not willing, however, to help the subpanel put together a pitch to the wider group that included a 'Muslims only' trip. Clearly there was my own and the project leader's desire to use the research as an opportunity to foster diversity and inclusion, combined with fears of possible headlines in Britain's right wing and openly Islamophobic *Daily Mail* newspaper. But there was also the impact that such a proposal would have on other panel members. Knowing that the African Caribbean debating society subpanel were putting together a much less expensive proposal, the idea that a large portion of the overall budget should be allocated for Muslims only would have resulted in a catastrophic breakdown of relations across the wider panel – a panel that we had explicitly set up in the hope that it would bring the neighbourhood's different ethnic groups together.

I brokered a compromise that I felt could be 'sold' to the male African Caribbean members of the panel. Two trips to the Lake District were planned, one open to anyone but with a second that would only be open to women and children. Although this would not be ethnically exclusive, in effect this would be a Muslims-only trip in the way that it was organised and participants recruited. We held individual conversations with the African Caribbean panel members to explain that those women would not be allowed by their parents/ husbands to travel if there were unknown men present – avoiding raising the explicitly racialised framing that underlay this compromise.

The compromise made me uncomfortable, particularly so as the two teachers who led the subpanel were only willing to organise the women and children trip, that is the one that effectively only served people from their own ethnic background. The 'open' trip was thus somewhat orphaned and ended up being poorly attended, lacking a community champion who had a stake in encouraging people to take part. On some levels, however, the women and children trip was a huge success. A group of people who had little-to-no engagement with the English countryside were given the opportunity to visit a very beautiful region and engage in adventurous activities such as tree-climbing and kayaking. Despite this, I felt a lingering sense that this was a missed opportunity and a disappointment that the subpanel leads were not willing to take ownership of *both* Lake District trips, despite the fact that without an 'open' trip, it was highly likely that the panel would have reacted with hostility to their proposal.

Conclusion: cohesion or disadvantage?

A 'community turn' has been evident in the aims and objectives of social policies under successive UK governments. From New Labour's 'community cohesion' policies, the coalition government's 'Big Society' agenda, to Prime Minister Theresa May's vision of creating 'a country that works for everyone', public institutions have grappled with idealistic, even utopian visions of citizenship built around shared values and experiences. Through the *Connected communities* programme, academics have joined the government in aiming to foster research with communitarian and collaborative objectives. In striving to ensure that research can make a positive impact outside academia, however, it is easy to lose sight of the need to critique our own engagement as researchers.

There is no question that our well-intentioned actions to drive a community cohesion agenda through our fieldwork had both constructive and disruptive consequences. We can, of course, point to positive moments of crosscultural learning within the project, for example white and African Caribbean participants becoming much more understanding about the mobility constraints faced by their Muslim neighbours. Rather than present a celebratory account, however, I think it is important for us to critically examine the moments where attempting to drive inclusion among our participants simply resulted in lost opportunities for engagement with culture and creativity – nominally the heart of the research.

Since 2010, the community cohesion agenda has largely been reduced to a narrative of preventing extremist behaviours, with police and other interventions almost exclusively targeted at Muslims (O'Toole et al, 2015). Indeed, even where projects have made concerted attempts to bridge gaps between people from different ethnic backgrounds, it has become clear that this is more successful with some groups than others (Phillips et al, 2014). This reiterates the fact that 'communities' are facing very different challenges even in the same geographic spaces and that simply getting people from different backgrounds to talk to each other is nowhere near enough to tackle wider problems of poverty and multiple deprivation.

Fundamentally, by focusing on cohesion rather than disadvantage and access, I am concerned we are missing the wood for the trees. The agenda of inclusion and diversity across ethnic groups tends to be played out in the poorest communities – there is very little handwringing in policy or academic circles about, say, middle-class Hindu and white populations not having a greater level of crosscultural dialogue. There is a danger of losing sight of the fact that the poorest communities face significant problems around lack of employment opportunities, low self-confidence, poor health outcomes, struggling schools, limited support for skills and career development and a range of other socioeconomic concerns. Solving these kinds of entrenched problems is well beyond the scope of any attempt to foster 'community cohesion' through dialogue across ethnic groups, requiring a significant rethinking of the role of the state in tackling poverty. From a neoliberal policy point of view, however, it is much easier to place responsibility on different minority ethnic communities, blaming them for not 'integrating', rather than tackling underlying drivers of inequality (Cowden and Singh, 2016). As academics optimistically and somewhat naively attempting to foster community cohesion we run the risk of becoming complicit with the neoliberal agenda that we so vehemently disavow.

References

Beal, J. F. (1973) 'The dental health of five-year-old children of different ethnic origins resident in an inner Birmingham area and a nearby borough', *Archives of oral biology*, 18(3): 305-12.

Benoit, C., Jansson, M., Millar, A. and Phillips, R. (2005) 'Community-academic research on hard-to-reach populations: benefits and challenges', *Qualitative Health Research*, 15(2): 263-82.

Cantle, T. (2001) *Community cohesion: Report of the Independent Review Team*, London: Home Office.

Chan, W. (2006) 'Re-scripting the character of Birmingham's ethnic minority population: assets and others in the stories of a multicultural city', *Area*, 3(1): 79-88.

Collins, S. and Page, D. (2010) *Superprix: The story of Birmingham's motor race*, Poundbury: Veloce.

Cowden, S. and Singh, G. (2016) 'Community cohesion, communitarianism and neoliberalism', *Critical Social Policy*, 37(2): 268-86.

Dhaya, B. (1974) 'The nature of Pakistani ethnicity in industrial cities in Britain', in A. Cohen (ed) *Urban Ethnicity: A.S.A. Monograph (12)*, London: Tavistock Publications.

Gale, R. (2005) 'Representing the city: mosques and the planning process in Birmingham', *Journal of Ethnic and Migration Studies*, 31(6): 1161-79.

Hubbard, P. (1997) 'Red-light districts and toleration zones: geographies of female street prostitution in England and Wales', *Area*, 29(2): 129-40.

Hubbard, P. (1998) 'Sexuality, immorality and the city: red-light districts and the marginalisation of female street prostitutes', *Gender, Place & Culture*, 5(1): 55-76.

Isakjee, A. (2016) 'Dissonant belongings: the evolving spatial identities of young Muslim men in the UK', *Environment and Planning A: Economy and Space*, 48(7): 1337-53.

Isakjee, A. and Allen, C. (2013) '"A catastrophic lack of inquisitiveness": a critical study of the impact and narrative of the Project Champion surveillance project in Birmingham', *Ethnicities*, 13(6): 751-70.

Lentin, A. (2014) 'Post-race, post politics: the paradoxical rise of culture after multiculturalism', *Ethnic and Racial Studies*, 37(8): 1268-85.

Lewis, H. and Craig, G. (2014) '"Multiculturalism is never talked about": community cohesion and local policy contradictions in England', *Policy & Politics*, 42(1): 21-38.

McGhee, D. (2003) 'Moving to 'our' common ground: a critical examination of community cohesion discourse in twenty-first century Britain', *The Sociological Review*, 51(3): 376-404.

O'Toole, T., Meer, N., DeHanas, D., Jones, S. and Modood, T. (2015) 'Governing through Prevent? Regulation and contested practice in State–Muslim engagement', *Sociology*, 50(1): 160-77.

Ouseley, H. (2001) *Community pride not prejudice*, Bradford: Bradford Vision.

Phillips, D., Athwal, B., Robinson, D. and Harrison, M. (2014) 'Towards intercultural engagement: building shared visions of neighbourhood and community in an era of new migration', *Journal of Ethnic and Migration Studies*, 40(1): 42-59.

Ratcliffe, P. (2012) '"Community cohesion": reflections on a flawed paradigm', *Critical Social Policy*, 32(2): 262-81.

Robinson, D. (2005) 'The search for community cohesion: key themes and dominant concepts of the public policy agenda', *Urban Studies*, 42(8): 1411-27.

Sanders, T. (2004) 'The risks of street prostitution: punters, police and protesters', *Urban Studies*, 41(9): 1703-17.

Sharp, D., Atherton, S. and Williams, K. (2008) 'Civilian policing, legitimacy and vigilantism: findings from three case studies in England and Wales', *Policing and Society*, 18(3): 245-57.

Williams, P. (1978) 'Building societies and the inner city', *Transactions of the Institute of British Geographers*, 23-34.

Worley, C. (2005) '"It's not about race. It's about the community": New Labour and "community cohesion"', *Critical Social Policy*, 25(4): 483-96.

TWELVE

Intervention: *Force deep*

Chris Jam

Like Skywalker the force is deep in Balsall Heath
Torrents of thoughts unique fall like Autumn leaves

Feed the soul supplant the holes in the whole
Steep the heaths peeps in a shoreless floral peace

Some say after good days first they play
And then – and only then they lay to sleep on astral beams
And that some dream of glorious auroral themes

Many vaunted schemes of Balsall's luminaries
Morphed and preened by mawkish teams
Of careering career politickis; the self styled Elite
Into policies as ambiguous as one of Morpheus's dreams
Meager morsels of morphine for communities ravaged by
  austerity

With temerity and tenacity the heaths inhabitants
Transcend the banality of these patently patronizing fallacies
Rouse their innate virtue verve Zirconic-zeal & cobalt-
  creativity
Adeptly think on their feet with the dexterity and grace of
  Zorba the Greek

Rejuvenate the jaundiced mortal sheath
That cyclically haunts and seeks us bought to our knees
By I not we philosophies and initiatives
Viciously viscous bitumen instilling recidivism
Nibbling at the very fabric of Balsall's tapestry
Prompting tempestuous mavericks who treat such despotic
  deviousness
With the lightness of a Waldorf salad
To challenge the talisman of established practices

Reimagining growth absent of environmental damage
Fertile forward facing frankness absent of anguish
Mediation rather than malice altruism not avarice

Neither chained by nor afraid of the omnipresence of
  change
For the chains change yet something intangible yet
  substantial remains

And yes the words with which I express what I observe
Are peppered with romanticized hyperbole yet my purpose
Is to celebrate the Heaths intuition & ingenuity

Her eternally palpitating purple perdurability
For I know this is something Heathonians
Will never do due to their implicit humility

Look at how Dr Atkinson and Anita Halliday in the 70's

Nurtured the birth of critical thinking for Balsall's
  burgeoning progeny
Creating through play in playgrounds that give the youth
  a say
And were swiftly mimicked across the UK
And when one is upset or want to lash out
Don't abandon; find him or her a space that suits their way

Engendering the essences of our shared
Opulent cosmology ardently humbly locally

Puncturing the presence of the parochial
Proffering pleasure and practicality
As a magical marriage of the matter and the imaginative

Sanctioning fantasy as a manner of extrapolating
  reinvigorated realities

When you reach the heath you will meet
Real leaders and find the sheep mainly confined to
The farm on Malvern street

Interdependent individuality All etched unto the DNA Of
  Balsalls
Phalanxes of passionate colour blind inhabitants

Even the havoc the Tornado wreaked was turned into
Just another opportunity to master and demonstrate the
  spirit of adversity

Like Skywalker the force is deeper than deep in Balsall
  Heath

THIRTEEN

Strategies for overcoming research obstacles: developing the 'Ordsall method' as a process for ethnographically informed impact in communities

Jessica Symons

Introduction

This chapter provides insight into the development of the 'Ordsall method', a step-by-step guide to community-led research activity. The method was developed in collaboration with local organisations and individuals in Salford, NW England, during the *Cultural intermediation: connecting communities in the creative urban economy* project. It emerged during a community engagement phase in an attempt to overcome obstacles such as power imbalance, stifling bureaucracy and local indifference.

The method's design was informed by an ethnographic approach which helped identify the critical challenges in the project and work out ways of stimulating enthusiasm and interest in project activities. It focused on existing priorities and interests within the community and, when people's responses changed dramatically from hostility to enthusiasm, we decided to record and share this method as a positive example of research-oriented engagement. The subsequent 'Ordsall method' provides a process for others to use when developing research projects in communities.

The method emphasises two key components for participatory research: first, develop research activities in conjunction with the aspirations of people in the target community; and, second, work with local intermediaries to support and enthuse people about the project. The step-by-step approach provides a structured framework to build new research projects.

This chapter describes the maelstrom of local angst about disappearing communities, rising property prices and avowals of alienation in a backdrop of national austerity and rapidly shrinking public sector services. Developed in the 2010s, the research period took place during the international conflicts that stimulated national and local debate about incoming migration, refugee and asylum seekers 'escaping' to Britain. The research ended just before the vote for Brexit (the UK leaving the European Union) and echoes of these anxieties appear in the project findings.

While the *Cultural intermediation* project began as an enquiry into the role of cultural mediators, austerity Britain in the run-up to Brexit forced a different kind of enquiry – one focused on people's understanding of culture itself. We went into the community expecting conversations about culture as art, theatre, music and performance; we left again with a new framing of culture as how people make their lives meaningful (Symons, forthcoming).

This chapter demonstrates how anthropological methods such as participant observation generate understanding of local priorities in areas targeted for research. Ethnographic fieldwork combines with strategies for community development and social entrepreneurship to stimulate enthusiasm for academic research rather than suspicion of researchers' motives. The chapter concludes by arguing that alignment with local objectives is not just a nice 'add-on' for social science projects but an ethical obligation for committed researchers.

For discretionary purposes, the names of people and organisations in this chapter are pseudonyms. The 'project team' combined university academics and local intermediaries who participated in the research project by supporting the idea development process.

Designing a research project in Ordsall, Salford

Salford is a city adjacent to Manchester and shares its history of rapid boom during the industrial revolution followed by slow decline in the twentieth century as mining, shipping and manufacturing sectors disappeared from the area (Peck and Ward, 2002; Lewis and Symons, 2017). The district is an amalgamation of five towns merged together in the 1970s with the city of Salford (Eccles, Worsley, Swinton, Walkden and Irlam). Over the past decades, Salford has remained high on the UK deprivation index with substantial areas of unemployment and associated health and social problems (see dclgapps.communities. gov.uk/imd/idmap.html).

Ordsall was the target 'field' for research, a four square mile area and Salford's largest sub-district. In the nineteenth and early twentieth century, Ordsall housed dock, factory and mine workers but from the

1970s onwards, the area had primarily low-income households with many people claiming state benefits. In 2010, over 25% of the working-age population were on income support, with half of the children and pensioners living in poverty (Symons, 2018; see also partnersinsalford. org/ordsallandlangworthy-neighbourhoodprofile-i.htm).

The district was situated in a prime property development area, however; by 2014, significant new residential developments had changed the demographic balance, particularly in the regenerated docklands now rebranded as 'MediaCity UK'. This new 'cultural quarter', and anchor for Salford's regeneration strategy, housed a thriving mix of TV production companies including BBC North and ITV, a theatre and art gallery, restaurants, shops, a public space hosting outdoor events and gardens.

Two main areas of social housing lay adjacent to MediaCity UK and these were gradually becoming interspersed with new property developments in a deliberate move by Salford City Council to encourage a more balanced combination of people on benefits with workers and students moving in from outside the area (interview, Salford planning officer, 2014).

Rather than generate excitement, however, ethnographic fieldwork in the area established that the influx of new workers and residents on higher incomes was stimulating anxiety among existing residents about their ability to continue living in the increasingly affluent area and frustration that their own circumstances had not changed or improved. As the research project got underway, these tensions had a significant impact on our ability to carry out activities as intended.

'I hope this project fucking fails'

The *Cultural intermediation* project included a community engagement phase of the research project which began in 2014. Distinct from the approach taken to the Balsall Heath area of Birmingham (see Chapter five), the first step in Ordsall was to appoint two community organisations to identify what kinds of cultural activities were already ongoing and what additional activities people would like to see happen. Emulating existing ways of resourcing cultural practices, the intention was to set up a 'panel' of local people using £50,000 of project money to commission new cultural activities. These activities would inform the overall research objectives of 'exploring the effectiveness of intermediation activity from a community perspective' and developing 'new forms of intermediation through a series of practice-based interventions' (as stated in the project proposal).

As an anthropologist on the project, I began participant observation working alongside these 'community researchers', joining in with their engagement in the area and discussing what exactly 'cultural activities' might mean. I also carried out the usual ethnographic practice of 'hanging around' the area, volunteered at the local Lads Club, a kids' club and a photo club, and spent time in the two community cafés, library and other public areas. I interviewed people who lived, worked and volunteered in the area, including council officials to find out their perspective on cultural activities and the community dynamics. Gradually an impression of community dynamics emerged which was to prove quite challenging in these early, and sometimes fraught, days of developing the project.

In many instances, I encountered local suspicion about my motives. One woman asked me 'Are you a spy?' and another muttered 'Who is she and what does she want?' to the community organiser at her church in front of me. Conversations would often turn to how dangerous Ordsall was, with its reputation for crime, drugs and violence. People would volunteer stories about how family or friends had been injured or killed by criminal activity.

During interview, Hannah, a community organiser described the situation as follows:

> Even if you show yourself to be the kind of person who might be the kind of person who would go to the police, then that ... do you know what I mean? So you just keep quiet, you live within your own networks that you don't ... there's so much that happens that, I understand that people don't want to talk about it, and they don't want other people to know it. Everything's sort of kept quiet really. (Hannah, community organiser in interview)

She went on to explain how people lived under 'shields' that protected them from becoming known as people who *might* go to the police. Silence and obscurity were valued and sought after – not willingly perhaps, but necessarily. Hannah described the research project as disruptive, because it proposed to carry out participant observation and, through close attention to the mechanics of this community, stimulated the possibility of change and through that opened up avenues that before did not seem possible. Some people in the community welcomed the intervention, others were much more wary.

As the community researchers talked to local people about cultural activities, they also experienced difficult conversations. Questions about 'culture' generated anger about local changes in the area. The researchers reported back to the project team that one woman had exclaimed 'I hope this project fucking fails!'. This response and the discussions about violence in the community indicated a heightened sense of anxiety and fear.

'Culture? They've taken it away'

This fear of speaking out was also compounded by a frustration that change may be happening all around the community, but not to them. Hannah explained:

> The only way in which local people's perspective of the government will change is if their real experience changes. It's just getting worse. So they are rightly suspicious, generally insulted and oppressed by the nature of that relationship and the 'tokens' of support and funding offered by government. (Hannah, community organiser, in interview)

Where we had intended to support people to commission cultural activities such as artworks or performances through the panel, local responses to the question 'what does culture mean to you' had brought out angry answers: 'Culture! *They've* taken it away' one local woman exclaimed. This emphatic exclamation that '*they*' had 'taken away' culture was indicative of many concerns that kept bubbling to the surface during fieldwork conversations about local activities, indicating a sense of loss about the changing neighbourhood and how people's 'real experiences' were of violence, poverty and frustration.

In this context, the £50,000 project budget was an embarrassment of riches perpetuating the sharp distinction between affluent bureaucrats from the university, who seemed to be indulging themselves in 'research' focused on 'poor' people in a 'hard-to-reach' area. At times, it seemed a wonder that people were willing to speak to us at all. However, through persistently friendly conversation and demonstrable sensitivity to local dynamics, people started responding to attempts at engagement and engaging with the research themes on culture and what activities they wanted to see happen in the area. We learned what was important to them and worked to reshape the project accordingly.

'Culture is everybody'

The research question 'what does culture mean to you?' may have brought out anger but it also delivered an answer. "My understanding of culture is everybody, just community; people living in a community" (Karen, community researcher, in interview, 2014). In response to the negativity about 'culture', community researcher and local resident, Karen retreated from asking people direct questions and instead considered how cultural activities were communicated through noticeboards, online and via the council. She would stay on longer at the school gates after dropping off her children or hang around chatting at the newsagents when buying milk. She let conversations about social activities develop naturally. In interview, she described 'culture' as people living together in a community.

This interpretation of culture also emerged during fieldwork. The area was alive with small groups operating with little or no funding as sites of cultural activity. There were art, music, photography, poetry and kids' clubs, a community café, a mental health group, church groups and groups led by the local NHS Health Improvement Team. While some had been started by government organisations, others were set up by individuals.

In particular, there was a strong sense of local pride in the new allotments; it had taken seven persistent years' work by key individuals to persuade the council to hand over land in perpetuity right opposite the community café. The community researchers celebrated these allotments by making giant *papier-mâché* sculptures of vegetables together with pea and carrot costumes for the children to take to an annual community festival. These allotments had become a community hub, and I spent many hours at the allotments and café, chatting in particular with the lead organiser Bob about the area and the challenges people faced.

Here was a 'culture' enmeshed in daily social practice rather than separated out into specific sectors such as art, music, theatre or performance (see Chapter three). Locally, people emphasised caring for each other and how socialising was a critical part of being a community. So, building on the observation that the proposed 'cultural activities' should respond to culture as 'just everybody', we determined to focus project funding on these local priorities rather than have a 'panel' commission work from outside artists or cultural producers.

A conversation with Karen, the community researcher, and Bob, the lead allotment organiser, precipitated the final decision on redesigning the approach to the project. We were standing in the park talking about how long it had taken to persuade the council to support the allotments. When the council finally agreed to provide land, they also insisted that their contractors delivered the project and as a consequence the allotments had cost considerably more than budgeted. In conversation,

Bob expressed frustration at 'the suits' who 'come into the area and take our ideas away. They don't allow us to develop them ourselves'.

Bob had focused on the right to self-determination. People wanted to have support to develop their own ideas rather than attend focus groups or workshops where their comments or observations were 'taken away' by officials and they were never sure what happened to them afterwards. It gradually became clear that part of the refusal to cooperate with the project was due to 'stakeholder fatigue' developed from too many of the wrong kind of consultations and not enough actual real change.

Adapting the research process

The research team responded to tensions in the community by reconsidering the original project design. We talked to people individually and ran workshops asking local organisations and individuals what modifications should be made. We asked: How could a 'panel' of local people be more broadly interpreted? What kinds of cultural activities would people like to resource? Are the research questions the right ones? How should the £50,000 be spent?

At one event exploring possible ways of setting up the panel, an experienced community organiser in the area exclaimed 'rather than set up new projects, we should maximise what is already here'. He expressed frustration that existing activities in the area struggled for funding, while new projects such as this research project were well resourced. This exclamation on supporting existing activities, together with Bob's observation that people wanted to support to develop their own ideas, became the two central pillars of the revised research approach (see also Symons, 2018).

Gradually an approach emerged where we would work with local cultural intermediaries to support individuals with ideas that needed a 'boost'. These two components formed the basis of the research activity in the Ordsall area and also sit at the heart of the subsequent 'Ordsall method'. After a six-month period of fieldwork and discussion, we had designed a new research approach which accommodated feedback from the community. We had shelved setting up a 'panel' of local people to commission cultural activities and instead were considering how to distribute the funds and who would spend them.

Working with local intermediaries

We put out a call for expressions of interest to support individuals in the community with their own ideas for cultural activities. Three organisations and one independent artist replied and we accepted them all. This focus on working with intermediaries was informed by discussion with experienced community development workers in Salford who described a progressive approach to develop people's 'capacity to respond effectively to events and issues that affect them' (Gilchrist, 2003: 13). In interview, one community worker recently retired after 40 years in Salford said:

> Community development is a much more personalised approach, a holistic approach. It's not looking at whether somebody is smoking but at what they're bothered about; to see what interests and hobbies they've got and how you can nurture them. Then perhaps you use that in an activity which propels them to become more confident and perhaps set up a playgroup or a holiday scheme. And from there, once people have got a bit more confidence and they know how the system works and where the funding comes from, then they're usually on the next step, the confidence will push them through. (Community worker, in interview)

It was this sophisticated understanding of how to support people that we aimed to access as part of the research project. However, it turned out that the emphasis on supporting people to develop ideas was a new approach for community organisations. Normally, they worked in groups and often came up with a theme and plan for developing an activity and then invited the residents to take part. Since the expression of interest required identifying and working with four individuals within the community, the intermediary needed sufficiently close and genuine relationships to be confident of identifying four specific people with ideas to develop.

Supporting people to develop their own ideas

The four intermediaries set about identifying people who had specific ideas that needed development. However, rather than work collectively (as one intermediary said, "we always sit together in our group and discuss what it is that we're going to do"), the research project was explicitly focused on individuals and supporting them to develop their own idea.

This approach was influenced by Bob's observation that people's ideas should be supported. It was inspired by UnLtd (unltd.org.uk), a national organisation that explicitly funds individuals for cultural projects as social entrepreneurs. This organisation provides small amounts of money and supports people with a specific idea to improve a particular social or environmental problem. The UnLtd North West coordinator provided insight into administering the £50,000, which we decided to split evenly between the four intermediaries, encouraging them to decide how to share the money between the individuals they were working with.

The intermediaries quickly found individuals with ideas and brought them together into a group to decide how to allocate the funding and to establish a rapport as people worked to develop each idea. While three intermediaries worked with four or five people, one decided to support seven individuals, all with an idea each. The process of supporting the development of ideas was open and fluid – responsive to emerging criteria and opportunities, including the personal circumstances and interests of the participants (Symons and Hurley, 2018).

'Time consuming, challenging but also highly productive'

After a nine-month enquiry and feedback period, the idea development phase launched in January 2015 with a specific timeframe of six months in which university resources and support were provided to the intermediaries and their 'Ideas People' as they came to be known. For the launch event, each person prepared a presentation or short film about their idea which they shared one by one in a community space in the area. The atmosphere in the room was excited and hopeful – people were delighted to have an opportunity to share thoughts and ideas about what should happen in their community. The framing of 'giving people's ideas a boost' was a novel approach in an area where people were more used to being asked to participate in predefined projects or initiatives.

Over the following months, the four intermediaries ultimately supported 25 people to develop ideas for cultural projects. The ideas ranged from a social history play to art collective as illustrated in Figure 13.1 and described in more detail in Chapter three. Some of the 'Ideas People' put in more time than others but all did something. For that six-month period, there was a real buzz in the community as people turned out to support each other's projects.

The project design emphasised autonomy for the 'idea person' and situated the creative practitioners as facilitators rather than authorities. For example, when Sadie, a retired older woman, said she had 'always wanted to write a play', a playwright was hired to help develop her

Figure 13.1: Local people's ideas for cultural activities in Ordsall

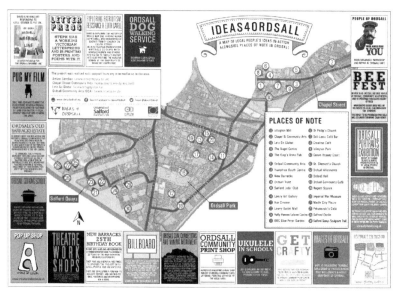

Source: Ideas4Ordsall

idea for a play about the area's local history to be performed at the local community club. Sadie retained final say throughout the project, often overruling the playwright to pursue her own vision. The intermediary involved supported Sadie when the playwright tried to change certain aspects, arguing that this is 'Sadie's idea' and 'she has final say on what happens'.

This approach contrasted with another theatre project in the area which captured people's memories about the docklands and developed a play scripted by a playwright and performed by local people. Here, the authority remained with the theatre company and producer rather than with a local person whose vision for the story had ultimate priority.

This approach also caused problems in the relationships between the intermediaries and the Ideas People. In some cases, the initiator of the idea rejected the support offered by the intermediary, preferring to carry out the project in their own way and actually missing out on opportunities as a consequence. In a few instances, personality conflicts and misunderstandings demonstrated the challenges of asking people to work together differently. The notion of supporting people to develop their ideas was new to both intermediaries and Ideas People alike in this particular community.

The project also introduced local people to each other, many of whom remain in contact and continue to collaborate. It stimulated a sense of ownership and pride about the area, particularly when the older participants shared their passion for social history and the area's industrial heritage. Sadie's enthusiasm for Ordsall's past, Paul's knowledge of Salford's mining history and the solidarity that came from it, Tony's interest in a World War I war heroine: these all stimulated a sense of connection between the participants and Ordsall as proud and productive working-class communities.

By identifying people who cared about the area, by supporting and promoting their ideas for cultural activities, the project demonstrated respect for local values and opinions. The intermediaries also reported a sense of positivity and value gained by their participation. They expressed an appreciation of the opportunity to reflect on their practice, revealing how they were challenged by a different approach to community engagement than they had previously experienced. Chapter three outlines in more detail how this community's ideas about cultural practices present a very different social dynamic to the one of deprivation used by the UK government.

A summary of the 'Ordsall method'

This chapter has described how a collaborative effort between local people, community organisations and academics turned a fraught and challenging experience into a productive and collegiate set of activities. By the end of the project, people were proud of their participation and celebrated at a well-attended community event hosted by the university and attended by the mayor of Salford.

When reflecting on the project experiences, the redesign phase emerged as a key finding since it demonstrated how to tackle mistrust, frustration and stakeholder fatigue in communities targeted for research. In the process of writing about the research, the process of engagement itself was converted into a 'method' that others could use to develop research activities that incorporate participants' needs and priorities. The subsequent 'Ordsall method' is introduced in *Maximising what is already there': Increasing research impact in communities using the Ordsall method* (Symons and Perry, 2016) and accompanied by a website and several short films (see ideas4ordsall.org).

This method comes at a time when 'impact' is an increasing priority for academic research while also undercritiqued as a process (Stein, 2018). Established practices of community development which emphasise the need for working alongside people and attentivity to emotional and social barriers to participation are often not part of a researcher's epistemological repertoire. Nor do academics necessarily appreciate the subtlety and depth of insight that informs the activities of a community organisation. These issues emerged in many projects related to the *Connected communities* programme (Facer and Enright, 2016) and form part of an ongoing debate on how to carry out research with impact but also with integrity.

The 'Ordsall method' is not a recipe, rather an approach that had a sufficient amount of success to be worth sharing. It is split into three stages:

1. identifying community partners for a research project (identify);
2. supporting the development of ideas as part of the research process (develop);
3. celebrating individuals' ideas as part of research-sharing stage (promote).

In this way, it situates communities as coproducers of research knowledge and gives the participants equal status in the research enquiry process. It insists on a symbiotic relationship where research ambitions run alongside those of the participants. It recognises that some people may not care about the research findings but still want to participate and have something to gain from the project.

The 15 steps of the 'Ordsall method' are shown in Box 13.1:

Box 13.1: 15 steps of the 'Ordsall method'

Phase 1: Identify a community for collaborative research
1. Map: explore area dynamics of people, activities, processes and relationships
2. Understand: identify key organisations and individuals with influence in target area
3. Stimulate: identify intermediaries to support the project
4. Accept: recruit intermediaries and co-develop action plan

Phase 2: Develop co-research activities
5. Find: support intermediaries to recruit people for research project
6. Cohort: group people into cohorts led by their intermediary
7. Plan: work with intermediaries to define budget, working process and timeframes
8. Encourage: support development of ideas for research
9. Independence: emphasise the autonomous nature of the idea development

10. Gather: monthly sessions bringing the cohort together
11. Network: use connections and resources to support ideas

Phase 3: Promote ideas
12. Promote: share ideas through social media, decision makers and others
13. Celebrate: hold event at a prestigious location,
14. Befriend: stay in touch and look for opportunities to develop ideas and people further
15. Share: pass on the learning to nurture community independence elsewhere

Source: Jessica Symons

The project's summary findings are shown in Figure 13.2. Elements of this method are already used in other contexts, such as supporting students to develop research projects, informing the development of cultural strategy at Salford City Council, and designing software as a research capture tool.

Figure 13.2: Summary findings of the *Ideas4Ordsall* project

(continued)

Figure 13.2: Summary findings of the *Ideas4Ordsall* project (continued)

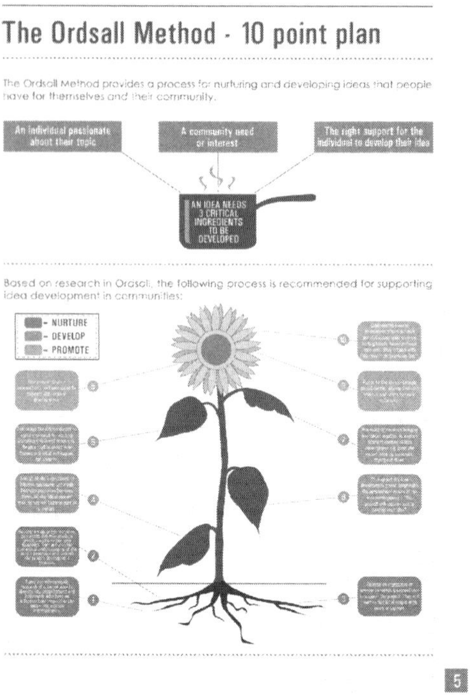

The Ordsall Method · 10 point plan

Source: Symons & Perry 2016

Conclusion

This research project, with over £1m in funding, was focused on exploring the role of 'cultural intermediaries' and how 'hard-to-reach' groups of people engage with cultural activities. A low-income community in Salford, NW England, was a prime target for research. However, questions about 'culture' among those already living precariously on very limited incomes and with few options for work produced a strong and negative reaction. These perceptions stimulated a project redesign to match local priorities and so ultimately generated enthusiastic engagement and participation in the research. The adaptive and responsive approach to project design and delivery helped achieve impact through our research activities and the 'Ordsall method' was born from that experience.

While these strong reactions unsettled the project team at the time, in post-Brexit Britain, they were early indicators of a schism growing in communities across the UK about the changing dynamics of British society (Adler-Nissen et al, 2017). Enquiries about people's preferred cultural activities came up against processes of regeneration and the related frustration, anxiety and fear about losing homes and close family networks. The extent of this angst emerged in the 2015 elections, when UKIP came second in every borough in Salford, and in 2016 with Brexit, when just over 50% of those who voted opted to leave the European Union, with Ordsall one of the Brexit voting areas.

Culture in this context is 'just everybody' – people living together and supporting each other where they can. When ideas in this community *were* expressed as art, theatre, music and performance, they were defined and led by local people on topics of their choosing. As the project sought to enable people's cultural activities on their own terms, it explored cultural intermediation by supporting and 'maximising' what was already going on in Ordsall.

The challenges involved in developing research with communities requires an attentiveness to the experience of participants, a process usefully informed by ethnographic engagement. A willingness to adapt the project design is supported by 'aha!' moments that emerge through fieldwork, where local experiences can reshape and optimise projects. The ultimate goal for the academic community must be for research to be led by communities who will directly benefit from the insights gained.

This project inspired a step-by-step guide to coproducing research with communities. The 'Ordsall method' presents three key stages:

1. *identify* existing local activity and priorities and look to align them with the research project;
2. *develop* and support community aspirations alongside the research;
3. *promote* community activities together with research outcomes.

It is critical to develop both local requirements for insight and activity *and* research objectives alongside each other, even if they are not directly connected (Symons, 2018).

These insights point to the need for *all* research to start from community priorities rather than from within academic institutions or in response to funder requirements. Recent initiatives in academic funding, such as the Global Challenges Research Fund (GCRF), bring together aid and research to benefit the global south and so put impact aspirations at the centre of their funding requirements (see rcuk.ac.uk/funding/gcrf/). For GCRF, successful projects are required to demonstrate thought leadership from participating countries in the global south as an integral part of any research project design. It seems inevitable that this agenda will reach UK communities as well.

References

Adler-Nissen, R., Galpin, C. and Rosamond, B. (2017) 'Performing Brexit: How a post-Brexit world is imagined outside the UK', *British Journal of Politics and International Relations*, 19(3): 573-91.

Facer, K. and Enright, B. (2016) *Creating living knowledge: The Connected Communities Programme, community-university relationships and the participatory turn in the production of knowledge*, Bristol: University of Bristol/AHRC Connected Communities.

Gilchrist, A. (2003) 'Community development in the UK – possibilities and paradoxes', *Community Development Journal*, 38(1): 16-25.

Lewis, C. and Symons, J. (2017) *Realising the city: Urban ethnography in Manchester*, Oxford: Oxford University Press.

Peck, J. and Ward, K. (2002) *City of revolution: Restructuring Manchester*, Manchester: Manchester University Press.

Stein, F. (2018) 'Anthropology's 'impact': a comment on audit and the unmeasurable nature of critique', *Journal of the Royal Anthropological Institute*, 24(1): 10-29.

Symons, J. (2018) '"We're not hard-to-reach, they are!" Integrating local priorities in urban research in Northern England: an experimental method', *The Sociological Review*, 66(1): 207-23.

Symons, J. (forthcoming) 'Culture as meaning-making: a new-old paradigm to reconcile working class priorities with creative hubs and cultural industries' in G. Evans (ed), *Post industrial precarity: New ethnographies of urban change*, Delaware, UK: Vernon Press.

Symons, J. and Hurley, U. (2018) 'Strategies for connecting low income communities to the creative economy through play: two case studies in Northern England', *Creative Industries Journal*, 1-16.

Symons, J. and Perry, B. (2016) *Maximising what is already there': Increasing research impact in communities using the Ordsall Method*, Salford: University of Salford.

FOURTEEN

Intervention: street art, faith and cultural engagement

Mohammed Ali

I used to describe myself as an artist – a visual artist in particular: I'm known as a graffiti artist, or in more refined terms as a 'mural painter' or any other posh term that you might use. If I am honest, nothing beats painting: taking over a big concrete wall in a public space and creating something meaningful, I enjoy that. I am also the founder of Soul City Arts, a cultural organisation located in the Sparkbrook area of Birmingham that serves the locality and city while working with an international scope.

In this chapter, I want to give an account of my origins, motivation and work as a creative worker and intermediary. I have found it difficult to capture what I do as where I started in cultural work and where I am now has expanded in productive and rewarding ways. Nonetheless, it is a useful exercise to take stock of this process in order to offer insights and reflections on the nature of such work in the context of this collection, the wider project framed by it, and the general field of policy support, directives and expectations. Some of this detail may resonate with the broader themes identified by the scholarly work collected here as well as with the wider fields which it references. I would like to hold onto the particularity of what I do, however, which I hope I have conveyed here.

Although I excelled in art from an early age, I rebelled against the idea of a career in fine art, although I did gain a degree in multimedia design. I was very much focused on the kind of paying job I could get, influenced to a great degree by growing up in a working-class family of Bangladeshi origin and the expectations of security to be garnered from education. At the time, I never understood why my parents wanted me be a doctor, engineer or whatever rather than indulging my creative instincts. As they used to say: "We want you to be well paid. We don't want you to struggle like we did". Now I get it: being in the arts world and trying to make a living, reputation and to produce meaningful work is a challenge. The path to security, let alone success, is unstructured and insecure and, as numerous accounts have demonstrated, not always conducive to enabling the kind of creative vision individuals might like to pursue.

While I thought of myself as creative, I wasn't sure what kind of artist I was. This is reflected in the degree course I took, which encapsulated typography, video, sound design and visual communication, working across different media. The early work I did obtain after that was relatively commercial, across what was becoming to be known as 'the creative industries': I worked as a designer for a bhangra record label, as a designer in a studio specialising in the diamond industry, then in gaming for five years.

Working in gaming was a dream come true, but I came to question the purpose of what I was doing in the industry. My concern was with how I was using the skills I had and the way in which I thought of the value of art, my potential as an artist and my confidence as a creative. Friends of mine had become teachers and doctors, teaching children or saving lives. And me? I felt that I was turning kids into zombies in front of video screens. The one ability that I had, I felt insecure about, worrying that: "Oh my god, I can't do much else". I thought about how I was using visuals and sounds and the one thing I knew how to do was to compose these things in the right balance to create an experience. These thoughts were also prompted by the fact that I was juggling an emergent identity and career as an artist on the side. I had to, to keep me going, a means of expressing my own thing.

It's a sad but significant marker, with no little resonance for my work, but this moment came around the time of the 9/11 attacks on New York. In terms of developing my art and reputation, I gained benefit from my digital skills and the take-off of the internet. I had a head start in understanding how the web worked, and it was such an incredible thing, allowing learning and connection in ways and at a speed not previously available. I could make my own website, and I was putting my personal work out there with immediate results. I was getting calls while I was at work from all over. I remember CNN calling me saying, "We've seen your work". They were interested because, at that time, I was exploring my faith and issues around being a Muslim through my identity as a street artist, a quality that seemed original and worthy of interest.

From about the age of 16, I was a regular graffiti artist. I was just painting around the town, none of what I did said anything in terms of social messaging in any way at all. As with much of the graffiti work then, it was focused on my name. The change came with one of my first socially conscious pieces which was in Balsall Heath Park: 'United Cultures of Birmingham'.

I had a scene of the city centre tower, the Rotunda, and there was someone of black heritage alongside someone of white heritage. That image might seem a cliché now, but I recall it was a play on the then current United Colours of Benetton campaign, so I put 'United Cultures of Birmingham' across the top, and it said 'Unity.' This work and others that followed that I made in the area, were ventures into something that was more meaningful than simply painting my name, with which I was no longer content. I started kind of exploring issues around my faith, thinking about my identity as a Muslim living in the UK, in the West, seeking to celebrate that fact in graffiti with Arabic script, Islamic messages and iconography.

This kind of expression was not apparent across the world of street art in the magazines or websites I read that documented graffiti scenes from around the world – *Graphotism* or *12ozProphet* or online at artcrimes.com. Remember, this was before rich kids were studying it at college, so the pursuit of knowledge was very street level but in reports from Taiwan or in the slums of Brazil there would be pictures of incredibly creative graffiti. Yet images always appeared to be influenced by an American experience: a guy with a baseball cap turned sideways, a ghetto blaster, a big car in the background.

For me, graffiti is an art form centred on script and the way letters interlink and lock together. So street art, graffiti art was essentially calligraphy – street calligraphy, right? While there are figurative forms and decorations, the centre was always your word – your tag. Islamic art is the beautification of the word of God, while street art is the decoration of the word of man. When I started bringing these together it felt like no contradiction and suited me as, at that time, I was very devout and had abandoned even figurative painting such as creating human forms in painting as it was taboo. Of course, this was not easily reconciled for me or for some observers who would challenge me: "How can you put that there? What if a dog comes and urinates on that script? This is sacred script that you're putting onto street walls." Nonetheless, I do all I can to ensure that the script is respected.

In the development of this work, while it was firmly located on local walls, I also sought wider attention for it and my approach. It was never by accident that it went global which itself was a means of demonstrating to doubters – myself included – that I could achieve something significant. I consciously and strategically said, "You watch. I'm going to make sure the work that I do gets seen in every corner of the globe." I put my work online, contacting journalists: CNN, BBC *Newsnight*, literally crossing them off a list thinking "Yes, done, next, next, next". As a result, I received invitations from universities and city authorities around the world to come and paint. I had commitment and developed confidence, telling myself, "You're going to reach the globe". It was borne out of memories of school and insecurity about my abilities when people would tell me: "You're not going to do [anything] with yourself". A lot of it was also about identity; being the son of an immigrant, born and partly raised in Sparkbrook, battling and wrestling with this idea that, "I'm different. I'm a Bangladeshi immigrant. I'm a Muslim. I go to the mosque."

I was travelling, gaining experience and a profile in Melbourne, Chicago, New York to Singapore, Kuala Lumpur. As a result people would ask why I was still based in Birmingham, but I am rooted in and committed to this city. Of course, this is partly because of my connections – my family, friends and culture – but it's also based in a sense of duty. I need to contribute, I need to give back to my home and I didn't want to be a nomad. I was kind of travelling and gathering, but it was only short-term. I still say that this is my city and I'm staying put. Admittedly, I would come back from New York, you'd come back from Melbourne and Chicago and you come to Birmingham, and you felt like, "Wow, I'm feeling suffocated as an artist here because there aren't the opportunities". But it felt like that's exciting as well, this city was an open canvas for me to create in, bringing back my experience and learning.

Out of that vision and commitment to Birmingham, from travelling and meeting wonderful artists, and being hosted by organisations around the world, Soul City Arts (SCA) was conceived. It was nine years ago when I went to Chicago and I saw an organisation called IMAN, which was an acronym for Inner City Muslim Action Network. As it states at IMAN's website, it is 'a community organization that fosters health, wellness and healing in the inner-city by organizing for social change, cultivating the arts, and operating a holistic health centre. IMAN incorporated as a nonprofit in 1997 through the drive of people directly affected by and deeply invested in social issues affecting communities of colour living on Chicago's South Side' (imancentral.org/about/).

This was an organisation borne out of the Muslim community, but that was serving all. For me, the organisation produced inspiring work that was not tokenistic, which you sometimes see in work across the interfaith world in which I'm involved. This felt like a real, sincere, genuine kind of effort to contribute to society and the city, their city. I felt like, I want to try and recreate this. So that's why I came home and established Soul City Arts which was also a means of addressing my feelings that, as an individual artist, there was only so much I could do to impact on my environment when I was interested in nurturing other artists. As an individual artist, I can mentor them, I can support them, but it didn't feel like I was doing *enough*. I wanted to create space for them, a centre to which they can come, even to build a physical site. Either way, I felt that even the knowledge that this site and group exists would give confidence and comfort for individuals who needed to know that there was something behind them.

Whatever the importance and success of places associated with the city's creative sector such the Custard Factory or Jewellery Quarter, my aim was to bring this organisation, this activity, this buzz, to very localised communities – to Sparkbrook, in particular. In this sense, it emulated the spirit of graffiti that was about making things accessible, to make art in the neighbourhoods where we live, in the places that are neglected rather than in remote galleries. For me, street art, graffiti and the spirit of graffiti were art for the people, art bursting outside of conventional art spaces and becoming accessible to the regular people. This commitment to accessibility was a practical matter for me, as a street artist you are pretty visible to the audience. I would always get support from everybody, people honking their horns in approval as they drove past a site. I've had people jump out their car to ask, "How much do these murals cost?", then put their hand in their pocket and give me a wad of cash for that expense. Such experiences helped me realise that communities were crying out for work that connects with them. It does so as a result of the ways in which, when you put something in the public space on a street corner, it feels like the people speaking, the city speaking, the real people and the real soul of the city as opposed to art sanctioned by city authorities.

This is an approach I've taken at home and abroad, and it has proven to be effective everywhere although it involves honestly answering questions from locals about my purpose. At home or in neighbourhoods around the world, people will often come and say to me and those artists I work with, "Why are you doing this?". And we respond "Well, why not?". A follow-on question usually asks, "Is this community service you're doing?". Because they think that we are undergoing some form of punishment! "Why are you here, then?" they ask. "Because we wanted to be here," I respond. Often, they cannot get their head round the fact that we *chose* to be there. They think inner city Birmingham – Balsall Heath, Sparkbrook – are neighbourhoods that they feel nobody gives a toss about. As a result of Soul City Arts, we have artists spending three, four days at work. Locals might watch you the first day and think, "What's that?". Then they'll come again and they'll see that you're committed and you're here and you're here for a reason. Then they'll pluck the courage up to come and engage with you.

Often on projects, I feel parachuted in and out, which a lot of arts organisers will do because they can't afford to have you there for a longer period of time. But it's not even about the time. Even if I'm there three, four days, I want to ensure those days are meaningful experiences, and I always insist on immersing myself in the community, spending time with its people. It's important that I'm not seen as an interloper who's just in and out, but rather someone who's made an effort to come and talk and listen to the people, who interviews them so that the art that I make is drawn from the community. That's become a fundamental part of my practice now, and I see too many a time an artist, where you see in the social media they've very selfishly just dropped in and out and imposed their art on people.

With the mentoring from SCA and it allowing its Hubb space to be used, it's important to note that we're not a regularly funded organisation. If we were, who knows? Maybe we'd do ten times the work for a bigger impact. Soul City Arts has been the first of its kind. The Hubb in Arabic means 'love', but it has this double meaning, one to which many have responded. When we set up the Hubb there was no such thing in inner-city parts of Birmingham, but it is also identified an absence amongst Islamic communities around the world who heard about it online. I had emails from people in Perth, in Mexico, queries from the US. After 9/11, diaspora communities that were maybe largely immigrant communities, second and third generation, were struggling to work out how to navigate the resulting suspicion of, and attack on, their faith.

What was unique about our space was it was in a largely Muslim neighbourhood but programmed for all. For me, if I didn't see a 50/50 split in the audience space, in my space, I'd ask myself "Why am I preaching to the converted here?". I want people from Solihull to be coming, and that's what we were getting, people saying, "We've never had a reason to come to Sparkbrook or Balsall Health, and now we have because your space is here". International queries asked: "What's the model of The Hubb? How did you do it? We want to do the same in our neighbourhoods". There are many others now; you can go to Sydney, Australia, Melbourne, London. There are similar spaces there now.

I would say with confidence that the Hubb and the Soul City Arts model was definitely part of the pioneering movement of people from inner-city sites around the world. Likewise, the art that I do as a graffiti artist, which explores religious ideas and Islamic script and iconography, it's common all over the globe now. Being part of a global movement excites me as an artist in engaging with it, and in coming back to Birmingham and creating a buzz as a result. Feeling like you have sparked a movement, where you have contributed to something where there was nobody, it very fulfilling.

Already underway or on the horizon are major heritage projects such as *Knights of the Raj* which documented the stories of Bangladeshi restaurateurs in Birmingham and which was featured in the Birmingham Museum and Art Gallery from September 2017 to January 2018. This activity opened up an important space for a largely undocumented aspect of the city's and nation's history (there are around 30,000 'Indian' restaurants in the UK) and brought in significant new audiences to the museum. This has allowed me to develop as a storyteller and cultural intermediary, capturing histories in creative and engaging ways. I am particularly pleased that the local story translated to a global stage as I was invited to develop the project for the Museum of Food and Drink in New York where it ran in the summer of 2018. I should note that I'm now a trustee of my city's museum: a graffiti artist who was shunned by the arts establishment but who's now at the heart of a representative institution. This position says something about the progress made.

The final thing to say then is that "I'm done there now. My work is done. I need to move on." I feel like I've tackled neglected audiences, managed to win them over, and they get the value of the arts now. But now I feel like I've had a different role, and now that's evolving. As the recent successes with *Knights of the Raj* demonstrates, I'm onto my next challenge now, which is to explore how I'm not just a graffiti artist. I don't want to be described as 'the Muslim artist' and the audience that I want to appreciate and engage with my work now needs to encompass more than the Islamic community. Otherwise this is, again, preaching to the converted. To move beyond this excites me now.

FIFTEEN

From the inside: reflections on cultural intermediation

Yvette Vaughan Jones

Introduction

Founded in 2010, Assemble is a London-based architectural collective. In 2015 it originated the *Granby four streets* project in Liverpool based around the renovation of a series of houses and empty shops. The project enlisted local people by offering them training and building jobs and included the creation of a workshop selling home goods created in collaboration with local craftmakers and artists. To the surprise of many, not least all the members of Assemble themselves, the project was awarded that year's prestigious Turner Prize for art. As Rosamund (2016: 119) relates, this award provided recognition of an uncomfortable sort 'as if to wave a magic wand that turns "projects" into "art"'. The result of nomination by a curator, she suggests how this bestowal manifests the conflicting nature of relations between the professional field of art with works expressing social objectives. While practices such as that of Assemble are a riposte to familiar expectations of creative work and the special status of the creator, the award evinces the art world's 'appetite for outsiders, for impact, for the look and feel of social engagement' (Rosamund, 2016: 119).

The nature and recognition of Assemble is a signal moment on a long trajectory of social engagement and cultural intermediation that, most of the time, has merited little attention of this kind from an art world of markets and celebrity artists. Whether art or not, the conception of *Granby four streets* and its relationship with the local environment, culture and community in which it was located resonates with contexts and projects described across previous chapters which also speak to a wider field of intermediation. As detailed by Long and Warren (see Chapter five in this volume) and Symons (Chapter thirteen), activity in Balsall Heath and Ordsall evidences the range of ways in which cultural projects might be conceived when originated among communities themselves. At the periphery of a cultural sector, let alone the creative industries, they challenge traditional expectations and parameters determining the nature of 'art' and indeed the role of the intermediary.

The moment of Assemble is a prompt for the contribution of this chapter, which draws upon the author's personal experience gained in a career as an arts practitioner, between the production of performance and other forms of production as well as policy formulation and analysis. I seek to reflect upon and assess intermediation processes 'from the inside', reflecting particularly on the culture of the art world and the aesthetics of cultural production – in intent and outcome. I suggest that this is an issue often neglected in discussion of the politics, policies and practicalities of participation and intermediation. This chapter surveys the context of policy impulses and what has been experienced as a movement from a concentration on process to 'product' among socially committed artists as a means of conducting their work. It commences with a reflection on the culture of practice that has nurtured social engagement in the arts. It then focuses in on the work of Visiting Arts, where I am Executive Director, reflecting on the evolution of the $1mile^2$ project. This venture is international in scope and gives a wider perspective on intermediation and engagement and the particularities of those projects and milieus dealt with so far.

A socially engaged arts?

The tradition and meaning of artists working outside of their studios/place of making and in collaboration with non-artists is one that has changed radically since the 1960s and 1970s. In its first flush, allied with the nascent community arts movement, this practice was one defined as an adjunct to 'education and therapy' in which creative work was enlisted as an instrumental tool (for instance, see Clift et al, 2009: 8). This framing and the prioritisation of a functional quality to art (making people better, didacticism) had a limiting effect on the ways in which practitioners and their work were regarded as legitimate in relation to the conventions of the art world.

The move beyond an association with education and therapy into a practice that made socially engaged arts visible came into being with a politically motivated set of artists and companies such as Welfare State Theatre, founded in 1968, or Greenwich Mural Workshop, that started in 1975. Such organisations used 'agit prop' techniques to give voice to a set of issues and values that artists themselves felt were hidden, stifled or at best underrepresented in the cultural sphere. They were focused in the first instance on two drivers. The first aimed to facilitate access to the arts for ordinary people. While 'ordinary' can be taken as a synonym for working-class communities and others generally outside of the regular constituency of high culture, 'the arts' were defined in more plural fashion in breaking with conventional boundaries. Taking a cue from art in the public realm – from equestrian statues to park benches, from bandstands to street theatre – the motive was to break down the cultural barriers that sustained perceptions of the 'hallowed halls' of art galleries and theatres and so kept potential audiences away. This drive sought to liberate art and culture from formal institutions and onto the streets in the belief that this is where ordinary people would see and be inspired by it. In so doing, a second driver was to give voice to hidden and silenced voices in culture, such as the voices of working-class people and those at the margins of society, such as new migrant communities (Khan, 1978; McGrath, 1981).

This aspect of the development in the community arts movement was spearheaded by artists acting in intermediary roles, advancing policy into organisational practice in and above their concentration on creative output. They took it on themselves to voice issues concerning the democratisation of culture to act on behalf of the people whom they felt were disenfranchised. The work they produced manifested itself in community murals, community filmmaking and, most prominently, through theatre in education (see: O'Toole, 1976; Jones, 1988; Goldbard, 1993). The theatre in education movement, in particular, rallied around ideological orthodoxies that were to a large extent shared and promulgated through organisations such as the Standing Conference on Young People's Theatre (see Vine, 2013).

Participatory arts?

One long-term outcome of this movement towards increasing access to art was that the practice of many artists in community-focused organisations became increasingly participatory in name and nature. As Matarasso (2013: 16) comments, by the 1990s this movement 'marked and allowed a transition from the politicised and collectivist action of the seventies towards the depoliticised, individual-focused arts programmes supported by public funds in Britain today'. One consequence of this shift was how creative work became increasingly process-driven to the extent that its final performative aspect and the artist's aesthetic expertise were deconstructed, if not totally absent. From my own perspective, this often left audiences, participants or collaborators with no common shared experience or anchor: in theatre there was no fixed output in the form of a performance, but a series of linked individual experiences in which participants worked through a series of instructions to come up with a self-curated piece of work. Of course, the motivation for this situation was, in part, to give agency to the participants, to give young people the excitement of discovery and creation of a memorable narrative. At its best, this outcome was achieved, but it required total engagement from participants (not all of whom, in my observation, were dedicated enough to the idea to pursue it with much vigour) and guidance from the 'actors', many of whom were themselves young, inexperienced and not at all skilled in facilitation. While the ideas of empowerment, agency, cocuration and collaboration were nascent and exciting, the skills and training of the actors in such engagement activities were often absent. Drama schools did not focus on this kind of work and many of the young actors had scant understanding of children's learning styles or psychology. Ultimately, this context posed questions for me about the value of the outcomes from this process and about the meaningfulness of 'participation' and the nature of collaboration and creative opportunities for participants.

An example that is typical of this approach was manifest in theatre-in-education piece by Spectacl Theatre, *Erasmus* at Cyfarthfa Castle, Wales, in the early 1990s (I was Drama Officer, Arts Council Wales in this period). In this piece, primary school students were given a short presentation and told that they were now part of an 'Erasmus Society' and their task was to uncover the truth about the lives of the people who contributed to the collection of the castle's museum. The castle was built by powerful ironmasters who founded the Cyfarthfa Ironworks in Merthyr Tydfil. The stories uncovered concerned the lives of working people in the mining areas of the region.

The young people who participated ended the day with a good knowledge of the history and politics of the area mediated through the questions posed by the theatre company and by the answers that they uncovered. Here, the process of engagement and sense of cocreation were anticipated in the rehearsal room of the theatre company, highly directed by the company; yet the 'product' was the interpretation of each of the children. The intermediation was thus *dirigiste* and, while the actors and directors were open to discussion and debate about the process, the narrative of 'discovery' was pretty much set by the theatre practitioners themselves. The outcome was that the young people 'discovered' the story that was determined by the players. This example is not to pinpoint a fault in the work of this company but rather to indicate the ways in which intermediaries have understood and explored the possibilities of engagement beyond its confirmation by the conventions of the art world. Significantly, theatre practitioners of this kind have tended to work within a network of other theatremakers across the UK (and sometimes internationally), taking the lead from pioneers in participatory and political theatre (see: Boal et al, 2000; Snyder-Young, 2011).

Although many enterprises in this field have been locally based, their regional networks have been comparatively weak: company members have tended to mix with other theatremakers and artists in the wider region – or in London – rather than with local businesses, educators and so on. I'd suggest that weak connections beyond the world of theatre and arts of this sort have tended to contribute to a general trepidation about handing over more fully the reigns of creativity in processes of intermediation. Nonetheless, in some instances, concern for the real needs of local people allowed for some innovative activity and tangible results. For instance, for Valley and Vale Community Arts' 'Sell Out' was the ironic name they gave to the commercial arm of the organisation. It was committed to developing long-term solutions in the community and also to investing in the skills and personal development of participants in its activities. It recognised that participation in the creative arts process *could* be the start of small local enterprises generating income, if not full-time jobs. This was the embryonic Community Interest Company (CIC) or social enterprise. Initiatives included the creation and sale of postcards of local historical and geographical interest and the production of publications for sale such as books of local stories and creative writing, photography and so on, as well as films. Such pioneering work developed into small businesses and enterprises that clearly relied on participation and a group or consortium approach to developing new skills among participants – and indeed, among intermediaries themselves.

The work of Valley and Vale, and others of this ilk, was also a step away from the *dirigiste* approach to the arts in order to explore an authentically cooperative/collective decision making. However, such activities are still a way away from the kind of cocreation where artistic and editorial decisions are made in a collaborative way in order to deliver *aesthetic* outcomes. In my experience, where community and participatory arts practice became more and more involved with the process and the participation of local people, often the nature of the aesthetic 'product' appeared an irrelevance when compared to other possible outcomes. These outcomes have included concerns for 'wellbeing' or a general sense of engagement and empowerment rather than an investment in creative objectives.

The lineage sketched above alongside these specific instances illuminates the context for my own struggles as an intermediary in dealing with a genuine dilemma around parity of esteem between participants in cultural projects and artists. By way of illustration, my own encounter with concepts of cocreation has been with large-scale community plays where professional actors worked alongside non-professionals. In some cases, the resultant performance may, at best, have displayed seamlessness between the contribution of both groups, making it difficult to discern who was professional and who was not. Behind any successful activity, however, is a wealth of issues indicative of practical challenges to collaborative approaches. For instance, rules and conditions determined by the actors' union Equity have made the experience of professionals and non-professionals working alongside each other problematic in the extreme. This is not just about ensuring proper payment to the professionals (although this begs the question of whether participant collaborators should be paid), but about attitudes and equivalent recognition in creation and the kind of aesthetic sensibilities and satisfactions sought in resulting artwork. In my experience, the relationships of cocreation have also been imbalanced in that the presumption has been that professionals know best and have greater skills by virtue of that status and experience. This dilemma continues to present issues of parity in each instance where professionals work alongside participants in the process of co-creation, an ethos that has become increasingly foregrounded in cultural intermediation. Recent examples of such collaborations include *Stories of change*, where Louise Osborn 'curated' the stories and testimonies of local participants to produce a half-hour theatre piece, or the 2017 National Theatre production of *My country* in which 'real testimonials are interwoven with speeches from party leaders of the time in this new play by Carol Ann Duffy, Poet Laureate, and director Rufus Norris' (nationaltheatre.org.uk/shows/my-country).

The basis of this critique concerns both the purpose of creative work for itself and its relationship with a genuine desire to connect in meaningful and authentic ways with those constituencies deemed 'hard to reach' by cultural policy makers, intermediaries and analysts. Here then, I turn to detail my own involvement in attempt to deal with this issue in my work with Visiting Arts.

Visiting Arts and *1mile²*

Visiting Arts (VA) has a forty-year history of working with artists across the world. It has specialised in brokering relationships between artists, producers and audiences and, as such, has positioned itself as an intermediary in cultural production. Established in 1977, it has worked with a global roster of innovative contemporary artists in formulating programmes that bring international and culturally diverse work from overseas to UK audiences.

Originally established as a department of the British Council, the organisation seeks to nurture cultural understanding through a process of international artistic exchange – working abroad as well as at home. In so doing, it seeks to engage and inspire young people, communities and future professionals. Its work is defined by three core themes: information and knowledge sharing; creating new connections for artists and cultural professionals; and providing training and professional development. Visiting Arts has conducted research that assesses trends in and barriers to international work, collaborating with a range of partners including the Department for Culture, Media and Sport, British Council, the Calouste Gulbenkian Foundation and ministries of culture across the globe.

As Chief Executive, I took over 10 years ago and have worked to refine its role as one focusing on the engagement of artists with their audiences, addressing issues outlined above. This takes place, in particular, by working closely with people and neighbourhoods in participatory programmes of work facilitated by or enhanced by varied artists' practice. A key example is *1mile²* which emerged as a counterbalance to the importation into communities of creative ideas from 'outside' and the notion that people needed to learn from experts elsewhere. Our approach to *1mile²* took the view that people learn from each other and that expertise can, in the most part, reside within the local community.

1mile² is a residency programme that prompts international artists to create and connect interpretations of a place, its people, its ecology and diversity. To date, *1mile²* projects have engaged 42 artists, 18 ecologists and 14 creative organisations, reaching over 13,500 people in 10 countries. Artists spend extended periods in a defined area in order to facilitate collaborations with local artists, ecologists and residents. In workshops and field sessions, they devise ways for the production and placement of art in both cultural and public infrastructures, working in partnership with local authorities and cultural, environmental, regeneration and social cohesion organisations. As we state at Visiting Arts' website:

> 1mile² inspires communities to explore the cultural and
> ecological diversity of their neighbourhoods through artistic

engagement. Artists and ecologists collaborate and lead activity that enables vital dialogue and knowledge sharing within and between cultural and geographic communities. (visitingarts.org.uk)

The character and direction of the *1mile²* project was born out of a reflexive critique of the impact of our own work launched against the backdrop of the London bombings of 5 July 2005. On the one hand, VA's work had involved contemporary artists from Pakistan, Afghanistan, Iraq, Iran, India and so on, yet the audience for this work was the white middle-class group familiar with cultural provision. On the other hand, and as part of our need for audience expansion, we were concerned about our engagement with young people of migrant backgrounds (whether first, second or third generation) who might be connected with those very countries and whose links with them were often framed from without by a simplified narrative of radicalisation, otherness and threat. Certainly, we did not feel in this moment that we were engaging young people of diaspora communities in particular with programmes that might have relevance to them and their identity. We were aware of a need for a greater understanding in the UK of their position and how this group might benefit from contact and interaction with the complex narratives and innovations produced by the international artists VA had worked with. These stories and such connectivity might act as a rejoinder to both stereotypes at home as well as to the limited narratives available at propagandist internet sites seeking to recruit those of the diaspora.

The process of developing a framework for the programme that resulted was collaborative and research led. Three roundtables were organised where a wide range of stakeholders were invited to contribute views, advice and guidance on both what was needed but also what had worked and crucially what had *not* worked in the past in programmes of engagement and participation particularly with migrant groups. Participants were drawn from specialist agencies with experience of engagement with diaspora and black and minority ethnic (BAME) communities, from arts and cultural organisations, and from local authorities. Each roundtable looked critically at the role of Visiting Arts itself in intermediation processes as both the broker between the public participants and the artists and also between the artists and the cultural sector, funders, local authorities and so on. The roundtables made a variety of observations but in common was an acknowledgement that none of the individual players could work effectively without intermediation to coordinate practice and ethos.

In developing the *1mile²* project, one of the first principles resulting from the consultation was that any project should evolve from a consortium approach. The direction of each project would be steered by a multiplicity of voices and disciplines with a stake in each locality in which work was pursued. This would avoid the dangers inherent in a single-issue focus under the direction of any one artist, director or other creative voice. The stakeholders involved in the pilot projects in the UK included environmental scientists, community activists, artists, third sector agencies and local authority officials from a wide range of departments, as well as teachers, local professionals, young people and other locally based agencies. Behind this consortium approach was the sense that there will always be a multitude of opinions, approaches and solutions to local issues. In the process of debating them, new ideas and learning can take place rather than a transfer from without of existing positions and expectations of what kind of learning would result.

Detailed objectives of the *1mile²* programme that emerged from research, assessment of the needs of young people and project development can be summarised as follows:

- to inspire participation in and appreciation of the arts and enable learning for communities and artists;
- to increase a shared understanding of biodiversity and sustainability through exploring our connected local and global environment;
- to improve understanding between people of different cultures through increased dialogue within and between communities;
- to measure and promote a better understanding of the relationship between culture and the environment through social-action research.

Initially, the project took place in six UK cities and six overseas cities all linked through a website (http://www.visitingarts.org. uk/programmes/exchange/1mile%c2%b2/). The idea was to share approaches and ideas, to have access to thoughts, celebrations and solutions to problems. The programme consciously addressed the issue of equitability and there was a real attempt to redefine the terms that had been formulated in art engagement. 'Cocreation' became the term to describe the way that the consortium worked together in the identification of issues to explore, the scope and pattern of activity, as well as the selection of a local artist and recruitment of international artists in residence. These were all agreed in discussion with the consortium or partners and, in particular, with local people involved in the programme. In addition, the work produced by participants was facilitated and in some cases augmented by the local artist, who acted more as a curator of the work rather than claiming sole authorship.

 With regards to the international artists, the brief invited them to 'do their own work' using material generated by the participants and the local artist as the stimulus. International artists defined this brief in widely differing ways. For instance, Xu Zhifeng from Shanghai working in Waltham Forest did not meet the participants who had worked with a local filmmaker, but instead created a new work out of his own interactions with people in the community. In contrast, in South Africa, local artists worked with the UK's Friction Arts (here acting as international representatives for that locality) as a seamless team and creative unit where it was impossible to discern from the outside where the input and identity of one began and the other ended.

 Xu Zhifeng used his residency to create a series of images of the locality made by gaining access to the codes for entry into a local tower block by befriending residents and taking aerial photographs from the top floor. He then described a circle on a 'map' created from that perspective and began knocking on the doors of the houses at its perimeter and talking to the residents. If they asked him in for tea (as many did) he asked if he could fly a helium balloon from the roof of their house. He then climbed the tower block again and took a photograph of the 'circle of friendship' that he had made, marked by balloons. This project was exhibited at the local community centre alongside the local filmmaker's work. The community participants loved the results, its artistic integrity and the clear inspiration that had come from their own contribution. In particular, they loved the fact that their community would subsequently be celebrated in galleries in China and across the world.

 The contrast with the *1mile²* programme in Johannesburg shows how cocreation can mean so many different things. On their blog, Friction Arts recalls their arrival in the city and how they made an impression on a major art gallery which, while initially suspicious, allowed the takeover of some space for a workshop for the period of their residency:

> Having the opportunity to make, what might be considered, a community arts project right next to their wonderful collection of contemporary artworks gave our project a legitimacy that is rare in an artworld that often seems confused by participatory approaches, based as it is on the existing model of art-lover as consumer. We took the bull by the horns and began to make a series of consecutive,

playful interventions to develop the project. (frictionarts. com/project/1-square-mile-johannesburg)

Friction worked with Anthea Moys and Kyla Davis in the Hillbrow area of the city, where they engaged with the area's young people and the trainers in the local boxing club. Among many artistic interventions that challenged local taboos, they created an installation out of the boxing ring. The ring was decorated with stories and flowers. The flowers were gained by asking for donations from the gardens of the affluent neighbours of the locality. The stories were elicited from the young people and the trainers at the boxing ring through a barter system. Vases and containers for the flowers were made from reappropriated alcohol bottles which had been discarded in the local park. The ideas and implementation of this intervention were cocreated by the two sets of the artists and the community itself. The resultant installation would have been an appropriate presence in any conventional gallery.

The *1mile²* project also looked at how there could be parity of esteem for art, artists and collaborators within the project and how this might be achieved. We looked at how projects needed to actively encourage voices from all members of the partnership, and beyond, to be heard and to feed into the planning, the delivery and the final showings of work. A good example of a successful process was the Big Art project produced in St Helens. Here, a group of ex-miners nominated their local park – the former site of the Sutton Manor coal tip – to be the site of a new piece of public art. The miners worked with a curator for some time in researching artists and looking at public art in different contexts. They selected the Catalan artist Jaume Plensa, who spent a long time talking to the community, the local authority and the miners (jaumeplensa.com). He heard from them of the importance of light and how the absence of light underground is one of the hardest things to come to terms with. When it came to the meeting where the artists showed his ideas, he showed a (beautiful) stylised miners' lamp that he felt would be iconic on the site. The miners subtly showed disappointment and articulated their feelings that the artist was trying too hard to see the world through their eyes rather than taking inspiration from them. He then said that his first idea had been of a young girl's head with her eyes shut lit from below to convey a dream of light and of the future. "That's what we want!" said the miners, and Plensa thus created *The dream*, a work that reflects less literally but more profoundly the search for light in the darkness (dreamsthelens.com).

The production of *The dream* describes the complex shifts and compensations as well as the difficult conversations and negotiations needed to ensure respect and parity of esteem between all involved in such projects. This specific case is indicative too of the importance of overcoming perceptions of groups imported from outside and layered onto artistic interpretations that might confirm stereotypes – whether of miners or the South African inner city. As Friction Arts reports of its intervention: 'It quickly became clear that people felt that the area of Hillbrow was considered a very dangerous area (this in a city recently cited as having the third highest murder rate in the world)'. Whatever the realities of crime or deprivation, these were not the things that participants sought to define themselves by or to explore in their collaborative works.

Nonetheless, what we have found to be most challenging in the *1mile²* project is the need to create shared values around the working practice and work produced. This is always a subjective judgement. To what extent is listening to the voices of partners enough in pursuit of equitability? What if those listened to distort the aims of the project and its outcome? There is an inherent tension in the desire for diversity and plurality of voices and sharing values. What if the voices are diametrically opposed, reflect taboos or antisocial or culturally antithetic tendencies? How can one give genuinely equal weight to elements of the work or practice that one feels to be weak or unrepresentative of the engagement or that confirms rather than breaks down negative stereotypes? These are issues that remain at the heart of collaborative projects and the most successful of them work slowly through differences looking at the common human values underlying the decisions and directions. Trust, respect, time and risk taking are the tools for this kind of working, which is why the cultural intermediation and the intermediaries are such an important feature of this approach.

Conclusion: the necessity of intermediation

Facer and Enright (2016) identify a range of roles that need to be played for a successful project, which indicate the various skills that are called upon in realising culture work such as *1mile²* and ensuring its values. These roles include: catalyst, integrator, designer, broker, facilitator, project manager, diplomat, scholar, conscience, accountant, data gatherer, nurturer and loudhailer. It is clear that these roles are interdependent, and creative artists, cultural intermediaries and others involved in promoting cultural activity are required to develop and share some of the skills required. In theory, all bases are covered in *1mile²* programmes but in reality the lack of time working with any community curtails the full exploration of the roles in pursuit and demonstration of outcomes that fulfil funding expectations. While any one *1mile²* team at work in the UK and across the world did not all have all the qualities outlined above, they worked to common goals with shared values. Clear and agreed objectives allowed people to negotiate from the particular and personal to the more general.

Ultimately, the question of the production of art and whether it was good, bad or indifferent was not part of the objectives of *1mile²*. This approach can be and has been criticised as allowing the art to be a less important byproduct of the process. However, our experience was that the integrity of the artists involved ensured that the works had great integrity and fulfilled the driving goals of the project. This may be because of the move away from the binary understanding of art as being defined by either participants or professionals and towards an understanding that great art emerges from a wide range of human emotions, dilemmas, conflicts, needs for recognition and visibility. Having emerged, art needs to be mediated in as varied a way as possible and through many different platforms and channels, so that it is both accessible to many different people and connects with them.

The experience of working internationally has shown how different cultures and, in particular, those in the developing world where resources are scarce are, in many ways, 'ahead' of the UK, Europe and the US in respect of cocreation. In our experience of international work in the developing world, the arts have not been separated and rarefied in the way that they have at home and the separation from quotidian culture, mores and customs is much less pronounced. This means that creative work is much more often collaborative and has always been so, and the social impacts are much more integrated into the work. In India, for example, the *1mile²* project is now part of the normal programme of residencies in Khoj and the work produced in the gallery as a result is judged in the same way as any work in any gallery. Issues of artists' exploitation of vulnerable communities or of crass appropriation of signs and symbols significant in cultures are, arguably, less intrusive in these cases as the practice is built on sharing and reciprocity rather than expropriation. The intermediation *is* the practice.

References

Boal, A. (2000) *Theatre of the Oppressed*, London: Pluto Press.

Clift, S., Camic, P. M., Chapman, B., Clayton, G., Daykin, N., Eades, G., Parkinson, C., Secker, J., Stickley, T. and White, M. (2009) 'The state of arts and health in England', *Arts & Health*, 1(1): 6-35.

Facer, K. and Enright, B. (2016) *Creating living knowledge: The Connected Communities Programme, community university relationships and the participatory turn in the production of knowledge*, Bristol: University of Bristol/AHRC Connected Communities.

Goldbard, A. (1993) 'Postscript to the past: Notes toward a history of community arts', *High Performance*, 16(4): 23-7.

Jones, B. (1988) 'The community artist as community development catalyst: an evaluation of a pilot project', *Community Development*, 19(1): 37-50.

Khan, N. (1978) *The Arts Britain ignores: The arts of ethnic minorities in Britain*, Commission for Racial Equality.

Matarasso, F. (2013). *'All in this together': The depoliticisation of community art in Britain, 1970-2011*, available at http://parliamentofdreams.com/articles-and-papers/

McGrath, J. (1981) *A good night out, popular theatre: Audience, class and form*, London: Eyre Methuen.

O'Toole, J. (1976) *Theatre in education: New objectives for theatre, new techniques in education*, London: Hodder & Stoughton.

Rosamond, E. (2016) 'Shared stakes, distributed investment: Socially engaged art and the financialization of social impact', *Finance and society*, 2(2): 111-26.

Snyder-Young, D. (2011) 'Rehearsals for revolution? Theatre of the Oppressed, dominant discourses, and democratic tensions', *Research in Drama Education: The Journal of Applied Theatre and Performance*, 16(1): 29-45.

Vine, C. (2013) '"TIE and the Theatre of the Oppressed" revisited', in A. Jackson and C. Vine (ed) *Learning through theatre*, London: Routledge, pp. 74-94.

Conclusion:
Where next for cultural
intermediation?

Phil Jones, Paul Long and Beth Perry

An obvious response to the variety of perspectives presented in this book would be to conclude that cultural intermediaries play a vital role in connecting communities into creative economic activity but that, without additional public funding being unlocked, their work is under threat in the UK. Indeed, there would be some truth to this claim as the exigencies of austerity have bitten hard and, in spite of considerable commitment, organisations and individuals have found it impossible to continue with their established work. What this book and the research project it was based on have unveiled, however, is a somewhat more complex picture.

As scholars have extended Bourdieu's notion of the 'cultural intermediary' (1984), so the scope of intermediation activity has significantly widened, but in doing so it has become more diffuse and somewhat less coherent or specific (for a critique of this diffusion, see Hesmondhalgh 2006). Nonetheless, for Smith Maguire and Matthews (2012), it is a term that is 'good to think with', foregrounding as it does qualities of agency and power. As detailed across these chapters, intermediaries can be seen to negotiate a role as interpreters of policy and proselytisers of the values of art worlds and the imperatives of the creative economy, in pursuing funding, determining where their work might be best located and engaging audiences, while often required to capture the impact of that work and thus to determine its value. In so doing, any sense that the core concern of the work of intermediation is with 'taste', that is the aesthetics and pleasures of expression, is tempered by administrative, political and economic priorities.

While we are in no doubt that there always been such an aspect to the work of intermediation (consider the account of Vaughan Jones in Chapter fifteen in this volume, for instance), this condition has been exacerbated by recent developments. In order to argue for higher levels of public investment, there was strategic value in blurring together different elements of the creative economy, cultural industries, formalised arts sector and work undertaken with (socially excluded) communities. The political atmosphere behind this strategy and in which this research project was born, however, was very different to the situation today. The project *Cultural intermediation: connecting communities in the creative urban economy* was conceived in 2011, at the point where the New Labour discourse of creative economy as economic saviour was still being deployed as a means to fend off the rapid shrinking of public spending as part of an austerity agenda pushed by a right-wing government – the Conservative-Liberal Democrat coalition. Reductions to public sector spending were complemented by a short-lived 'Big Society' agenda that sought to inculcate communities with a desire to fix their own problems – a fairly transparent neoliberal trick of shifting responsibility for structural problems onto the shoulders of the poor supported by relatively limited resources.

As Brook et al note in Chapter one, where New Labour wrapped different parts of the creative economy together, more recently there has been a disaggregation of those sectors that are conventionally profitable from those that fit into our more traditional, ghettoised, understanding of 'the arts' as usually reliant upon public subsidy. While the Warwick Commission (2015) report used an ecosystem metaphor to argue that the entire cultural and creative economy should be seen as an interdependent unit, questions arise about the utility of this idea. For instance, do those (predominantly white, middle-class men) who work in the less glamorous parts of the IT sector really have that much in common with artists eking out a living via occasional commissions to work in deprived neighbourhoods? What kinds of exchange actually take place in this ecosystem? What kinds of economic relations and hierarchies are exhibited between those striving for profit and those whose energies are directed to chasing an ever-dwindling pot of public funds? Indeed, if funding for the UK's museums and art galleries disappeared tomorrow, would that actually prevent, for example, Dundee's DC Thompson from continuing to produce a range of mischievous multimedia content around its *Beano* comics brand? What would community arts initiatives look like if required to optimise the intellectual property of their work as a means of sustaining their enterprise? On the last point there have certainly been initiatives to emulate a more market-driven approach to support with the exploration of American philanthropic fundraising models with Arts Council England importing Devos' Michael Kaiser, 'the turnaround king', to deliver workshops (DCMS, 2011).

As research for the chapters collected in this book was being undertaken, the divisions between different parts of the creative economy and arts sector were being thrown into sharp relief by the austerity-led cuts that have become the new normal for UK policy making. One of the intermediaries we worked with reflected angrily about the large amount of public money being spent to keep Salford's Lowry Centre afloat while their organisation, working closely with deprived communities in neighbouring Ordsall, was struggling to make ends meet. If a big arts centre and a small community organisation are seen as having the *same* intermediary function, then undoubtedly this would be a sound point. While large arts organisations do have outreach and engagement functions, a more significant reason why venues such as The Lowry exist is to produce a visible symbol that an area is 'on the up' – a redevelopment recipe that has been applied in cities as different as Amsterdam and Los Angeles, Guangzhou and Dubai. Arts and cultural venues as anchor points of redevelopment schemes became a regeneration cliché of the early 2000s, leveraging vast profits for the private sector. They do, however, still have to be funded by taxpayers long after the developers have made their money and moved on to the next city (Jones and Evans, 2013).

Despite the good work done by large cultural venues undertaking outreach to poorer communities, arguably their primary role in terms of intermediation is in encouraging middle-class and wealthy communities to consider using an urban locale they had previously ignored. At the start of the millennium, Richard Florida (2002) was leading the charge for investment in creative activity as part of driving economic growth in contemporary cities. In more recent years, however, even Florida (2017) has acknowledged that the processes he celebrated in the 2000s have led to increased social division, inequality and gentrification. Staring over the barbed wire fences that separate Ordsall from the Lowry Centre's home in Salford Quays, it is hard to disagree with the idea that the worthy activities as community engagement intermediary of the large arts organisations do not necessarily outweigh their complicity in wider processes of social segregation. Even at this end of the cultural ecology, one might pinpoint the obvious disparities between the eminently consumable qualities of sites such as The Lowry and the kinds of organic cultural projects embedded in the community of Salford. The kind of constituency each addresses, their function and meaning, is quite distinct. And indeed, intermediaries involved across this spectrum might accrue quite distinct economic rewards and cultural capital that reflects a particular hierarchy and any potential for movement across any ecological relationship. These dynamics are illustrated by Perry in Chapter seven, where she notes the value of locally embedded cultural organisations as intermediaries engaged in the making of meaning, community *and* markets, in a wider context of 'making do'.

Attempting to disentangle some of the different types of cultural intermediation, their function and meanings within a complex and diverse creative economy, is therefore very significant. In Chapter two, De Propris makes the case for disaggregating the different elements of cultural intermediation using a value-chain analysis. This sort of approach would make some in the sector nervous, particularly, as suggested, many intermediaries have activities cutting across creation, commodification and outreach. Nonetheless, by identifying the different stages in the process of moving from a creative idea to an engagement with a community, De Propris' analysis reminds us about the geographical skew within the sector. Stripping out those elements of cultural intermediation that focus on the more ubiquitous processes of commodification highlights just how unevenly the creative and engagement parts of intermediation are distributed. Fundamentally, these activities are disproportionately concentrated in London and in wealthier parts of other English regions.

This element of De Propris' analysis should come as no shock – the London-centric skew of the wider creative economy is well established (Oakley, 2006). What is significant is that even the *engagement* element of the intermediation value chain cannot be seen to be evenly geographically distributed. This gives a lie to the idea that cultural intermediation in and of itself would be able to play a significant role in combating poverty and deprivation – this kind of engagement activity simply is not located in the places where poorer communities actually live. Our research project used case studies within Birmingham and Greater Manchester; even within these large metropolitan regions, it is clear that the relative absence of the engagement element of the intermediation value chain places these areas – and the concentration of deprived communities within them – at a significant economic disadvantage. Let's be clear here and point out that intermediation activities, alongside the provision of cultural consumption – introductions to arts, drama and so on – also include support for galvanising skills oriented to the creative industries, nurturing business development, production and employment. As in any other sector of provision, the question of who is able to take advantage of such provision is inflected by a range of social variables and inequalities. In considering models of urban governance in Birmingham for instance, Cattacin and Zimmer summarise a policy shift focused on an idea of entrepreneurialism in the service and creative industries that might provide the city with new economic advantages. As they note however, any emergent social innovations:

are not likely to be able to surmount the decisive problems faced by a large segment of Birmingham's population that is not well educated and does not have the skills to work in the increasingly important creative sector. Therefore, it is most likely that the divide between rich and poor, and hence between the entrepreneurs and workforce of the new economy on the one hand and those who continue to identify with the way of life of the old working class on the other, will grow further. (Cattacin and Zimmer, 2016: 36)

A major theme that cuts through this book is the role of universities as key actors within local economies and the cultural life of regions. Birmingham City University (host for author Long), for instance, announces itself as the university *for* Birmingham, emphatic of how its mission extends beyond the concern of classroom encounters with its students. Reflecting on this activity is not simply navel-gazing by the academics who have put this volume together. In times of significant public sector cuts across the UK, universities are one of the few institutional actors that have continued to be *very* well resourced. Indeed, universities can be thought of as de facto policy organisations with regards to the cultural sector, supporting intermediaries betwixt and between education and projects, students seeking internships and, of course, graduating as emergent creative workers (see Ashton and Noonan, 2013). Where universities are directly engaged with cultural work, whether via research, knowledge transfer and so on, real tensions can emerge, particularly when working with smaller arts and community organisations. At the AHRC's *Connected communities* summit in Manchester 2012 the audience was split between academics and those from arts and third sector organisations. This led to the somewhat unedifying spectacle of people from community groups reacting in horror to academics casually saying "you can't do anything for forty grand" in response to a call being issued by the funder. While this may well be a reasonable response by scholars in the face of how university financing works, it only served to reinforce the impression of a sector awash with cash and completely detached from the realities of austerity Britain.

As a result of the resources it has available, however, the higher education sector really does have a potentially significant intermediating role for communities and culture. The Bristol Radical Film Festival (BRFF) discussed in Ager's Chapter ten is a really intriguing example of this. Rather than drawing directly on funding from the institution, instead the BRFF used the *social* capital of its organisers being associated with the University of West of England (UWE) to leverage buy-in to the festival. The fact that UWE did not subsequently use the festival as a means of demonstrating the institution's 'impact' on the wider world as part of the 2014 Research Excellence Framework (REF) says something interesting about the internal politics of the institutions. Scholars have become quite adept at doing things under the radar that rely on their institutional status but which managers in their institution might not necessarily be enthused about. As such, the effect universities are having as intermediaries is almost certainly being underestimated by way that the REF has been designed to evaluate impact activity.

Where researchers are working on funded projects, there can be an embarrassment of riches, but usually only for a fixed timeframe. Trying to explain to external partners that the money will disappear at the end of the project and that 'the university' will not provide ongoing resource is a challenge of managing expectations. For a few short years, the AHRC's *Connected communities* funding pot made a huge amount of grant money available to a relatively small pool of academics. The underlying motivation in the cultural budgeting work described by Jones in Chapter eight was to try to make sure that some of the 'communities' that were being 'connected' should actually get to decide how a portion of this money was spent.

A noble aim, perhaps, but as the chapters by Isakjee (eleven) and Symons (thirteen) highlight, the mismatch of the amount of money available and the capacity of communities to spend it on cultural activity was brutal, particularly at a time when austerity had made all too many people in the UK utterly destitute. From the point of view of a £1.5m project, £50,000 is a fairly minor spend, but as Symons demonstrates in Chapter thirteen, it is pretty insulting to the community organisations that work in a struggling neighbourhood if you turn up and appear to throw a lot of cash around on projects just because it is interesting to the researchers to see what happens. The model she highlights of 'maximising what is already there' represents a more humble way for university-led intermediation processes to take place.

As Isakjee highlights in Chapter eleven, questions of cultural engagement can also be problematically tangled up with the wider politics of 'inclusion' and post-2001 fearmongering about the status of Muslim 'communities' in the UK. It is far too easy to slip into the trap of a cultural deficit model, positioning communities as needing to be 'fixed', just as policies such as the Prevent strategy are designed to 'fix' Muslim communities. Indeed, notions of 'cultural deficit' originated in education studies as a way of asking why minority ethnic communities 'failed' to take on the cultural values of white, middle-class consumers and whether this could be used to explain segregation (Kirk and Goon, 1975). The question, then, is not whether the work being done by cultural intermediaries is helping to drive social cohesion in diverse communities, but whether this aim is, in itself, problematic. Furthermore, discourses of social cohesion play out in the poorest communities and thus potentially obfuscate some of the very serious question of social class and exclusion that was also highlighted by Brook et al in Chapter one.

One of the other major projects funded under the *Connected communities* funding strand looked at *Everyday participation*, pushing past the deficit model of access to cultural activities (Miles and Gibson, 2016). Long, in Chapter four, examines how everyday and amateur cultural production finds a space within communities, particularly examining the intermediating process he terms 'sponsored amateurism'. Public funding mechanisms are designed to force artistic producers to widen their audience, within the general idea that consuming art is *good* for people and thus reaching a socially excluded audience represents better value for money in a cultural spend. Long instead asks us to examine how intermediaries can encourage cultural production among communities as means of enabling expression and expanding the comprehension of culture rather than the model of passive consumption of what is deemed to be valuable. Many intermediaries work precisely in this field – witness Mohammed Ali's practice of working with communities in order to engage their voices and concerns in his work (see Chapter fourteen). Even more enabling is Chris Jam, who contributed his poem about Balsall Heath to this volume (see Chapter twelve). He has extensively worked with school-age children, encouraging them to write and perform their own poems. Jam argues that creative expression is a basic human right, not simply in the narrow sense enshrined in Article 19 of the International Covenant on Civil and Political Rights (United Nations 1966) around freedom of speech, but as an essential component of being able to live a rich and fulfilled life. Not all creative expression will be of familiar artistic merit, but it can have other important values to that individual. Indeed, as Burwood demonstrates in his reflections about the *Some cities* project (Chapter six), the 'sponsoring' intermediary activity can itself dissipate as those leading it move on to other interests. Often, however, the products of this amateur activity will be ephemeral and hard to capture in the kinds of evaluation processes about which the UK's public sector is inordinately enthusiastic.

As Perry and Symons note in Chapter three, however, there is still a tendency to privilege creative production where it generates economic value. As we have suggested, this was the way that the creative sector was 'sold' to the UK's Treasury in the late 1990s to justify public funding being unlocked. Indeed, the framing narrative which unlocked the funding for our research was built on the idea that the creative was a key driver of economic growth. Perry and Symons therefore elaborate a 'cultural ecology' model, not as a way of bundling together the highly diverse 'creative economy' but instead as a way of linking culture to questions of social justice. Thus, policy priorities around using culture to drive growth fade into the background as more bottom-up design of cultural activities blur the boundaries between expressive and instrumental production. Working with and through intermediaries gives a space in which to produce work that moves beyond narrow categories of being either of aesthetic or socially productive value.

Rounding out the book in Chapter fifteen, Vaughan Jones reflected on how the history of socially engaged arts has informed her own practice as an intermediary. The idea that art and artists can make a difference in society beyond simply the production of aesthetically pleasing products is, of course, not a new one. The move away from participatory and engaged arts practice as being solely a product of therapeutic spaces in the late 1960s was doubtless a signal moment. What is so interesting in her reflections is the extent to which she sees the mission of participatory work as having been somewhat lost in a funding climate from the 1990s onward that favoured the individualised experience over the collective, the depoliticised over calls for change. Her response, through the $1mile^2$ project, was to drive a more cooperative approach to arts practice, with communities working together rather than relying on an outside expert to *do* art to them. This model of collaboration, which placed a tremendous emphasis on *learning*, does the kind of blurring between instrumental and expressive work that Perry and Symons are calling for in their notion of a cultural ecology that combines the social with the creative (Chapter three).

This conclusion is framed as being a reflection on the future of intermediation. In truth, just as the 2000s notion of a creative economy has been disaggregated, so we need to break down our notions of what intermediation is *for*. UK policy now effectively considers the publicly funded arts as being something separate from the profit-making creative industries – something that the Warwick Commission explicitly sought to avoid. In line with this, however, we also need to split out cultural intermediation processes and objectives. On the one hand, it can be seen as a means of engaging individuals with particular creative products and processes that they might wish to consume or in which to participate. More importantly from the perspective of this book, other forms of cultural intermediation can be seen as an attempt to work with deprived communities to improve their lives.

The funding for the research that underpins this book came with an implicit idea that the benefits of the rapidly growing creative economy should be more equally shared with poorer communities. While one can point to individual exceptions to this rule, the better paid jobs within the creative sector are still overwhelming dominated by highly educated graduates from middle-class backgrounds. Those jobs are also predominantly located in London and the South East as well as the richer parts of other major cities. Realistically, therefore, only the very talented and the very lucky can count on the creative sector as a route out of poverty, no matter how many well-meaning cultural initiatives are run in deprived neighbourhoods. Indeed, Ali's account (Chapter fourteen) recalls some of the cultural barriers to imagining a creative career and the lack of available models or apparent practical value to families concerned to see an improvement in the next generation's fortunes.

Intermediaries who work to encourage communities to engage with arts and creative practice as a consumer, as non-professional or amateur producer, or in some kind of coproducing role can have a major impact on an individual's confidence, capacity to express themselves or simply bring some pleasure into an otherwise difficult life. It should be noted that, in spite of the aim for *collective* impact, transformations are often mapped at an *individual* level because of the way in which the world of culture is predicated. Nonetheless, intermediaries doing this work are to be unambiguously applauded. In the contexts of austerity economics and as outlined across this book, the commitment shown by many individuals – to specific communities and to their faith in culture – is a mark of their integrity and authenticity.

Fundamentally, however, there are much bigger issues at play that throw into relief the concern with culture and the potential of the social remedies placed upon it. Savage cuts to education and training since 2010 have pulled up a ladder that was already out of reach for many, if not most people in the UK. Dramatic regional imbalances in employment opportunities make a mockery of the idea that the creative economy can be any kind of saviour for those living in poverty. In this situation, intermediation and claims for its virtues appears to be a sticking plaster over these much more serious wounds to the UK's national wellbeing. In future, cultural intermediation will doubtless continue to play a small role in building confidence and skills among a relatively limited number of people, but in the face of a right-wing agenda that seems determined to entrench inequality, the capacity of intermediaries to help make the world a better place remains, as it always has been, highly limited.

References

Ashton, D. and Noonan, C. (2013). *Cultural work and higher education*, London: Palgrave Macmillan.

Bourdieu, P. (1984) *Distinction: a social critique of the judgement of taste*, London: Routledge & Kegan Paul.

Cattacin, S. and Zimmer, A. (2016) 'Urban governance and social innovations' in Brandsen, T., Cattacin, S., Evers, A., and Zimmer, A. (eds) *Social innovations in the urban context*, Cham: Springer International Publishing, pp. 21–44.

DCMS (Department for Digital, Culture, Media and Sport) (2011) 'Arts fundraising seminars from the "turnaround king"', 26 May, https://www.gov.uk/government/news/arts-fundraising-seminars-from-the-turnaround-king, accessed 9 July 2018.

Florida, R. (2002) *The rise of the creative class and how it's transforming work, leisure, community and everyday life*, Basic Books, New York.

Florida, R. (2017) *The new urban crisis: How our cities are increasing inequality, deepening segregation, and failing the middle class – and what we can do about it*, New York: Basic Books.

Hesmondhalgh, D. (2006) Bourdieu, the media and cultural production, *Media, Culture & Society*, 28(2): 211-31.

Jones, P. and Evans, J. (2013) *Urban regeneration in the UK, second edition*, London: Sage.

Kirk, D. H. and Goon, S. (1975) 'Desegregation and the cultural deficit model: an examination of the literature', *Review of Educational Research*, 45: 599-611.

Miles, A. and Gibson, L. (2016) 'Everyday participation and cultural value', *Cultural Trends*, 25: 151-7.

Oakley, K. (2006) 'Include us out: economic development and social policy in the creative industries', *Cultural Trends*, 15: 255-73.

Smith Maguire, J. and Matthews, J. (2012) 'Are we all cultural intermediaries now? An introduction to cultural intermediaries in context', *European Journal of Cultural Studies*, 15: 551–562.

The Warwick Commission (2015) *Enriching Britain: culture, creativity and growth. The 2015 Report by the Warwick Commission on the Future of Cultural Value*, Warwick: University of Warwick.

United Nations (1966) *International Covenant on Civil and Political Rights*, New York: United Nations.

Index

Note: Page numbers for figures and tables appear in italics.